Dear Reader:

The book you are about to read is the latest bestseller from the St. Martin's True Crime Library, the imprint the *New York Times* calls "the leader in true crime!" Each month, we offer you a fascinating account of the latest, most sensational crime that has captured the national attention. St. Martin's is the publisher of perennial bestselling true crime author Jack Olsen, whose SALT OF THE EARTH is the true story of one woman's triumph over life-shattering violence; Joseph Wambaugh called it "powerful and absorbing." Fannie Weinstein and Melinda Wilson tell the story of a beautiful honors student who was lured into the dark world of sex for hire in THE COED CALL GIRL MURDER. St. Martin's is also proud to publish two-time Edgar Award-winning author Carlton Stowers, whose TO THE LAST BREATH recounts a two-year-old girl's mysterious death, and the dogged investigation that led loved ones to the most unlikely murderer: her own father. In the book you now hold, AN HOUR TO KILL, Dale Hudson and Billy Hills investigate an appalling murder performed by the *last* person anyone would suspect of the crime.

St. Martin's True Crime Library gives you the stories *behind* the headlines. Our authors take you right to the scene of the crime and into the minds of the most notorious murderers to show you what really makes them tick. St. Martin's True Crime Library paperbacks are better than the most terrifying thriller, because it's all true! The next time you want a crackling good read, make sure it's got the St. Martin's True Crime Library logo on the spine—you'll be up all night!

Charles E. Spicer, Jr.
Executive Editor, St. Martin's True Crime Library

Knowles felt the anticipated shock through his forehead as he saw the foot sticking up beyond the side of the ditch. Moving down, to his left, he stepped over a clump of weeds growing in the bottom of the ravine and eased forward. He squatted to take in his first full view of the mutilated corpse. A numbing heat through his entire body quickly replaced the relatively minor shock of seeing the foot.

"Oh, my God," he said softly.

Knowles had apprised himself early in life of the rigors of his chosen profession and understood and accepted the unknowns. But even as a boy, he didn't like surprises. No matter how they turned out, surprises usually started poorly and usually got worse.

When he became a police officer, he had found that the job included something that can only be understood by being there. The experience of homicide detectives with hardcore evil is immediate. They look at it . . . they smell it . . . they touch it . . . they have to explain it. They see and know things other people don't know, don't want to know, and usually wouldn't believe anyway. Because of his training, though, and particularly his experience, Knowles had begun to feel there wasn't anything he hadn't seen or couldn't handle.

Until that moment.

AN HOUR TO KILL

A TRUE STORY OF LOVE, MURDER, AND JUSTICE IN A SMALL SOUTHERN TOWN

DALE HUDSON
AND BILLY HILLS

St. Martin's Paperbacks

Published by arrangement with McGregor Publishing, Inc.

AN HOUR TO KILL

Library of Congress Catalog Card Number: 99-042210

ISBN: 0-312-97835-9

Printed in the United States of America

McGregor hardcover edition published 1999
St. Martin's Paperbacks edition / March 2001

St. Martin's Paperbacks are published by St. Martin's Press, 175 Fifth Avenue, New York, NY 10010.

10 9 8 7 6 5 4 3 2 1

To our fathers

NOTE

This is a true crime story. It has been pieced together from interviews, detectives' notes, memos, freedom of information requests, newspaper articles, and numerous readings of the 3,204-page transcript of the murder trial.

The problem in telling a story like this is what to exclude to keep the story flowing and the reader actively engaged. The investigation into the rape and murder of Crystal Todd remains the largest undertaking in the history of the Horry County Police Department. The police spent countless hours tracking down dead-end leads. Hundreds of people were interviewed. Numerous reports were written and filed. Thousands of pages of documents resulted from the work of the homicide task force.

Only a small fraction of those efforts, however, bear on the discovery and arrest of Ken Register. That's what you'll find in this book. But make no mistake. This is the story of a murder and the investigation and arrest of the person responsible.

The reader should also note that this book is not a simple recitation of the facts of the case. Where we knew the setting of a conversation and who-said-what, we painted the picture by putting the events in story form. Elements of setting, such as weather and physical structure, are based on fact and were derived from extensive research. Dialogue was only created when we knew a conversation took place and the content of the conversation. To the fullest extent possible, original quotes were maintained as the backbone of that dialogue. Exact phrasing was used throughout the book when quoting from documents and was only modified for clarification in accordance with traditional standards. Names of characters in the story were maintained or changed based on our assessment of the person's involvement. For example, Ken Register's girlfriend was not named Tammy, but we changed her name to protect the privacy she now desires.

PROLOGUE

The afternoon sun sat low in the winter sky. The glare inside the truck was blinding. The small, tow-headed boy stretched his neck to peer over the vinyl dashboard. The sight of familiar trees or his road would have been nice, but he especially hoped to see his house. With the sun shining brightly into the window, he could do little besides shield his face with his hand and wait.

Daddy gripped the steering wheel and grinned at the boy's struggle. "What's wrong?" he asked, as the strong six-cylinder engine pulled the bouncing vehicle on the country road. A steady rumble from the truck's oversized tires mixed with the whining sounds of the radio and filled the roomy cab. A screeching metal-on-metal noise sounded sharply each time the boat trailer bounced through a patched pothole. The red-faced man smiled and adjusted his visor.

"Look here, boy," he said, raising and lowering the visor a second time.

The boy smiled and again covered his eyes from the sun. He didn't ask how much further they had to go. Daddy didn't like when he did that.

The rugged man alternately glanced down at his small son and out to the road ahead. "You have fun today?" he asked hopefully.

Squinting, the boy nodded. He did have fun, at least most of the time. Spending time outdoors seemed to please Daddy. Then, suddenly aware of the smelly stains on his shirt, the boy held the back of his small hand to his nose.

"Don't worry, Son," his father said reassuringly. "You'll get over that." He patted his shirt pocket and snaked a callused finger into a pack of cigarettes, counting by feel. Smoothly pulling the pack up, he used a well-practiced wrist motion to deliver the filtered end of a smoke to his lips.

The boy quickly grabbed the matches on the seat and held them out. He liked the smell of the cigarette as it was first lit, but what he really liked was that it masked the lingering odor of the fresh duck meat that had earlier clung to his body. Just a brief memory of that experience was enough to produce an acid taste in the boy's mouth. He cleared his throat.

"Don't start that, now," his father said gruffly.

"I'm not," the boy replied weakly, grimacing as he swallowed.

The man cracked his front window and smoke swirled through the truck. The boy was grateful for the refreshing cool air and breathed through his mouth.

Glancing again at the boy, the man shook his head in thought. He didn't know why his son had such a reaction to smells. He had wanted to make hunting and skinning a part of the boy's upbringing, as it had been a part of his, but with an important difference: The days of hunting to put food on the table were over for his family.

He had given his son his first shotgun, a .20 gauge, the year before. The boy was only seven, and although he wasn't big enough to shoot the gun, he would be before long. The man was hopeful that he and his son would soon routinely rise early in the morning, suit up, and head out together on the hunt.

But then, during that first deer skinning, the boy got sick. As the razor-sharp blade peeled back the underbelly of a warm buck and the smell of blood assaulted his nostrils, he experienced waves of nausea and then vomited. Relief came for the boy only when he moved away from the rough men who worked efficiently to remove large portions of the dark, bloody meat.

The man was sure the boy would get past this strange reaction, but he was concerned. He hadn't experienced anything like that as a boy, and had taken naturally to the rigors of hunting. He was dismayed by his son's reluctance to rejoin the skinning.

Drawing deeply on his cigarette, he watched as the boy tried to not look at the stains on the front of his clothes. The day's hunt had been for duck, even though the season had recently ended. He had shown the youngster how to quickly skin the duck over the mouth of a brown paper grocery sack, separating flesh from bone and stringing tendon, keeping only the meat. Extra time was taken to show the boy how to avoid cutting into the animal's intestines, the source of the smells the boy seemed not to like. Unpleasant interactions with the game warden, he had explained, could be avoided by dumping the contents of the bag, and the bag itself, if it became too messy.

Late that afternoon, the boy had been standing in the front of the boat, fixing to empty the feathers and innards into the river, when a gust of wind blew the sticky debris back into his face. He immediately dropped the bag in alarm and panicked as the bloody guts clung to his mouth and arms. The man quickly cut the motor, fearful that his son might fall into the water, and moved forward to help. Fighting to control his anger, the father held his sputtering son as he leaned over the side of the boat and used his small hands to rinse his mouth with the brown river water. In the end, his son had calmed down, but he was still covered with stains and the pungent scent of the game meat. The boy had gagged off and on since then.

Rounding the final curve, the man said, "We're here." He started to say that he would need help with the boat, but stopped short, knowing the boy would run to his mama at the first chance.

The boy sat up abruptly. Seeing the one-story brick home rapidly approaching, he put his hand on the door handle.

"Wait until we stop, Son. Don't be jumping out."

"There's Mama!" the boy blurted out when his mother appeared at the screen door off the carport.

"Mama," he said excitedly, bouncing up and down on the front of the seat in anticipation, his hand still firmly clenching the door handle.

As the truck rolled to a stop, the boy braced his feet on the floor and leaned into the heavy door. Then he jumped to the ground and ran directly to his mother's embrace.

The woman held her son tightly as her husband stepped out of the cab.

"We got some ducks, here, Mama," the man said, brushing aside a little brown dog and kissing his wife.

The boy stiff-armed out from between the adults and ran through the open screen door into the house.

"How did he do?" the woman asked tentatively.

"Oh," the man drawled, removing his cap and scratching his head. "Everything was fine until near the end, when I was having him empty the bag. I know the hammerhead don't like the smell, so I was trying to help him. I run the boat a little, thinking the wind would blow the smell back, but a daggone gust whipped some of the guts up on him, instead." He took a deep breath and looked at his wife. "Then it just weren't good at all."

She nodded, sizing up her husband's mood. "He had something all over him, all right," she agreed. Reflecting for a moment, she said, "Bless his heart," and turned toward the door. "I better go help him. He'll be done out of those clothes by now."

The man watched his wife go into the house and stood thinking about his son. "I don't know what's wrong," he muttered as he tended to the boat. "But I'll make a man out of him yet."

Ten years later
Conway, South Carolina

PART I

THE CRIME

1

"**Y**ou gotta help me, please, I can't find my daughter!"

The frightened caller shrieked into the phone line of 911 Horry County Emergency Medical Services. The lone dispatcher on duty, Mike Hill, fielded the call crackling over his headset at 3:30 a.m. on Sunday, November 17, 1991.

Glancing at the clock, Hill jotted the time in the log and listened to the panic-stricken voice. Unable to determine whether the voice was male or female, he interrupted.

"I'm sorry, but I am having some difficulty following you. Could you please speak more clearly into the phone?" Muffled, fumbling noises over the line suggested to Hill that the caller wasn't alone.

"There, that's better," he said after a brief silence. "Now slow down, caller, and, first off, tell me your name, please."

Hill was used to responding in emergency situations and listened attentively to the caller's labored breathing. "That's right, slow down," he said reassuringly, "and go ahead, please."

The caller stammered, making guttural, low-pitched noises as she tried to calm herself and organize her thoughts.

"Uh, all right," she mumbled. Hill recognized the distinct local accent and thought the caller was a woman.

"What's your name, please?" he asked again.

The caller ignored the question. "My daughter went to a party tonight and she ain't come home yet," she blurted out.

"Caller, please tell me your name."

The caller intermittently cried and coughed deeply in raspy spasms.

"Caller," continued Hill patiently, "please help me by answering a few questions. Can you tell me your name?"

"She was with her friend, Carla Allen."

OK, he thought, noting the name of the friend, *we'll do it your way.* "When did you last see your daughter?"

"They went to a party together, then left there and drove back to the mall at about 11:15 so Carla could get her car, and then my daughter drove off and that's the last time anybody seen her."

Certain the caller was a woman, Hill listened to the anguished voice.

"I called Carla," the woman continued. "She ain't seen her, and I called her friend, Ken Register, and he said he ain't seen her neither."

"Ma'am, what's your daughter's name?"

"She's driving her brand new car that I give her."

Thinking that maybe the woman had a hearing problem, Hill said loudly, "What kind of car is it, ma'am?"

"It's blue, a new car, one of them Toyota Celicas. I just got it for her as a graduation present. She's got her name on the back of it, uh, on the license plate. It says, 'C TODD.'"

Hill quickly made the connection.

"Mrs. Todd? Mrs. Bonnie Faye Todd? This is Mike, Mike Hill, remember me? I taught Crystal piano when she was just a little bitty thing. Remember, she wanted to play for the church?"

"Oh, yeah, Mike. Well, good." Bonnie Faye breathed heavily into the receiver. "I'm sure glad I got somebody I know. I'm worried sick about Crystal. Do you think you can help me find her?"

This wasn't the first time Hill had received a plea for help from a parent worried about a tardy child. Hearing Bonnie Faye's sobs, he patiently worked through the standard information in a soothing voice he had developed through similar experiences.

"I drove everywhere and called 'em all and ain't nobody seen her," Bonnie Faye said, pleading with Hill to send someone to look for her daughter. "I just know something has happened to her, and if she is dead or something, I'll kill myself."

"Now, now, Bonnie Faye," Hill interjected, "let's not get carried away. I'll tell you what, as soon as she comes home, call me and I'll see if a patrolman can come out there and we'll give her a good scare, just in case she ever thinks of pulling a stunt like this again."

"Would ya, Mike? Oh, that'd be so nice."

"You know I will, Bonnie Faye," he said, hoping that would be the end of it. "Let me ask you, Miss Bonnie, just how old is Crystal now?"

"She's seventeen, a senior in high school."

"Can you believe that?" said Hill. "Why, it just doesn't seem possible, her all grown up. I bet you're so proud."

"Well, I mostly am, but I'm sure worried now."

"I know you are, but now that we're aware of this, maybe you can relax some. First thing you know she'll be home and you give her a big hug before you scold her, OK?"

Hill felt there wasn't much more he could offer Bonnie Faye and was relieved that her voice had evened a little. "I'm going now, but you give me a call back when she comes in, you hear? Everybody knows Crystal, Miss Bonnie, and she's a good girl. She's not the type to get involved with trouble or somebody up to no good."

Although Bonnie Faye dismissed the soothing words, she thanked Dispatcher Hill. As she hung up the phone, she was still terribly worried for her beloved only child.

Hill thought about all of the parents he had consoled. Even though teenagers got into mischief and, sometimes, even trouble in the small town, things had a way of working out. For parents, the dark makes everything scarier. The cold of the middle of the night is a time of worry. But, thought Hill as another call lit up the switchboard, everything always looks brighter in the morning light.

Bonnie Faye made several more calls that morning to Crystal's friends and became more desperate and frantic with each one. Finally, at approximately 8 A.M., she called 911 with an unrestrained plea for help in finding her daughter.

"I can't take it no more," she cried into the phone. "Why won't you do something? I'm about to go crazy for worry. She ain't come home yet and I know that somebody's got her somewhere and she's dead. I just know she's dead."

The morning dispatcher asked Wade Petty, a uniformed officer with the Horry County Police Department, to drive out to

Ms. Todd's house and talk to her. Though Crystal was overdue by only several hours, a missing persons report could be filed to console the distraught mother.

At 8:44 A.M., Officer Petty left the police department in downtown Conway, South Carolina, and headed west on Highway 378. He had no idea that what began that brisk November morning as small town, routine police assistance would quickly become the largest investigation in the history of the county, an investigation into a crime not thought possible in the rural town of Conway. Officer Petty, as it turned out, was only the first of many who would make the eight-mile trip through the countryside to Juniper Bay Road and the home of Crystal Faye Todd.

2

The temperature had dropped and Ken Register's thin cotton shirt provided little protection against the cool evening air. The blond, blue-eyed young man's bare ankles flashed stylishly above his Docksiders as he shifted his weight in a futile effort to stay warm.

"Tammy, I'm cold," he said again, jamming his balled up hands into his pockets. His elbows hugged his sides, making it difficult for his girlfriend's hand to slip around his arm without him squeezing it and preventing her from pulling away.

"OK, I know you are," she said, turning toward him. "But there's just a couple more races and I want to stay. I can ride home with Misty if you want to go on." The pretty, blond teenager nuzzled his neck and placed her chin on his shoulder.

The go-cart track in Aynor, South Carolina, always buzzed with excitement for the Saturday night races, but tonight it was especially busy. The extra prize money of the upcoming Thanksgiving weekend races was a lure and had drawn the attention of well over a hundred carters, some of whom trailered their homemade machines hundreds of miles to reach the remote Dodge City Park Raceway. All were eager to fine tune their driving styles to local conditions and stood close together in the small pit areas, awaiting their turns, enjoying a chance to talk racing.

Fans standing around the outside of the track moved in synch with the nonstop action, stepping forward to the track fence for the heats of their favorites and then back to the staging area to talk with the drivers and watch the next group get ready. Even though it was getting late, pickup trucks and hot cars continued to jam the parking lot as the whine of the two-stroke engines filled the air, reverberating off the pines at the perimeter of the dirt track.

Ken turned his head quickly in Tammy's direction and then looked at the crowd milling around the concession stand.

"What is it now?" she said. Her voice reflected her growing irritation.

"Stop looking over there," he said sharply. "You were looking over my shoulder."

"I was not," she sighed. "I was looking at you." Pushing away from him, she folded her arms across her chest.

He glanced again toward the concession stand and scowled. "Why don't we just go?" he said. He shivered with exaggeration, demonstrating his desire to leave.

"I told you, I'm not ready to go yet." She turned and smiled in the direction of a couple she knew from high school. "Hey, y'all . . ." she said. She abruptly walked toward them, leaving Ken standing by himself.

Although Aynor was only twelve miles from Conway, the small towns' social circles didn't completely overlap. Ken knew almost everyone around Conway, where he had gone to high school, and a lot of people from Aynor, where his mother's family lived. But he didn't know all the boys and men that frequented the go-cart track and had told Tammy the track wasn't a place to go to by herself. Though she lived next door to the track and had family that worked there, she had to agree. Her family had always been cautious because of the track's rural locale, and though she had been there numerous times when her father or her aunt was working, always checking in as she arrived, she wasn't allowed to simply hang around the track.

Ken was upset because Tammy had recently gone to the track not wearing his ring, even though they were going steady. In all fairness, he knew she had been a racing fan since long before they started dating thirteen months before, and that she thrived on the social scene the track afforded young teens in the small country town.

Tammy walked back over and nestled her face into the front of Ken's shirt. "Ken, it would really be all right if you don't stay," she said, looking up at his rigidly set jaw. "Misty came over by herself and wants me to ride home with her."

"Tammy, you know I don't like that," he answered. His eyes softened as he looked at her upturned face. "You rode with me up here and I'll take you back." Although Tammy's house was visible from the track, the dirt road winding around to it was dark and isolated. She never walked to or from the track at night. Shortcuts in the country could be dangerous.

"Ken, I'd rather stay up here than go home and be bored," she said. Her curfew was normally eleven o'clock, acceptable for a fourteen-year-old, but she was allowed to stay out later if she was at the track, where her family could watch over her.

"I'll be with you," he said, looking at his watch. "It's already after eleven."

At eighteen years old, Ken didn't have to be home until 12:30 and usually left Tammy's house close to twelve to allow for drive time. Tammy knew if they left the track to go to her house, she would be stuck with nothing to do, able to hear the excitement nearby, but with no way to get back.

She knew Ken was cold, though, and hadn't planned on being outside without a coat or socks to keep him warm. Earlier, they had tended to her mom, who had been injured in a car accident a couple of days earlier. When some other family showed up to visit, Tammy took advantage of the additional mom-sitters and asked if she and Ken could ride over to the track and see what all the excitement was about. Her mom, surprised that Ken agreed to go, said it was all right with her. They arrived at the track a little before ten o'clock and had been there over an hour.

"This might be the last race, anyway," Tammy said loudly over the din of the revving machines.

The burst of sound as the high-pitched engines accelerated filled the night, stopping, for the moment, any possibility of further conversation. One by one, the carts slid around the dirt turns and sped along the straightaway as the wide-eyed spectators turned their heads in unison.

Tammy leaned on Ken, enfolding his thick arms around her for warmth as they watched the carts on the final lap. As the screaming carts rounded turn four and slowed to file into the weight stand area for the final check, another group moved out of the staging area to the starting line.

"I guess that wasn't the last race, darling," Tammy said, noting the continuing pit area activity. "There sure are a lot of people still here tonight."

"We could just go on now," Ken said determinedly.

"You'll just have to go if you're ready," she said, determined not to leave until the very end. "I'm staying. I'm going to tell Daddy I'll be here." She skipped away before he could protest.

Ken gritted his teeth. Dad gumit! This was just the kind of situation he hated. If it wasn't so cold . . .

Ken's sunburn made the November air feel much colder than it really was. He'd spent the afternoon, as he did most Saturdays, racing his boat with friends down at the river landing. Because of the unseasonably warm weather, the boys stayed longer than they had planned, but Ken had dutifully left in time to make preparations for his date. Following a quick stop at his house to shower and get his shotgun, he'd driven to Aynor, picked up Tammy, and gone to a turkey shoot. He wasn't in the mood for shooting, but a friend had asked that they drop by.

Ken had been glad when they finally got back to Tammy's house and thought they'd stay there to watch television and sit with her mom. But then Tammy wanted to go to the track, and he'd agreed, and now he was stuck. "Come on, girl," he said under his breath. "Do you have to stop and talk to everybody here?"

Tammy worked her way through the crowd to the concession stand, where her aunt was doing the bookkeeping. "Tell Daddy I'm gonna stay and ride home with Misty," she said, popping her head in the door.

"What's wrong, honey?" her aunt said without looking up from her task. "Isn't Ken here?"

"Yeah, but he's cold and I'm gonna get him to go on."

Her aunt looked into her eyes. "You kids aren't fighting, are you?"

"No, ma'am," Tammy said thoughtfully. "Not really. I don't want to go yet. And he's just being Ken."

"All right, I'll tell him, but we're fixing to get real busy tallying up, so keep an eye out."

"I will," she said, turning to leave. "See you later."

Tammy made her way through the crowd and found Ken talking to an old friend through the staging area fence. Seeing her approach, Ken said, "Now can we go?" loudly enough to turn nearby heads. Recognizing from the others' reaction that his question probably sounded like a threat, Ken lowered his voice. "This is the last race, you know."

Tammy dropped her head at the comment and stepped close to Ken. "I'm going to stay, darling. But I want you to go on and get warm." She tugged gently at his arm, trying to get him to turn toward the parking lot. "You're going to be so handsome in the morning leading the music and you don't need to catch a cold now."

Ken planted his feet. "I'll watch the last race and then we'll go," he said stubbornly.

Tammy pulled her hand away and looked at the track as the race began, purposely avoiding looking in his direction.

As the carts crossed the finish line several minutes later and yet another group filed from the staging area to the starting line, Tammy tugged firmly on Ken's arm. His skin felt cold and she thought of the heater in his car. He slowly relented to her insistent stare and moved with her toward the car, his arm muscles taut against the thin fabric of his shirt.

"I'll wait with you as your car warms up," she said softly. Ken unlocked Tammy's door and then hurried around to slide his shivering body onto the cold seat. He turned the key in the ignition and hunched forward, rubbing his hands together between his tightly clenched legs.

As they waited for the car to warm, Tammy leaned across the center console and lay her head on Ken's shoulder. Feeling his cool face, she placed her lips against his cheek and nibbled at his skin, coaxing him to turn toward her. Gently placing her warm hand on his cheek, she felt his resistance lessen. The teens kissed. Ken sighed as his body quaked from the cold and the mounting excitement of Tammy's warm embrace. Ten minutes passed as Ken warmed with the car. The couple talked, kissed some more, and made plans for the next day.

The Register family's church was meeting in a new building for the first time the following morning. Ken had spent Saturday morning putting the finishing touches on an altar he and his father had built for the sanctuary. The small church of thirty-five members relied heavily on member participation and always found that the Registers could be counted on when something needed to be done. Ken had also scrubbed floors at the church and made preparations to lead the music the next day for the opening service.

"Remember, it's Harvest Day tomorrow at my church," Tammy said, "and you're invited to come and eat with us."

"Yeah, I remember, but I don't know when I'll get out," Ken said.

"That's OK, call my house when you're ready to come and if I'm not there just come on to the fellowship hall."

"All right," he agreed. "Do you want me to call you when I get home tonight? In a little while?"

"Well," she hesitated, "I'll probably be down here until late."

"You be careful, now," he said sharply. "Don't get hurt."

"I won't, darling." She kissed his cheek. "I'm going back over now."

Tammy pulled away, got out of the car, and walked back toward the track. Ken watched as Tammy joined her waiting cousin, then he put his car in gear and backed out of the parking space. He looked at the fancy paint jobs on the sticker-laden vehicles as the heater blew hot air onto his face. He felt considerably better in the heated car than he had out in the night air. Reaching the edge of the lot, he looked at his watch and realized he had about an hour before he had to be home.

He slipped the heater down a notch, slowly pulled the car forward, and decided to take the long way home.

3

The party at the pond house was loud and crowded. Crystal Faye Todd didn't hesitate to say, "OK," when her friend Carla said she had to leave to make her curfew.

Crystal smiled weakly at a passing friend as she placed her unfinished beer on the counter and followed Carla to the door.

"You look like you're about lit!" the friend said.

"No," Crystal responded matter-of-factly. "That's the first beer I've had."

"Gotta go so soon?" the friend asked. "Y'all just got here."

"Yeah," Crystal said, looking back over her shoulder, "Carla's got to be home by 11:15 and I'm driving." She scanned the room again to see if Sammy had reemerged from the back with the girl he had brought to the party. He hadn't.

"Are you coming back?" the friend added.

"Maybe," Crystal said loudly, trying to be nice. She would definitely not be back.

"Try to, won't ya? We need to catch up." The friend playfully slapped at the boy who had his arm around her waist. "Stop that," she said, laughing. "I'm trying to talk to Crystal. Where'd she go?"

Saturday night had begun for Crystal like any other Saturday. After an early dinner with her mother's family in the nearby town of Marion, Crystal had set out in search of her friends and something to do.

In Conway, where there weren't a lot of organized activities, teens traditionally gathered together to see what the night would bring. That meant showing up downtown at Minnesoda Fats, a local teen hangout, or over at the edge of town, a couple of miles away, at the mall. The half-mile irregular loop around the town's only mall had, for several years, been a cruising spot and all the kids knew that if anything at all was going on, the mall was the place.

Crystal wasn't in a party mood but, having recently regained her driver's license, she got excited when she heard about a get-together at a friend's house outside of town. Not wanting to go alone, she killed time around the mall and waited until her best friend, Carla, got off from her part-time job at Belk's.

Crystal had originally planned to meet her cousin, Kevin. But that fell through when he started partying with friends and forgot to call. She also didn't receive a call from Jamie, a boy she had recently started dating. As a last resort, she thought she might hear from a young man from the nearby aviation school. Crystal and a girlfriend had on several occasions gone out to party with some of the trainees and one of them said he would call if he could on Saturday afternoon. When Crystal left with her mom around five o'clock that afternoon to attend the family dinner, she hadn't heard from anyone.

At nine o'clock, Carla emerged from the mall and saw Crystal waiting by her car in the parking lot.

"Hey, Carla," Crystal said as she approached. "How's work?"

"Hey, Crystal," she said, flashing a tired smile. "Feels good to be off."

Although the seventeen-year-olds had known each other since childhood, they had only become best friends over the last couple of years. Now, as seniors in high school, they found themselves almost inseparable on the weekends and had started making plans for what they wanted to do after graduation.

"You want to go out to Dana's pond house to a party?" Crystal asked.

"I didn't think she was going to have any more parties out there," Carla replied. "I heard she was real mad when the last one got out of hand and the house got trashed."

"Well," Crystal said, shaking her head, "that's what I understood, too, so I called her. It's a surprise party for her boyfriend. She said only a select group was told, but that me and you can come, providing we don't bring a crowd with us."

Carla looked at Crystal. "What do you want to do?"

"I guess I'd like to go," Crystal replied uncertainly. "I feel like I should do something now that I have my car back. That's where everybody'll be, probably."

Carla eyed Crystal suspiciously. "Including . . ."

"Don't say it! I don't care if he's there." Crystal shrugged and looked away. Carla waited until Crystal added, "I just thought he might be, is all."

"Yeah, whatever," said Carla, looking at her watch. "I'd have to call home first. They're expecting me to come straight on from work."

"No problem," replied Crystal, smiling. "Let's take my car."

Following a quick call to Carla's mom, who imposed an 11:15 curfew, the girls drove out to the country.

At the party, Crystal sat on a couch with Carla the entire time and made small talk. Carla's boyfriend was there, too, giving Crystal bits of free time to visit with several of the fifty or so teens at the party. Crystal talked excitedly with her closest friends about having her car back. A car meant independence in the spread-out, rural community.

Crystal had been without a car since a collision with a telephone pole three months earlier. She was arrested and charged with driving under the influence of alcohol. The police subsequently told her she could become an informant to clear the DUI charge, but she refused, saying she wasn't the type to "rat on her friends." The charge was ultimately reduced to minor possession of alcohol. She lost her driver's license, but got it back four days prior to the party. Once again, she was filled with pride over her beautiful car.

Though Crystal did her best to hide her feelings, she stiffened when Sammy arrived at the party with another girl. Crystal had known Sammy for about two years and had had her heart broken by him several times. Sammy was a charming user who hooked up with Crystal when it was convenient for him, most typically for quick sex, only to subsequently ignore or openly shun her. Carla disliked Sammy tremendously and often said so to Crystal. Crystal, in turn, would resolve to stop seeing Sammy, only to find herself back with him when she got the chance.

Crystal had seen Sammy the night before in Aynor and had a good time cruising around with him and a male friend. Carla was suspicious of Sammy's motives and was only slightly placated when Crystal told her she didn't drink or have sex with Sammy. Carla was nonetheless dismayed at her friend's belief that Sammy had treated her nicely, and the half-hope Crystal expressed that she might see him at the party and continue building with him what she thought could be a normal relationship.

Carla became angrier at the party as Sammy ignored Crystal and refused to acknowledge her presence. Sammy's date, apparently unaware of any connection between Crystal and Sammy, actually sat down on the couch next to Crystal. Sammy intervened by signaling to the girl, who got up from the couch and accompanied him to a back room.

Just before eleven o'clock, Crystal said, "Carla, whenever you're ready, we'll go."

Carla looked at her watch. "I guess it's getting close if I'm gonna get home on time," she replied. Turning to her boyfriend, she said, "We got to go now. Walk us out?"

Following Carla's lead, the teens moved slowly toward the door. The party was in full swing and teenage bodies packed the tight space as rock music blasted from the stereo.

"Just a few close friends, huh?" Carla said in Crystal's ear as they moved through the surging crowd. There was a good chance the party house might get trashed again.

Carla was already at the car and locked in an embrace with her boyfriend when Crystal arrived. "Carla, you said you have to go," Crystal sharply reminded her.

Noticing that a boy had followed her out, Crystal turned and told him, "We're leaving."

"I'm waiting on him," the boy said, gesturing to Carla's boyfriend.

"Well, we can fix that," Crystal said. She unlocked her door, got in, and said loudly, "Come on, Carla!"

"Jeez," said Carla as Crystal's car door slammed. "I guess we're leaving right this second." She gave her boyfriend another peck on his cheek before getting into the car. He stepped back as she closed the door.

"Crank it up," she said to Crystal. "I want to roll down my window." Carla looked at her boyfriend and laughed as he pressed his lips to the glass. She kissed the inside of the window, but quickly pulled her face away as the glass lowered.

"Hey!" Carla said, frowning at Crystal.

"You said you wanted your window down."

"Good gosh, Crystal. Don't take Sammy out on me." Carla looked back out of her window and waved to her boyfriend as the car lurched forward. Crystal drove through the yard and up the dirt lane lined with cars. Reaching the blacktop, the tires spun briefly as the new Toyota sped forward. It felt good to be back in her car again.

Carla rolled up her window and felt the backward pull against her seat as the car accelerated. "Well, go ahead, girl," she said with mock excitement. "Let 'er rip." Settling back in her seat, she shook her head and added, "You should have let some of that out in Sammy's direction. He's a prick."

Crystal turned into the mall parking lot just before 11:15 and pulled up beside Carla's car. Carla looked at her friend as she pulled her keys out of her purse. "What are you gonna do now?" she asked.

"I don't know," Crystal said. "I'll probably get something to eat or find something to do for a little while. I've got until 12:30 and I don't want to go home yet."

"You're not going back to the party, are you?" Carla asked. "Tell me you're not."

"No, no, I promise," Crystal said. "That would definitely not be the right thing for me to do. I'm sure I'll run into somebody in town."

As Carla opened the door to get out, she felt a strange sense of foreboding and turned around. "Crystal, be careful. OK?" Carla said.

"OK," Crystal answered. "I only had one beer, you know?"

"That's not what I meant," Carla said softly. "I just mean, be careful."

"Don't worry about me, Carla," Crystal said, breaking into a smile. "I'll be fine."

The two teenagers exchanged a last look before Carla got out.

Crystal waited while Carla got in and started her car. Satisfied that her friend was tucked in, she put her car into gear and pulled forward to the edge of the mall parking lot. At that moment, and certainly without realizing it, she made the most important decision of her young life. Checking her watch again, Crystal noted that she had just about an hour before she had to be home, and turned toward the shortcut to downtown Conway.

Crystal sat at the stoplight and searched her glove box for her new tape. The residential shortcut was quiet, which wasn't unusual at 11:30 on a November evening in Conway.

Elm Street is a quiet, tree-lined avenue that flows at one end past a collection of old homes, some with large front porches where townsfolk sip sweet tea in the late afternoons, waving lazily as neighbors and cars pass slowly on their way to and from downtown. Cracked concrete sidewalks, uneven from burrowing tree roots, set back from the road, bustle in the daytime with children on bikes and mothers pushing baby carriages. Elm offers a quick alternative to Main Street, a block over and littered with traffic lights. Teenagers race down Elm, slowing only where the road narrows to one lane to accommodate a particularly grand live oak someone long ago decided was too nice to remove.

Crystal looked up when she heard the horn and saw a familiar car. The blue Plymouth Sundance looked dark in the moonlight as it rolled to a stop, and Ken Register rolled down his window. After a brief exchange, Crystal parked her car, and, taking only her keys and leaving behind her coat and purse, got in with Ken.

Ken and Crystal had known each other all of their lives. They had dated for a short time in 1988, but during Crystal's last year in school had gone back to being very good friends. Because they lived only one mile apart, it was convenient for them during high school to occasionally attend social and school events together. For a short time, Ken gave Crystal rides to school each morning, but stopped when some of the guys on the football team insinuated that there was more to their relationship than just carpooling. Ken denied having any physical attraction for her and didn't appreciate his classmates' taunts.

He considered his relationship with Crystal to be more like brother and sister, rather than boyfriend and girlfriend.

It was Crystal, however, who stopped their dating. "I don't want to date Ken no more, Mama," Crystal had told Bonnie Faye when Ken asked her out again, six months before getting into Ken's car that night on Elm Street. "He stinks like cigarettes, and all he wants to do is have sex, so I told him no."

Bonnie Faye wasn't disappointed with her daughter's decision, even though she liked Ken and had originally encouraged Crystal to date him. When Crystal told her that Ken only behaved nicely at home, Bonnie Faye told Crystal she was right to not go out with him anymore. "The ones who are nicest around home," she said, "are often the ones that're the meanest when they're away from other people."

Ken and Crystal occasionally saw each other. Ken was very busy. He had a new job with Santee Cooper Electric, attended evening classes at Horry-Georgetown Technical College, and had a new girlfriend in his life, a young cheerleader from Aynor. What little social time he had was typically spent with her at school athletic events, go-cart races, movies, and church.

Still, perhaps just to be neighborly, Ken continued visiting the Todds, sometimes when Crystal wasn't there. One route into town took Ken right past Crystal's house. He stopped by the day Crystal went to get back her license, but refused her request for a ride to the Department of Motor Vehicles. After washing her car to get it ready to drive again, Crystal went into the house and told her mother that Ken had again approached her about dating. "He must think an awful lot of you to want to go with you," Bonnie Faye told her, "and him already dating another girl."

No one will ever know everything that happened on that night to place two teenagers, each with an hour until curfew, together in a car on a dark and secluded country lane. Crystal knew that Ken seemed to have successfully removed himself from the party scene in Conway. He no longer drank or attended rowdy parties. He had told Crystal's cousin, Kevin, to get a good girl to help straighten out his life. Whether he spoke with Crystal about her behavior is unknown. According to Crystal's friends, she, too, was trying to straighten up. They didn't think she had been very successful.

Perhaps Crystal climbed into the car with Ken to persuade

him to divulge how he had broken away from his old friends and old habits. Perhaps she was curious about how he avoided backsliding in the face of the temptations offered by the home-town crowd. Perhaps he had some new knowledge of self-control or self-restraint. Perhaps it had something to do with his girlfriend. Perhaps she was just lonely and needed some company.

The car seat barely had time to cool from Tammy's warmth before Crystal was strapped in and traveling with Ken to a parking spot just outside of Conway. Following Crystal's directions, Ken slowed the car and made a turn onto a two-lane dirt road that appeared as a shared drive between two houses. Driving quickly down the road and over a little bridge, he pulled into a small opening to the right.

The dirt lane amounted to little more than a path, with a grass strip running between two bare treads. Scrub oaks and pines standing in raggedy patches along the sides provided a sparse cover typical of land that had been cleared and allowed to grow back naturally. Beyond the trees ahead, they saw what, in the moonlight, looked like an open field. Seeing no other cars as they neared the end of the lane, Ken suddenly cut the ignition.

Crystal looked at her watch in the dim light of the car and casually said, "Remember, we don't have long."

"Yeah," Ken responded.

Within minutes, Ken and Crystal were kissing, but what probably began as consensual sex for the long-time friends went terribly wrong. Something happened to release a deadly impulse. Adolescent games, fueled by fears and fantasy, suddenly turned into a frenzied assault.

Minute after unending minute, sounds of torment filled the night as a bloodied knife thrust forward again and again, past an upturned hand placed futilely in harm's way as a pitiful defense against a young man intent on silencing her screams. Even after the life force was completely drained from Crystal's crumpled body, the night continued to bear witness to the savagery of an unspeakable depravity, ending not with a sated need as much as a childhood aversion. What was left was cast aside without concern, only to become someone else's nightmare. What was left would forever change the life of a community.

Horry is a large, predominantly rural county with several small towns and one long border on the Atlantic Ocean. Occupying an area about the size of Rhode Island, this now-easily-accessible part of the Bible Belt was isolated during the first third of the twentieth century by the numerous, largely non-navigable waterways and rivers that crisscross the land. The Independent Republic of Horry, as it is still known by many, afforded the earliest settlers a lifestyle free of outside influence and rich with self-sufficiency. Bridges, woods, and many churches dot the landscape to this day.

Located in the heart of Horry is the small town of Conway, the county seat, just fifteen miles inland from Myrtle Beach, a rapidly developing resort. Known for family fun in the sun, entertainment, shopping, and, more recently, as the place to play golf, Myrtle Beach has seen constant change over the past several decades as its population seasonally swells to hundreds of thousands of visitors at a time.

Conway has been influenced in various ways by the continuing development at the beach, but has retained much of its small town flavor, despite being situated directly on the main access route to the coast. Two large highways, from northern and southern South Carolina and beyond, converge in south Conway into one large thoroughfare that delivers most of the fifteen million or so visitors to the beach each year. One consequence of packing so many people into the narrow coastal strip is the inevitable traffic trying to get into and out of the beach on big weekends and holidays.

Conway has prospered by developing the clogged artery. Restaurants, service stations, Wal-mart, a mall, and major shopping outlets stand side by side, tempting the tourists who have plenty of time to look around. Critics fear urban sprawl is changing the character of their small, sleepy southern town. But Conway still has beautiful old residential areas with traditional southern homes, and a downtown historic district where locals gather to swap stories, attend to their business at the courthouse, and eat. Folks still know each other and most simply go about their business each day, having long ago gotten used to the steady stream of traffic along the southern rim of town.

Officer Wade Petty had been with the Horry County Police Department for less than a year but was, nonetheless, a seasoned cop. At 6'1", 230 pounds, the thirty-seven-year-old projected an image that police departments like for their uniformed officers. That, and his fourteen years on patrol with a department in another county, helped Petty fit into a complicated network of men and women who watch over and try to keep order in the coastal regions of South Carolina.

As part of his acclimation to the Horry County Police Department, Perry had been apprised of the tensions between eastern and western Horryites. Operating primarily in the vast rural sections of the county, he had to familiarize himself with each of the little communities and the names of the families who had made their homes there for many generations. Because many of the communities have names not recognizable to a post office, the task of finding one's way around, he had found, could become tiresome and, occasionally, frustrating. A dispatcher's advice to ask for directions could produce varying results. Many of the country folks, while not necessarily suspicious of the law, were self-sufficient and needed to know that the status quo would remain intact. They were hardworking, God-fearing people who had lived their lives with minimal interference, and that's how they wanted it to stay. All in all, Petty had managed. His attention to detail paid off as he navigated the two-lane blacktops and numerous dirt roads coursing through the countryside.

Petty was particularly interested by police records which revealed that most teenage boys and adult men living in western Horry County still carried knives. He knew farmers needed them as tools for a variety of everyday tasks. Knives are certainly useful for hunting and skinning game, cleaning fish, and woodworking, and for just about anything else that needs doing on a farm. The best knives for farmers are the combination knives with a variety of blades fitting into a case that can be tucked away in a pocket or worn on a belt.

He had also learned, though, that many of the farms around Conway had long ago been divided, sold, subdivided, and sold again and again. In the modern era of big business farming, most of the county's residents no longer made their livings off the land. Many of the smaller operations had shut down, and people had to leave the land they so cherished to find gainful employment elsewhere. Riding through the countryside, one now sees but a few dilapidated, graying skeletons of tobacco barns and smokehouses remaining among the modest brick homes and mobile home parks.

An interesting result of this, police records show, is that most confiscated knives are lock blades. A single, long blade, very sharp, possibly serrated, locks into place when opened and folds away only when released. Perhaps most alarming is that the knives are no longer considered tools. They are now considered weapons. Records further reveal that most of the ol' boys in western Horry County know how to use them.

On Sunday morning, November 17, Petty slowed his cruiser as he approached a black and white mailbox posted with the numbers he'd been given and pulled into the yard of a gray trailer home with lattice underpinnings. He noted no visible signs of disrepair, although the house looked like it was more than twenty years old. The yard was small and bordered on the front by a six-foot drainage ditch and down each side by a hodgepodge of shrubs. On the front and side of the house was a narrow, wooden porch. Less than fifty feet away and adjacent to the trailer house was an older, weathered farmhouse, partially shaded by four huge red oak trees. The farmhouse had an open front porch with two red wooden couches. A hand-cranked water pump rose from a four-inch black pipe. Behind the house, Officer Petty could see a converted barn sheltering a rusting automobile, and directly behind that an old, splintered, broken-through tobacco barn. An old white dog, positioned to soak in the morning sun, lifted his head and briefly eyed the officer.

Bonnie Faye Todd stepped out of the trailer house and greeted Petty on the front porch. Petty's first thought was that she looked as if she hadn't slept all night. She appeared nervous and fidgety. With her short, tousled gray hair and leather-tanned skin, she looked more like the grandmother than the mother of a teenager. Her eyes were bloodshot from crying and she smelled of too many cigarettes and cups of strong, brewed coffee. The officer identified himself, stepped into the living area of the home, and began the standard interview process for a missing person's report.

Bonnie Faye described Crystal as seventeen years old with brown hair and blue eyes. She thought Crystal was about 5'3" and weighed around 112 pounds. When last seen by her mother the night before, she was wearing blue dungarees, a print top, brown shoes, white socks, and was carrying a brown leather jacket. She was driving her 1991 metallic-blue Toyota Celica with the personalized tag C TODD.

Bonnie Faye mentioned to Petty that she had called several of Crystal's girlfriends earlier that morning. The girls were eager to help and had ridden into Conway and driven to all of the places where they usually hung out. They had found Crystal's car parked at Conway Middle School off of Elm Street. Now that Bonnie Faye said so, Officer Petty remembered seeing a metallic-blue Toyota parked in the schoolyard earlier that morning. He hadn't seen anything suspicious about it, though, nor did he mention it to Bonnie Faye.

At 9:15, the phone rang and Bonnie Faye excused herself to answer it. "Maybe that's Crystal," she said excitedly.

Petty scanned the room and saw a large portrait of a pretty teenage girl. *That has to be Crystal,* he thought.

Several minutes later, Petty and Bonnie Faye were outside in the yard when a blue Plymouth Sundance pulled up.

"Here he is," Bonnie Faye told the officer. "That's one of Crystal's best friends. I just bet he can help us find Crystal."

When the car stopped, a tanned, muscular young man with a sunburned face and sandy blond hair got out and walked across the lawn. He embraced Bonnie Faye and kissed her on the cheek.

"I'm Ken Register," the young man said, introducing himself to the officer with a firm handshake and a tentative smile. "I was on my way to church," he added, glancing down, referring to his attire. "I'm a friend of Crystal's."

"Oh, I'm so glad you're here, Ken," Bonnie Faye exclaimed,

hugging the young man tighter. "Crystal still ain't got home yet, so maybe you can tell this policeman where you think we might could find her."

"I can't tell you much," answered Ken. "I graduated from high school last year and don't hang around with Crystal and her friends anymore. The only thing I might could tell you that would help you is about a few parties I heard about last night."

Ken and Petty leaned against the Plymouth Sundance and talked for more than ten minutes about the location of those parties and where Crystal might have gone the night before. As they talked, Ken lit two cigarettes. He kept one for himself and gave the other to Bonnie Faye.

"I don't know too much about those parties or the people who go there because that's not my thing anymore," Ken told Petty. "Bonnie Faye called me last night and asked me to go help her look for Crystal, but my mom didn't want me to go back out in the night air because I had taken a cold. I told her what I had heard about the parties. I also told her I would call the hospital and see if Crystal was there."

"And did you?" Petty asked. "Did you call the hospital?"

"Yes, sir. I called," he answered, "but they told me there was no one by that name in the emergency room. Then I called Miss Bonnie and told her that."

"About what time was that?"

"Oh, about 1:15, or sometimes afterwards," he recalled. "You can talk with my mom. She was there with me."

The officer thanked Ken and wrote down his phone number.

"I wish I could tell you more, Officer," Ken apologized. "But I don't know anything about where Crystal was last night, or anything about those parties either."

Before leaving, Ken shook Petty's hand again, embraced Bonnie Faye, and told her not to worry.

"Crystal is probably at a friend's house and just fell asleep. I'm sure she's OK," he said reassuringly. "After church, I'll come back and help you look for her."

Bonnie Faye thanked him and said she knew she could always count on him to help when Crystal was in trouble.

"You're the best friend Crystal has ever had, Ken," Bonnie Faye said. "I just don't know what she would ever do without you."

After checking to make sure he had enough information to complete the report, Petty left the Todds', drove back down Juniper Bay Road into Conway, and went straight to the Conway Middle School, where the blue Toyota was still parked. The trunk and car doors were locked, and inside he could see a pocketbook and several dollar bills and loose change in the compartment between the seats. *There's no mistake about it,* he thought, *this vehicle has to be the one that belongs to the missing girl.* To completely satisfy his curiosity, Petty walked to the back of the car and read aloud the bold black letters on the license tag: C TODD.

6

The autumn weather in the coastal regions of South Carolina brings relief from the heat and the bugs of summer and is welcomed by town and country folk alike. The thinning of tourist traffic and the cooler and drier fall air signals a return to a more normal way of life following the seasonal work schedule of the previous months. The children are back in school, church activities that had been suspended for the summer are planned, and friends and family members visit each other more freely.

Many of the locals stay off the well-beaten tourist paths during the spring and summer months, avoiding the theaters and their favorite restaurants. The hot months are when many in tourism work nonstop and make a large portion of their money for the year. Others are simply too tired after commuting to work through the summer traffic to go anywhere unless it's absolutely necessary. Fall in a resort area signals the beginning of rest, much as the summer season does in other parts of the country.

Late summer and the beginnings of fall have an additional and special meaning for many citizens of Horry County. Men and women take to the woods in search of the elusive whitetail deer. Hunting for deer is a time-honored tradition in the South and is a family activity throughout the rural areas of Horry County, which has an abundance of the beautiful creatures. South Carolina has so many deer that drivers in the rural areas need to be alert, particularly at night, to the large animals feeding along the sides of the road and the real possibility that one might bound suddenly into the path of an oncoming vehicle.

Deer hunters using primitive weapons are allowed into the woods in August for bow season. Compound bows and black powder guns shooting .40- to .60-caliber balls require hunters to stalk and kill their prey at close range. The regular deer season, which allows hunting with long-range weapons, opens around the middle of September and lasts until January 1. It is one of the longest seasons in the United States. Hunters are then permitted to use big, scoped rifles in the .30-caliber range and to drive the deer with dogs toward other hunters positioned with shotguns. Going out into the woods, one sees trucks with empty dog boxes pulled over on the side of the dirt roads and can sometimes hear hounds in the distance, a sure bet that hunters are close by. Locals generally know better than to go in the woods in the fall without brightly marked clothing.

For many families, hunting is more than a pastime or a sport. It's a way of life that sometimes supplements the family food budget. Young children are taught to hunt and some actually bring home food. During the season, many families fill their freezers with enough venison to satisfy their personal needs with enough left over to give away or trade for other game meats. Local schools are aware that some teenagers miss school to hunt and that sometimes parents will even lie by saying the youngster was sick. The teens joke that you can tell the real rednecks by seeing who's missing from school on the first day of hunting season.

Sunday, November 17, 1991, started for the Allen brothers much as did any other Sunday during deer season: with preparations for the daily hunt. Lloyd, 24, and his older brother, Willis, were descended from a long line of deer hunters and had been active in the sport for as long as they could remember. Going hunting was as natural for them as getting up and going to work.

Both were skilled and had an unquenchable love of deer hunting. They often stopped by the wildlife and outdoor equipment store to swap stories with other hunters. Savoring every minute of the season, Lloyd and Willis routinely spent their days off in the woods. Signs of deer energized them and drove them toward the possibility of carrying home something like the big, 12-point buck they were sure had left a footprint etched in the sandy soil somewhere beneath the wooded pines and hardwood trees.

The day before, Lloyd and his father, Lloyd, Sr., had been outside of Conway slowly riding the paths and trails looking for deer. Even though they hadn't actually seen any deer, when the day ended Lloyd decided to go back the next day with his brother to check on some tracks he had seen in one area.

Stepping out the next morning, Lloyd noted with satisfaction that the air was crisp and the sky was blue. A perfect day for hunting. Lloyd banged on the door of his sister's mobile home. "Tell Willis it's time to go," he said when she answered the door.

"Tell him yourself. I think he's still asleep," she answered. Lloyd was glad she was already up.

Willis was in bed and Lloyd wasted no time waking him.

"C'mon, man. Let's go," he said, shaking his brother.

"Go on, now," Willis said, covering his head with the pillow. "Man, I ain't had three hours of sleep."

"C'mon," Lloyd said insistently, "time to go."

"Go on, man," said Willis as Lloyd pulled the pillow from under him.

"You're wasting time." Lloyd threw the pillow back at him. "I swear, I saw tracks down that dirt road, next to that open field. Let's go look and see."

"My dawg'gone girlfriend kept me up half the night on the phone," Willis complained, pulling the pillow back over his head. ". . . a wild hair about something. I told her I had to get up early."

"Man, that ain't nothing," Lloyd said. "Let's go, now. Quit wasting time."

Willis yawned. "All right, but I got to get in the shower."

"No, you're not either," said Lloyd. "Did you get those shells like I told ya?"

"Yeah, yeah," Willis said, sitting up and scratching his head. "That's them, on the dresser."

Lloyd grabbed the box of shotgun shells and checked the gauge. "All right, c'mon. I'll be in the truck. Don't make me wait. That big one's got my name on him."

"You wish," Willis said. He made a halfhearted attempt to get up, but curled back onto his side. When he heard the horn, though, his sister yelled, "Willis!" and he rolled to his feet.

"All right, all right," he said, "I ain't responsible for his noise."

Although he felt like hell, Willis quickly gathered his clothes. The brothers' routine was timeworn. They were going hunting, and that's all that really mattered. In less than three minutes, Willis was slipping his shotgun into the rack of Lloyd's rusted, long-wheelbase, blue 1976 truck.

"I need to stop by Tommy's," he said, sliding into his seat. "I'm starving."

"All right," said Lloyd, "I could take a leak."

A little after nine o'clock, the brothers stopped at a country roadside store, where Willis purchased a soda and a corn dog to eat in the truck on the way to Collins Jollie Road.

"Man, it's a nice day," Willis said, wiping his mouth with the back of his bare hand.

Lloyd abruptly turned the truck down the dirt lane leading to the open field where he and his father had seen signs of deer the day before. "Keep your eyes open," he said.

"This it?" Willis said while glancing at his brother, who was looking ahead at the narrow lane. "This is private, Beau."

"We're just looking." Lloyd drove slowly. The truck eased along, rolling from side to side as the wheels tracked through the dirt treads. Neither brother spoke, their senses tuned to the slightest indications that deer were around.

Willis was scanning the tree line of the scrubby woodland on Lloyd's side when the truck suddenly slowed and stopped. Looking at a darkened spot in the road ahead of them, Lloyd pointed and said, "Look at that."

Willis looked where Lloyd had pointed and reached out the window to unlatch the broken door.

"Looks like somebody killed a deer here this morning," Willis said, leaning forward for a closer look.

Lloyd turned off the truck and climbed out.

Willis had already spotted a blood trail. "Somebody musta shot one and he run off over there in that ditch," he said. Stepping across the lane, he followed what looked like drag marks.

Lloyd moved forward to where Willis had first stood. "It's a damn lot of blood, isn't it?" he said, looking at the large, damp spot. Several small pools of fresh red blood were near the center of the saturated area.

Willis stopped suddenly when he saw a shoe on a slender ankle sticking up over the edge of the ditch. He remained motionless as he stared at the shoe, confirming to himself that he wasn't seeing things. His eyes followed the shoe to an ankle and, ultimately, to the partially clothed body of a mutilated human being sprawled on its side in the dry crimson leaves. He turned his head and started to call to Lloyd when the nausea hit. As he leaned forward to release the soda and corn dog, Lloyd approached and said, "What's going on here, Duke?"

Willis gasped between heaves. "It ain't no deer, Lloyd, it's a dead body!"

"Man, you're lying to me," he said, stepping carefully around his brother for a closer look into the ditch. *Willis has to be exaggerating,* he thought. He quickly stopped, though, when he saw the shoe.

"What in the hell?" Inching up sideways, Lloyd turned his head to look over his shoulder. It *was* a body! He looked back at Willis, who stepped forward again for another look, his hand covering his mouth and nose. Both brothers were transfixed and stared into the ditch.

"Well, I have never . . ." Lloyd said. "You think it might be a woman?"

Willis gagged again and turned away. "I don't know anything about that, man!"

"Look at that shoe and the clothes," said Lloyd, leaning over the side of the ditch. "It's got to be a woman."

"Dang, man, get away from that." Willis leaned forward, and, with his hands on his knees, took a couple of deep breaths. Straightening up, he moved toward the truck and, after stopping to heave again, said loudly, "Let's go!"

Lloyd studied the scene. Blood seemed to be everywhere, mixing as clumps with dirt and leaves in and out of the cuts on her body and face. The hair was so matted, he couldn't tell what color it was. Her lower abdomen, maybe her stomach, had been cut open and her guts looked like they were hanging out. "Jesus," said Lloyd, "that person was butchered up like an animal."

"C'mon, Lloyd," said Willis urgently. "In case you ain't thought of it, Beau, somebody or something done that, and I don't want to be here if it comes back."

That was all Lloyd had to hear. Looking around quickly, the brothers hurriedly climbed back into the truck.

"Let's go, man!" said Willis, "Crank it up!"

"I'm going, I'm going!" Lloyd shot back. Lloyd spun the tires in the sand and backed out of the lane. Willis watched out of the rear window as Lloyd drove back down Collins Jollie Road. "Ain't nobody behind us," he said in a relieved voice.

"Good," said Lloyd, focusing on the road.

When they arrived back at their sister's house, the brothers practically gasped in unison. "Quick, call the police. You gotta call the police. We found a body down in the woods. Hurry! Before somebody else finds her, or maybe the killer comes back!"

The call went into 911 Emergency Dispatch at 9:10 a.m. Shortly before ten o'clock, the police arrived at the trailer home and accompanied Lloyd, his sister, and Lloyd Sr. back to the site where the body had been found.

Willis wanted nothing more to do with the dead body and remained in the back bedroom of his sister's trailer until the police left. When asked afterwards about the experience, he said, "I was too scared and had seen all of that body in those woods I had ever hoped to see. You go huntin' all your life, and you don't never see nothing like that. When I seen them guts hanging out, when I seen her split open like she was, I said to myself, 'Willis, whoever did this was sick.' You know what I'm saying? Just very, very sick."

PART II
THE INVESTIGATION

7

"**C**'mon, y'all, we'll be late," Bill Knowles said loudly toward the hall entrance of his home. "Can't keep the preacher waiting."

Knowles had been ready for church for several minutes, but he waited patiently for his wife and children. The 34-year-old detective leaned over and pushed around the crumpled sections of the newspaper. Reading the paper in the morning was a rare pleasure.

Knowles slipped on his coat, patted his pocket for keys, and took a last look in the mirror by the door. Straightening his tie, he thought about how well the weekend had gone. Though he was the homicide detective on duty, everything had been quiet. He had caught up on his chores around the house and then, though he had napped through most of it, watched a football game like he imagined ordinary people did on Saturday afternoons.

He grabbed his pager and whistled as he stepped out his front door. The newspaper was right. One week before Thanksgiving and the day would be in the 70-degree range with a clear blue sky. Knowles opened the doors to the family car and waited.

His wife emerged from the house and called after their children. Two teenage girls and a young boy hurried out in their Sunday attire.

Knowles pumped the gas pedal a couple of times and turned the key. The car cranked just as his pager sounded. He looked at the code and turned apologetically to his wife. "Honey, y'all'll have to go on without me," he said.

He got out and slipped his arm around his wife's waist. "I'm sorry, honey. I'll know more in a few minutes. I hope to be home for lunch, but I can't say yet."

"That's OK," she said, running her fingers under his lapels. "I'll call the station when we get back if we don't see you."

"I'm gonna call in," he said. "Y'all go on, though. I'll join you if I can, but don't count on it." He kissed her and felt a firm embrace.

She watched him walk across the yard. "Hey, Knowles!" she called out.

He turned. She smiled. "It was a good weekend," she said.

Smiling back, he replied, "Yes, it was."

He wasn't smiling a minute later when he called his office.

"We got something real ugly, Bill," the dispatcher said. "You just better come on."

"What do you mean, real ugly?" he said into the police car radio as he watched his family turn the corner at the end of the block.

"Well, it's an apparent homicide, but . . ." the dispatcher hesitated. "A young female . . . it's terrible. That's about all I can tell you now. The things I've heard . . . I don't want to be the one to start rumors. Just come on as quick as you can."

"I'm on my way," Knowles said. *Well, that's certainly curious*, he thought. *Doesn't sound like I'm gonna make lunch.*

In his heart, Knowles had been a detective since boyhood. Law enforcement was the only career option he had even considered. In his thirteen years of actual police work, starting during college, he had moved efficiently through the ranks from patrolman to detective, and, over the prior six years, had personally investigated over a hundred homicides. One of only three officers in his department to finish the special three-month FBI Training Academy in Quantico, Virginia, Knowles was considered by his peers to be a better than good detective. In a career where results meant everything, he got the job done.

Knowles liked using drive time to the scene of a crime to mentally prepare for his task. A homicide means looking at a dead body. Drive time, if used properly, allowed him to brace for the first shock of seeing the remains of yet another cruel and twisted act. A good bracing, in turn, allowed him to quickly move beyond that first jolt to the detecting part of the job. Knowles couldn't have known that this scene of the crime wasn't far enough out of town for a proper bracing.

Officer Petty stood in the middle of Collins Jollie Road and motioned Knowles to a parking spot outside the bright yellow police tape.

"Morning, Wade," Knowles said tentatively, noting the grim expression on Petty's face.

"Bill." Petty nodded. His eyes appeared dark beneath his trooper's hat.

Knowles moved past the tape to where Lieutenant Gilbert Lewis and Assistant Coroner Gerald Whitley stood.

"This is a mess, Bill," said Lewis. "Wade filed a missing persons report on a young girl this morning, but we don't know if this is her."

"What do we already know?" Knowles asked.

"Nothing, yet. Wade cordoned the scene and we just got here, too. Evidence is on the way."

The perimeter of the crime scene included portions of Collins Jollie on both sides of the mouth of the dirt lane where the body had been discovered. At the far end of the lane, Knowles saw yellow tape, chest high, tied to trees.

"OK, so let's have a look," he said.

Knowles looked with dismay at the narrow dirt lane. They'd have to work from the outside in to preserve evidence on the path. He carefully picked his way forward, stopping to focus his thoughts as he began encountering evidence of the homicide. *Something there,* he thought, *in the dirt, beside the pooled blood. Marks in the road . . .*

Knowles felt the anticipated shock through his forehead as he saw the foot sticking up beyond the side of the ditch. Moving down, to his left, he stepped over a clump of weeds growing in the bottom of the ravine and eased forward. He squatted to take in his first full view of the mutilated corpse. A numbing heat through his entire body quickly replaced the relatively minor shock of seeing the foot.

"Oh, my God," he said softly.

Knowles had apprised himself early in life of the rigors of his chosen profession and understood and accepted the unknowns. But even as a boy, he didn't like surprises. No matter how they turned out, surprises usually started poorly and usually got worse.

When he became a police officer, he had found out that the job included something that can only be understood by being there. The experience of homicide detectives with hard-core evil is immediate. They look at it . . . they smell it . . . they touch it . . . they have to explain it. They see and know things other people don't know, don't want to know, and usually wouldn't believe anyway. Because of his training, though, and particularly his experience, Knowles had begun to feel there wasn't anything he hadn't seen or couldn't handle.

Until that moment.

The warm, fresh stench rose and stirred his stomach, forcing his head to the side. Holding his breath, Knowles realized he couldn't estimate the age of the victim. In addition to the blood that drenched the hair and clothes, and the pooled blood in the road, the blood-soaked earth circling the body made Knowles think there just couldn't be any more blood in her body. *Someone certainly wanted this person dead,* he thought, *but it didn't take all this to accomplish it. This was . . . way too much. This was overkill.*

A mutilated body presents the worst possible scenario for the police. Family outpourings for the death of a loved one are terrible to witness under normal circumstances. But a murder can often be understood in context and accepted over time as a tragic consequence of human failure.

There is nothing, however, that compares with family grief when a loved one has been ravaged. The police, always on the front line, feel a tremendous responsibility to provide answers and bring a semblance of order to the ensuing chaos. There is intense pressure to solve the case quickly to avoid having a panicked community. A person who is capable of this roaming around free . . . *Well,* thought Knowles, *no one wants to think of that. And then there's rumor control. And then there's the press, they'll demand to be told something. And lunatics who want to claim credit for the crime. And the possibility of copycats . . . Dear God.*

Standing over the mutilated homicide victim that clear Sunday morning, Knowles experienced the palpable evil that the Allen brothers had felt just before they dashed to their truck and sped away. He recognized the evil as an unwelcome acquaintance, an intruder who sought to indiscriminately sow sorrow and despair. There'd be no dashing away for him, though. Knowles had bested intruders before and he would another time—this time. That was the oath he had taken. Besides, he knew the demon had probably already left a clue that would be his undoing.

Feeling the familiar excitement build and urge him into action, Knowles looked for a moment at the small, bloodied figure. "I don't know who you are yet," he said aloud, "but I'll find out who did this to you. I promise."

8

The evidence team, directed by custodian Kelly Chestnut, was responsible for going to Collins Jollie Road and observing the body and the crime scene before any evidence was compromised. By the time Chestnut arrived at 10:45 a.m., a few on-lookers had gathered around the crime scene's perimeter.

Chestnut's assignment was theoretically simple and employed a formula developed from previous murder investigations: examine, sketch, and photograph the body and the crime scene, then collect as much evidence as possible. Chestnut knew, however, that what was theoretically simple wasn't really always simple. As he opened the trunk of his car to begin assembling his tools, he noted with concern that the crime scene included a dirt road that had probably been traveled on since the crime was committed.

"Can't really say good morning," Knowles said to Chestnut.

Chestnut nodded to his colleague and placed two large cases beside the road.

"Everything looks OK so far," said Knowles. "Don't know about the path."

The two men examined the surface of the lane.

"Those boys that found her . . ." said Knowles, looking at some papers he was holding. "Uh . . . Allen boys, they drove in here, and again when they came back. Petty ran the tape out where you saw it on Collins Jollie. There were two cars in here then, parked end to end there. Then they backed 'em out. They didn't come up this far, though.

"Footprints, too. We've been walking along here," he added, indicating a single lane passage along the edge of the bushes. " 'Course, the Allen boys probably walked all over it. And there's a puke spot that belongs to one of 'em."

"What about SLED?" said Chestnut, referring to the forensic assistance provided by the State Law Enforcement Division, located in Columbia, about two hours away. Horry, like most other counties in the state, didn't have a forensic pathologist who could be called to a crime scene. SLED provided specialized teams consisting of experts in fingerprinting, imprinting, tool and murder weapons, and the identification of hairs, fibers, and other substances, that could be sent to a scene upon request.

"I talked to Chief Harris and he called and requested a team," Knowles said. "They said they would be here, but not before about three o'clock this afternoon. He and I agree that we need to go ahead. There's preliminary evidence of a sexual assault and the longer she lays out there, the less chance we have of getting DNA. As it is, our luck is good that those ol' boys found her as quick as they did."

Chestnut looked up at the blue sky. "Going to get nothing but hotter today, in the seventies."

"Yeah, we gotta get her out of there," Knowles agreed.

"All right, let's have a look," Chestnut said as he and Knowles turned to approach the body.

Most people think of crime scene investigations as involving a series of reasonably well-defined steps—which is true—carried out by people who operate like scientists, which is only partially true.

Homicide detectives begin with collected evidence and then construct hypotheses and draw conclusions. The process employed by the police to solve crimes is similar to the process employed by scientists to solve problems, but differs in a significant way. Scientists develop the hypothesis, or the educated guess about the way things work, then collect evidence that directly bears on the hypothesis. In other words, the evidence gathering process is specifically directed around the hypothesis, and the actual evidence gathered is determined by the hypothesis.

The police face a different situation. A crime about which little or nothing is known is committed, and the police have a limited amount of time to collect as much evidence as possible to gain clues about the crime. Since the hypotheses aren't formed and followed until after much of the data collection has already taken place, the police collect everything they can and

hope they have what they need as leads are developed and followed.

The police don't have the advantage that the armchair critics
have of knowing which evidence was important. Many blind
leads are often run down and exhausted before something important is discovered. Looking for quick results, the public rec-
ognizes the work as useful only when it results in a solution to
the crime.

Knowles and Chestnut both knew that a crime scene is cor-
rupted the moment somebody invades the space, changing
blades of grass, the dirt, even the air. The very act of studying
something changes it in unknown ways. Nothing is perfect.

Given that, Knowles knew Chestnut would do what was
needed. His confidence in the tried-and-true process employed
by the Horry County Police Department was borne out with
their ninety-six percent success rate in solving homicides in
1991, well above state and national averages.

The two men had worked side by side many times and understood each other's work habits without a lot of small talk.
But, so far, Knowles knew, and Chestnut was about to find out,
that this case was unlike any of the others they had worked.

Judging from the marks along the dirt road, the victim had
apparently struggled with the assailant before she was killed.
Drag marks to the ditch, approximately ten feet from the bloodstain, indicated that the victim was dragged to the ditch while
dying or dead, possibly to forestall discovery. The position of
her body in the ditch indicated the victim was thrown or heaved
into the five-foot-deep ravine. There were tire marks in the dirt
and sand on the rutted road, possibly including those of the
hunters who had discovered the body. The packed soil would
probably make tire and footprint identification difficult, if not
impossible. The lack of tire prints through the blood in the narrow road indicated the probable stopping point of the assailant.
The position of the bloodstain relative to the probable parking
spot suggested that the struggle had started in one spot and
moved to the murder location.

A gold-colored herringbone necklace, probably lost when
the victim's throat was slashed, was found next to the bloodstain. A gold-colored earring was found on the ground close to
the body.

The evidence team discussed the possibility of the crime being sex-related. The victim had been found with her belt and blue jeans unfastened and pulled down around her hips. Her shirt was pulled open and torn and, along with her bra, was pulled up, exposing her breasts. The buttons from her shirt were missing.

There was a large amount of blood on her face and a gaping three-to-four-inch opening across the throat area. The victim's throat had been slashed, perhaps more than once. Small, black insect pods were lodged in the fleshy, purplish opening. There appeared to be several stab and slash wounds in the breast and abdomen area. She had a cut on the stomach and a ball of inner body portions protruding from her body. The victim's body appeared to have bloodstained fingerprints on her left side, under the arm.

Thirty-eight photographs of the body were taken from several angles. The body and crime scene was videotaped. Plaster casts were made of footprints and tire impressions in the road, and small envelopes of dirt were placed in plastic bags. Four swabs were taken from the blood in the road and additional swabs were taken from a brick found in the gully along Collins Jollie. Also found were two condom packages and one condom, and a black and orange piece of material. Because the crime scene contained signs of a struggle, hair and skin from the assailant possibly remained under the victim's fingernails.

Mike Hill, the EMS dispatcher who knew Crystal Todd, was called upon to make a positive identification of the body. Hill was led past the yellow tape and the gathering crowd to the half-naked figure that was partially covered by leaves. He grimaced when he saw the bloodied and torn corpse. Her hair was matted with sand and blood. Ripped and bloodstained flesh dispelled any preconceived notions he had about being able to positively identify the body. He covered his face with his hand and felt sick to his stomach. Still covering his nose, he looked again. The thought of Crystal sitting beside him on his piano stool with her little fingers dancing across the keys suddenly seemed very remote.

"It looks a little like her, but I can't tell for sure," said Hill, his words muffled.

He took one last look and turned away, sorry he'd looked at

all. He couldn't help but admit to himself that it probably was her, but he silently prayed that it wasn't. Otherwise, his memories of Crystal as the bubbly, laughing little girl, eager to learn piano so she could help at church, would be gone. He would, until his dying day, remember her as the poor, pitiable creature lying awkwardly in that ditch.

Fearing the worst, Hill passed Officer Petty on the way back to his car and choked back his emotions. He whispered in a shaky voice, "You can probably change your report on that missing girl, Wade. I think she's just been found."

Later in the day, the crime scene team removed from the victim's hand a high school ring engraved with the name Crystal Faye Todd. Knowles instructed Petty to update the status of the blue-eyed, dark-haired, seventeen-year-old Conway High School senior, Crystal Faye Todd, from "missing person" to "murder victim."

9

Knowles mentally rehearsed what he wanted to say to Bonnie Faye Todd as he drove to Juniper Bay Road. He dreaded the task. He stared out the windshield, numb to the colorful leaf displays of fall in the country. From what he'd heard of the limited interactions the police had had with Bonnie Faye so far that morning, he knew this wasn't going to be easy. It never was.

When they arrived at the Todd house, Knowles, Petty, and Whitley sat in the police vehicle for a couple of minutes. Bonnie Faye had been alone when the dispatcher had called, but was soon joined by her nephew, Kevin James. The three men took James's arrival as their cue and followed him across the lawn and to the small porch. From her window, Bonnie Faye thought that perhaps these men in Sunday suits were bringing her good news about Crystal. She had no idea that one of them was the assistant coroner; she thought they were just policemen.

Knowles watched Bonnie Faye through the doorway as her nephew entered. As he searched her eyes, he watched for some sign of how she was holding her emotions together. The piercing worry was taking its toll on her. She looked rough. Her eyes were red and dry with deep, dark blue circles. She hadn't slept in many hours and her gray, short-cropped hair was unruly and matted. Her mouth seemed creviced with uncertainty. Her voice was deep and scratchy. She looked like a person who had been dealt a tough hand.

Knowles tensed and took a deep breath. "I'm sorry to have to bring you this bad news, Ms. Todd," he started.

"You've found my Crystal," she interrupted, looking into Knowles's eyes, "and she's dead, ain't she?" Knowles saw the last glimmer of hope fade as Bonnie Faye listened quietly.

"Yes, it is my unfortunate responsibility to inform you that your daughter has been found dead."

"Y'all better come on in," she said, her lips trembling.

Bonnie Faye offered the men a seat. Two of the officers sat on seat edges, while she sat back heavily on the couch. There was a long, quiet moment.

"Well, if she ain't alive, then I don't want to live neither," she said suddenly. Crossing her arms on her chest, she began rocking forward, her sobs punctuating the stillness as the detectives watched. Her cries slowly accelerated and became screams that stunned the officers with their force. Two of the officers stepped outside, leaving only Kevin James and Knowles to assuage the tiny, anguished mother as her misery filled the living room. For ten agonizing minutes, they sat helplessly, offering meager sympathies, feeling increasingly inadequate. When Bonnie Faye's cries finally subsided, Knowles knocked on the front window and the two men reentered the house.

Knowles told the grieving mother what little he knew about Crystal's death. He hoped Bonnie Faye could provide some of the information they needed so they could get started on finding whoever was responsible for the murder. The window of opportunity for solving the crime was closing with every minute.

"Crystal attended a party with a friend," began Knowles, "and then dropped her off at the mall to pick up her car. That was the last time anyone reported seeing her alive. That's all we know, and you told us that. Is there anything else, anything at all that you can think of?"

"Crystal always loved parties," she began, handing Knowles Crystal's senior picture. "She loved to talk to her friends on the phone and ride around with 'em on Friday and Saturday nights."

Knowles knew to let Bonnie Faye talk. People grieving will often vent their feelings by talking. A skilled interviewer can guide the conversation and get answers to questions already anticipated and more information that arises out of unexpected revelations. Knowles knew he needed to cultivate a good relationship with Bonnie Faye and, so, he would prompt her only a few times if he sensed she needed to be quiet. He was relieved as she continued talking.

"Crystal didn't like for boys or girls to be jealous of other friends, because she wanted to have lots of friends. It didn't matter—she loved children and animals, people of all ages . . . they loved her, too."

Knowles felt sorry for Bonnie Faye and was ashamed that he had no information for her about the killer. "It sounds as if she was a wonderful person," he offered.

The girl in the picture Knowles held was cherub-faced with dark curly hair, tanned olive skin, and a bright smile. Knowles reminded himself to give his children an extra hug when he got home that evening. The beautiful, happy teenager in the picture was so unlike the horrible corpse he had seen lying dead in the ditch just an hour earlier. He tried to block out the image of the slain girl and turned his attention back to Bonnie Faye.

She described how Crystal, as a youngster, could cook her own breakfast, complete with grits, eggs, sausage, and coffee. He listened as the proud mother described how handy Crystal was to have around, doing the shopping, cleaning, and always straightening up.

The officers were shown through the house as Bonnie Faye talked. Pictures of Crystal were on almost every wall. In one, she was a drooling infant; in another, she was a shy, innocent child; in still another, she was a vivacious, laughing teenager. Many other mementos and keepsakes were placed neatly around the house. Bonnie Faye would be reminded of Crystal no matter where she looked.

Bonnie Faye gave Knowles permission to look through Crystal's room. As she sat on the bed, the detectives moved through the small room. Crystal obviously was fond of clothes. Her closet and clothes chest were stuffed. The officers found the contents of her undergarment drawer curious, and Knowles exchanged a puzzled glance with Petty. All of her panties, bras, and lingerie items were fancy and expensive. Most were silky or satin and trimmed with lace and frills. They appeared to the detectives as the type one would find in a Victoria's Secret catalogue, not in a seventeen-year-old's dresser drawer. All kinds of teddy bears were on Crystal's bed, dresser, and the floor. Other items were ordinary and identified the occupant of the room as feminine and a high school student.

"Crystal especially liked to go shopping for clothes," Bonnie

Faye said. "She loved blue jeans, makeup, and jewelry, and she loved perfume and to smell good. She liked to go to parties, too."

Knowles picked up and examined an unopened pack of gum from Crystal's top dresser drawer. "She liked Big Red, too," said Bonnie Faye.

"Don't get me wrong," she continued. "It weren't all good times for Crystal. Her daddy was sick when she was a little ol' bitty thing, and she helped take care of him. She watched him die, ya know. It was so bad, I had to take her to the doctor and get somethin' on account of her nerves. She had a sick uncle and got a sick grandma, too. She lives next door. Crystal hauled 'em back and forth to the doctor for me. Both of 'em was crippled up real bad." Bonnie Faye's face turned ashen. Her eyes brimmed with tears. "Seems like all she's ever known was suffering."

Taking a deep breath, Bonnie Faye wiped at her eyes with a tissue. "She liked everything clean. That's why she cleaned this house all the time, did the cooking and the washing, the mopping. She even cut the grass. It was like she always wanted it. She didn't like for me to smoke, especially in her car. If I did, she'd clean out the ashtray right time we got home. She ain't gone with boys that smoke, either."

"What time was your daughter's curfew last night, Ms. Todd?" asked Petty.

"Her regular time was 12:30 and I got a good bit worried when she didn't at least call. I knew something had happened when she didn't let me know . . ."

The officers finished searching the bedroom, setting aside Crystal's address book, several items of paper, hand-drawn maps, and loose-leaf school notebooks.

"Is there anything else you can tell us, Ms. Todd, about your daughter, that would help us find her killer?"

"No . . . uh, nothin', but she used to be the assistant piano player in church . . . but she didn't want to no more. I believe some of her friends coulda made fun of her . . . uh . . . I don't know. She didn't like too many black people . . . she liked to go to movies . . . and eat out . . . and she didn't like anyone to stare at her when she was busy, which she got honest from me." Bonnie Faye was rambling. Knowles knew the interview was effectively over.

Moving again through the small house, he stopped to shake Bonnie Faye's hand and again apologized for the bad news. The three men left. Once inside the car, Knowles ran his hands through his thinning hair to the back of his neck. "You know," he said, "I can't wait to sit face to face with the sorry bastard who killed that poor girl. This could have been one of our kids, just as easily."

The three men sat quietly for a moment.

Bonnie Faye watched as the gray police car backed out of her yard and onto the road. Excusing herself to her nephew, she then walked back down the hall to Crystal's bedroom, opened the door, and stared inside. Although the detectives had thoroughly searched the room, nothing seemed to be out of order or missing other than the few things she knew that they had taken. Sitting on the edge of the bed, she picked up the phone and dialed her niece's home, thirty miles away in nearby Marion, South Carolina.

The day before, she and Crystal had agreed to ride to Marion on Sunday to eat dinner at her niece's. When Crystal didn't come home, Bonnie Faye had called her niece that morning and canceled. She had told the detectives just a little while earlier that she had gotten angry with her niece for taking the news of Crystal's absence so lightly. The niece, who knew Crystal well, had insisted everything would turn out all right, and that Bonnie Faye should just come to Marion. The niece assured Bonnie Faye that when she returned home, Crystal would be there, safe and sound.

Bonnie Faye sat on Crystal's bed and listened to the phone ring.

"Hello," Bonnie Faye said into the receiver. "I called to tell y'all . . . to let you know that the police just left my house . . . and, uh . . . they found Crystal."

"She's OK, isn't she?" her niece asked.

"No, she ain't," Bonnie Faye said, holding back her tears. "They found her dead . . . laying in a ditch . . . down in the woods somewheres."

Her niece gasped. "Oh, no, I'm so sorry, Bonnie Faye. We'll

be right there. Don't you go nowhere. Will you be all right 'til we get there?"

"Yeah, Deena's boy is here, Kevin. He'll stay with me."

"Oh, Bonnie Faye, I can't believe it. Oh, no, we'll be right there, honey."

When Bonnie Faye heard the line click, she looked around the room at Crystal's things. Holding onto the cord, she let the phone slip out of her hand. Her mind slipped back to the first day she and Crystal had a phone, just a couple of years before. They used to have to go next door to Crystal's grandma's house to make a call, but Crystal complained that she didn't have any privacy for her conversations with friends. When Bonnie Faye's boyfriend said that every teenager needs a phone, she finally relented, called the phone company, and had a phone line installed in Crystal's bedroom.

Bonnie Faye had admitted it would be nice to have a phone so she could reach Crystal at night. She worked the night shift at AVX, a microcomputer component manufacturing plant in Myrtle Beach, about a forty-five-minute drive from home. She hated to be so far away, but she had to work.

"I don't know what I'm going to do with her," Bonnie Faye had told her niece. Crystal had been resisting going next door to her grandmother's and uncle's each night. "She wants to stay home, by herself. I'm kinda 'fraid for her to do that, but I guess I ain't got no choice."

So, she decided to get a phone for Crystal. She made it a surprise, a present, and remembered how happy Crystal had been when she saw the phone. Bonnie Faye had never been phone shopping and was intimidated when she saw the large selection. But then she saw it: Bonnie Faye chose a princess phone for her little princess.

Bonnie Faye slid down off the bed and onto the carpet. She grabbed her hair, pulling at it with clenched fists, and started to sob. Her wails accelerated from a barely audible murmur to a heaving moan that shook her body each time she gasped for air. Stiffened legs thrust outward as her arms flailed and unconsciously assaulted the bed and floor. Her hand instinctively grasped the telephone receiver and she relentlessly slammed it to the floor, over and over, again and again, until she finally collapsed face down on the carpet.

Within minutes after Crystal's body was positively identified, word of her death spread through the rural community. The Todds' small trailer home was soon overrun with family members and well wishers who spilled into the yard and road. Trucks and cars parked up and down the drainage ditch, slowing traffic and forcing neighbors and late-arriving relatives to walk in. Rumors of the heinous nature of Crystal's death had already leaked out into the community and were fueled by the little information offered by the police. Just what had happened? No one seemed to know anything, but everyone had heard something. The location of the crime scene had also leaked out and some people jumped right back into their cars and raced off toward the Maple community and Collins Jollie Road.

A murder in a small town stuns the community. The rare event forces each citizen to face the possibility that life might not be so predictable. The close communication network buzzes with talk of whodunit. Townsfolk look over their shoulders and lock their doors. Regaining a sense of personal safety and comfort usually doesn't require much more than the quick apprehension and harsh punishment of the criminal. Citizens associated with the murder are affected, but the ripples tend not to spread far from the source.

But when the murder involves a young person, the fear is intensified and exaggerated. The murder of a child tears at the very social fabric of community life as each parent faces, at least for a moment, the question, "What if that had been my child?" Restrictions and curfews are put into effect, straining family relations to the breaking point. A heightened sense of suspicion tears away at community life.

The murder of a child in a small town came to Conway, South Carolina, on November 16, 1991. Only hours had passed since the discovery and the identification of the body when the collective voice of the stunned community started asking: "Why would anyone want to murder such a kind, sweet, fun-loving, innocent person? Why would anyone want to murder Crystal Faye Todd?"

10

Knowles returned to the crime scene and took a last look at the pool of blood. The surprise was over, he realized. The feelings of shock had passed. "I won't forget my promise," he said out loud, not as much to remind himself as to declare himself.

Taking a deep breath, he abandoned his inner focus and opened his senses to the outside world. He saw blue sky and the movement of evergreen branches as the wind blew the trees. A few birds flitted through partially bare branches. Dried leaves stirred in the hardwoods and rustled, then floated gently to the ground. The breeze on Knowles' cheeks brought an unidentifiable, yet familiar, blend of wood smells. *Winter's coming on,* he thought. *How appropriate.*

Carla Allen's father met Knowles at the door and asked to speak with him outside.

"I guess you're here to see Carla," he said, standing in the sun at the edge of the carport.

"Mr. Allen, we need to speak with your daughter about the death of Crystal Todd," Knowles said.

"We heard about it already. Tell me why you need to speak with Carla, if you would. She's pretty torn up right now."

Knowles understood his concern and appealed to him as a father. "I have teenage daughters that I would want to protect, too, but in this set of circumstances, I would want them to speak with the police," he said. "As you probably know, Carla was the last person that we know of to see Crystal alive, so it's critically important that we find out anything we can as quickly as possible. If it could wait at all, we would, but we just can't. We have to cover as much ground as possible before too much time has elapsed. And I have to tell you that we may need to speak with her more than once. If this thing resolves quickly, then maybe not."

Knowles looked closely at the concerned father and sensed he wasn't convinced. Rather, he appeared to be weighing the benefits of what Carla might know against the possibility of her getting more upset by the ordeal. Knowles took a calculated risk.

"Mr. Allen, I know people are already talking about the terrible way Crystal died," Knowles said. "But I can tell you that almost nobody really knows anything, and we, of course, don't want them to. This crime is going to require special attention the likes of which has never really been seen before around here. I've been a detective for years, but Crystal's murder is the worst I've ever seen."

Knowles allowed his words to hang for a few moments and then continued. "I'm going to show you something, sir, not to shock you, but to convince you that we absolutely have to speak to Carla about this. I apologize in advance, and you understand this is done in the strictest of confidence." He then slipped a Polaroid from his shirt pocket and offered it to the father. Mr. Allen took the picture and looked at it for a long moment. Lowering his head, he said, "Are you sure that's Crystal?"

"Yes, sir, there's no mistake."

"I understand."

Knowles put the picture back in his pocket and waited while Mr. Allen lit a cigarette and took several deep draws.

"Carla can't see that," he finally said.

"No, sir. She won't," replied Knowles.

"Under no circumstance."

"No sir," said Knowles. "You have my word that I'll do my best to protect her through this in every way possible."

"And I'll be with her at every moment. Do you agree?" Mr. Allen's piercing eyes fixed on Knowles.

"Agreed," Knowles said, resisting the urge to look away.

Carla was in the living room, crying on the couch with some of her and Crystal's friends.

"Excuse me, Carla," Knowles said softly, "I hate to interrupt y'all, and I know this is a difficult time, but I'm Detective Knowles of the Horry County Police Department and I need to ask you a few questions about Crystal."

Carla looked to her father, who nodded yes.

"Yes, sir," she said, her voice trembling.

"If the rest of you could just wait in another room for a few minutes, I'd appreciate it. We won't be long." One by one, the girls hugged Carla and stood up. When the room cleared, Knowles sat in a chair facing the couch. Carla sat beside her father and held his hand.

"I'm so sorry your friend is dead, Carla," he began. "I can understand what you might be feeling."

"Thank you, sir." Carla held a box of tissues in her lap.

"Carla, can you help us reconstruct last night so we can try to figure out where Crystal might have gone after you and she split up?"

"Well, you know she came by where I work. I work at Belk's at the mall, and she said, 'Let's go to a party out in the Punchbowl section, at a friend's pond house.' So I said OK."

Carla recounted for the detective the events of the early evening.

"So," said Knowles, "you then went to the party, at nine o'clock. Do you remember what you talked about on the way there?"

"Nothing, really, that I can remember. She said it felt good to have her car back. She was in a pretty good mood, I thought, at least until we got there."

"What happened then?"

"Oh, this boy was there, but he wouldn't talk to her. I told her he was no good, but she likes . . ." Carla caught her mistake and started sniffling again. A tear rolled down her cheek. Mr. Allen put his arm around her and looked at Knowles.

"I'm sorry, sir. I don't mean to cry."

"You're doing fine, Carla. You take your time."

"She liked him a lot for some reason," Carla continued. "I never could figure out why. Sammy Byrd is his name. He was there with another girl and didn't even say hello to Crystal. The girl even came and sat on the couch where we were, right beside Crystal. But I don't think she knew anything. Crystal certainly didn't say anything to her. It was shortly after that that

Crystal told me she was ready to leave whenever I was. So when I told her a few minutes later I needed to go to get home on time, she jumped out and practically ran out the door."

"What time did you leave the party, Carla?"

"I was supposed to be home by 11:15, but I was a little late. We left at eleven o'clock and got back to the mall to my car at 11:13, according to Crystal's clock. And then I came home."

"So, you say Crystal was upset by seeing Sammy. And she didn't talk to him or argue with him at the party?"

"No, nothing. That's what upset her. She saw him the night before in Aynor and rode around with him and a friend of his, I don't know who. She said he was real nice to her then. I think she went to the party hoping to see him."

"Was there anyone else there that Crystal talked to that she might have wanted to see later?"

"Nobody that I saw."

"She didn't have words or anything with anybody that you know of?"

"No, sir. Nobody really seemed to pay much attention to her at all so we just left."

"Was Sammy still at the party when you left?"

"Yes, sir. He went into the back of the house with his date earlier on and that's the last we saw of him."

"Do you remember what you talked about on the way home?"

"Just the regular. I tried to get her to not be upset over Sammy. I thought she was some better, 'cause we laughed a little." Carla's eyes again brimmed with tears. "I knew she was sad, though."

"Did Crystal say anything to you about what she was going to do when she let you off?"

"No, sir, she usually likes to eat or something like that. She didn't have to be in until 12:30, and she just said she was going to look for something to do. I don't think she wanted to be by herself. If I had just . . ." Carla's voice trailed off.

Knowles hesitated, unsure whether to continue.

"Is that all?" she suddenly asked.

"One last question is all, Carla. Do you know anybody that Crystal hung around with that would do anything like this, like maybe somebody in a gang or a cult of some kind?"

Carla gave the detective a puzzled look and turned toward her dad. "No, uh . . . I don't understand the question." Carla hadn't been told the details of the murder and believed Crystal had been run over by an automobile and left to die in a ditch. She wouldn't learn how her best friend had died until the visitation at the funeral home.

"I wish I could help you, but I don't have any idea who would want to kill Crystal. She had so many friends." Carla covered her eyes. Unable to hold back her tears any longer, she sobbed and buried her face in her father's shirt. Knowles stood, thanked them, and excused himself. He didn't have much, he knew, but it was still very early in the investigation.

Later, Knowles visited Kelly Chestnut of the evidence team.

"Give me some good news, Kelly," Knowles said hopefully.

"Well, I hope I can," he said. "We got some loose hairs, including some dark pubic hairs, looks like, and some clothing fibers. There weren't any obvious signs of sexual assault, besides what you saw, but the full autopsy will determine that. We completed a rape kit, including vaginal, anal, and oral swabs, and fingernail scrapings from fingers on both hands, for forensic analysis in Columbia at SLED's new lab."

"When's the autopsy?"

"She'll stay in the freezer at the morgue tonight, and then go to Charleston to the Medical University tomorrow morning for the full deal."

Knowles knew that state law mandated an autopsy for any wrongful, or even suspicious, death.

"You going down for that?" he asked.

"Oh, yeah, a couple of us will."

"What about prints, Kelly? Were those prints on her that we saw?"

"Not enough ridge detail," he said. "Looked like a palm and a couple of partials, but we got nothing."

"What about the car?"

"Nope, doesn't look like anything there, either. You know, the family went and got it and drove it home before we found her. But it hadn't been wiped down or anything."

"I guess that about does it for now, Kelly," Knowles said as he closed his notebook and looked at his friend. "How does it look to you?"

"It looks OK, Bill. We've got some solid stuff to go on, and then, of course, we hope the forensic analysis will tell the tale."

"Yeah," replied Knowles. "Maybe it will."

Knowles went to his office and sat down. So far, he thought, it'd been a hell of a day, and it wasn't over yet. "What have I missed?" he said to himself as he went over the case from the beginning. He spent the next hour poring over his notes and preparing assignments. The homicide task force would meet together for the first time at the crack of dawn. Apparently, there were plenty of leads.

Satisfied with the progress so far, he allowed a nagging thought in the back of his mind to crawl forward. Somewhere out there, on the street, was a maniac. Even if it was a first-time experience for the murderer, going through the actual motions of the kill might have stirred something evil deep inside him. Knowles added books on sexual and fantasy killing to his list of materials to read immediately.

Maybe it was more than one person, he thought. *Two maniacs!* This type of crime, he admitted to himself, definitely put him and his colleagues in new territory. *Thank God for SLED. Whoever did this was going to remain unknown to the police and the public for . . . for how long?* he wondered. *Maybe he'll just walk in and give himself up. Fat chance. No, whoever did it was probably either very scared or not worried about it at all.* He contemplated the difference and couldn't decide which would be better. The scared first-timer would make errors of judgment and give himself away. The hardened sociopath usually identified himself in other ways, typically through carelessness. The first-timer might be panicking and thinking he had made a very big mistake. Knowles wrote "motive" with a big question mark on his list of things to think about.

Whoever committed the murder was still out there. The thought of another mutilated teenager sent a shudder through Knowles. He stood abruptly.

I need to call my wife, he thought. *It's going to be a long night.*

11

Southerners traditionally flock to the home of the bereaved to help ease the family's suffering and facilitate the healing process. This formalized etiquette of condolence allows all those affected by the loss to reconnect with the departed through shared pain and regret, to offer what comfort they can to the family, and, in return, to find absolution for the guilt from what they should or could have done.

Carla needed nearly an hour after speaking with Knowles to compose herself enough so that she could visit with her deceased friend's mother. Bound by the loyalty of true friendship, she was determined to speak with Bonnie Faye and express her sorrow.

"What will I say to her?" Carla asked her father as they traveled the long stretch of open road to Juniper Bay. "I feel like it was my fault. If I had just done something different . . . asked her to spend the night, something, just anything but what I did."

Carla's father ached from his daughter's distress and sat quietly while she condemned her behavior of the previous night. Choosing his words carefully, he said, "Carla, honey, one of the things that we love about you so much is your ability to feel so deeply for your friends and those you love. But you know you aren't any more responsible for her death than you are for the behavior of the one that killed her."

"I know you're right, Daddy, but I just can't believe this is happening," she said. Carla sat and sniffled as her father reached and reassuringly patted her on the shoulder.

As they approached the Todd residence, Carla saw vehicles parked on and around the yard. "Aw, Daddy, this doesn't feel right," she said anxiously. Carla hadn't counted on so many people being there. She chewed nervously on her bottom lip.

"What do you want me to do, honey?" her father asked quietly. "We can come back another time." Slowing the car to a crawl, he calmly waited as his daughter eyed the people standing in the yard and on the porch.

"No, I want to go be with Bonnie Faye," she said decisively, holding a wadded tissue to her nose.

"All right, I'm right here with you, honey. I'll pull around the back of the house. Less people will see you go in."

Carla got out of the car. A familiar voice surprised her at the door. She saw Kevin James standing by the shrubs bordering the back of the house, as well as the silhouette of another person kneeling in the bushes.

"Hey, Carla, how's it going?" Kevin asked.

"Hey, Kevin. OK, I guess, considering the circumstances." Carla smiled weakly, recognizing that the depth of his loss matched her own. Looking down toward the kneeling person, she asked, "What are you doing? Who's that?"

"Oh, that's Ken, throwing up in the bushes."

"Ken? Is he sick?"

"Yeah, said some lady gave him some punch that made him sick." Kevin approached the stairs where Carla stood.

"Is there anything I can do?" she asked.

"Nah," he replied. "Ken's a big boy. He can take care of himself."

Carla felt close to Kevin and the two expressed their heartfelt sentiments for their lost friend. They were among the last people to see Crystal alive and felt an unaccountable responsibility for the events surrounding her death. Kevin was heartbroken about not contacting Crystal as he had planned and prayed for forgiveness for his sin of omission. Carla was heartsick for not altering the course of Crystal's last movements and prayed for forgiveness for her sin of commission. Both understood, though, that their anguish was but a shadow of the misery Crystal's mother had to withstand. They agreed it was time to visit Bonnie Faye.

With Kevin close on her heels, Carla moved past the people blocking the doorway and walked into a thick cloud of cigarette smoke being pushed around the room by an overhead fan. Rubbing her eyes, she worked her way through the living room and into the kitchen, where small card tables had been set up to hold the overflow from a kitchen table covered with casseroles, various meats and breads, an assortment of pies and desserts, pitchers of sweet tea, liter bottles of soda, and a four-quart urn of black coffee.

"Wow," said Kevin, in surprise. "There's enough here to feed an army."

Carla nodded. "And any other time I'd have made a dent in it myself," she said.

"I know exactly how you feel," Kevin agreed.

Kevin and Carla remained positioned by the kitchen door and talked for more than an hour to each other, classmates, and friends. Bonnie Faye had taken sanction in Crystal's room and people walked back to pay their respects and share in her affliction.

Carla recognized Shirley and Kim Register as the mother and daughter filed through the front door and moved toward the kitchen. Although Carla didn't know Ken's mother well, she had seen her numerous times at ball games and school functions.

"Hello, Mrs. Register," Carla said.

"Hello," Shirley said, barely above a whisper. "I brought these casserole dishes. Would you mind sitting these on the table for me?" Handing the dishes to Carla, she then opened her arms and summoned Kevin to her for a hug.

"Thank you, ma'am," he said, embracing her warmly. "We appreciate you coming over." Kevin took Carla's arm and pulled her closer for introductions. "We're close, you know, this lady and I," he bragged to Carla. "Why, I practically lived over at their house for a while when my family was going through some rough times."

"What do you mean practically?" Shirley said, grinning. "You did live over at my house."

"I know, you were like a second mom to me," Kevin acknowledged. "I don't know what I would have done without y'all."

Shirley wandered to Crystal's room, where she found Bonnie Faye flanked by teenagers and talking on the phone. Two of the teens were Ken, her son, sitting on the floor adjacent to the bed next to Bonnie Faye, and Ken's girlfriend. A hush fell over the room as Bonnie Faye waved her arm for everyone to be quiet.

"Now, which one of the brothers are you?" Bonnie Faye asked into the phone. She was talking to the Allen brothers, who had discovered Crystal's body.

"And when was it you found her?" The grieving mother, desperate for information about her daughter, repeated out loud, word for word, everything the Allen brothers told her.

"Younguns, he says she was butchered like a hog," Bonnie Faye said while Ken and the others listened intently.

Shirley motioned to Ken that she was leaving. Ken immediately excused himself and followed. As Ken watched his mother and sister drive away, several friends, including Kevin, came out of the house, talking animatedly.

"Hey, Ken," called a friend. "We're gonna ride over to Collins Jollie, where they found Crystal this morning. Want to go with us?"

Ken hesitated. "No, I don't think so," he said. "Y'all go ahead."

"How come you don't want to?" asked Kevin.

"I just don't," he replied. "I don't think I can handle it."

12

Sunday evening, Knowles and his partners went to the Coastal Mall, the last place Crystal was seen alive, and found teenagers parked in cars and trucks and riding around the parking lot. Several years earlier, the mall had inadvertently become the place to go and Knowles hoped some promising leads could be developed.

The Coastal Mall is an outdoor shopping center with awnings that make it appear enclosed. The cluster of stores, centered in the middle of a large piece of land on the edge of Conway, is surrounded on all four sides by parking lots. Through the haze of dusk, it resembled an island of brick and glass floating in the middle of an ocean of concrete and black asphalt. Knowing the area as the perfect spot away from the beach to cruise, young folks from all over the county drove in to make the loop around the perimeter, honk their horns, and blast their music.

As they entered the parking lot, the detectives noted that the festivities were like any night, despite the tragedy of that morning. They showed the teenagers pictures of Crystal and her car, but none of them remembered seeing her on Saturday night. One of Crystal's classmates gave the detectives the name of one of Crystal's last boyfriends, Davey. Davey lived in Aynor and drove a black, two-wheel drive Chevrolet truck with SS written in red on the side.

"If he had wanted to get hooked up with Crystal," the teenager told the detectives, "the place to find her would most likely be the mall. That's where everybody goes that goes anywhere in Conway. They usually end up there, or go by there on the way to somewhere else. Or they might stop by there on their way going back home."

According to Crystal's classmate, Davey had a mean streak

and was known to get violent. She had heard a rumor that he was at the party Crystal had attended the night before, and that he and Crystal had been seen arguing. She said that Davey wanted to get into a deeper relationship, but Crystal had turned him down.

The detectives left the mall and radioed ahead to the Aynor Police with a description of Davey and his truck. By the time they rolled into the small neighboring town, the Aynor police had already found Davey riding around and had asked him to follow them to the station for questioning.

During the interview, Davey appeared to be very nervous and made limited eye contact with the detectives. He said he had called Crystal at about 1:30 p.m. on Saturday and asked her out for a date, but she refused, saying she had other plans. The last date he had had with Crystal had been two or three weeks earlier, when they went to a movie. He had been dating another girl, who he had seen the night before.

Davey had a pocket knife in his right rear pocket and gave it to the detectives. He also let them search his truck. The officers noted that while the outside of the truck was very clean, the inside was absolutely immaculate.

"Sir," the officer asked, "when was the last time you washed your truck?"

"Uh, last night about dark," he answered.

"Do you always clean your truck so thoroughly?" the officer continued.

"Yes, sir," Davey responded without hesitation. "Taking good care of my ride is important to me."

When they searched behind the seat, the detectives found a condom package in a cup and a wooden hammer handle partly wrapped in duct tape.

"Sir, we advise you not to plan on going anywhere for a couple of days," the officer said. "We are giving you a receipt for your knife and want you to come and see us at the Horry County Police Department to answer a few questions about Crystal Todd. Do you think you can do that for us?"

"Yes sir, I think I can," he answered.

Davey was interviewed at the Horry County Police Department on November 25, 1991, eight days after Crystal's death. He said he had first met Crystal four years earlier at a homecoming football dance at Conway High School. She was about thirteen or fourteen years old, he remembered, and he had given her a ride home from the football game.

The next time he saw her, she was seventeen. She told him she didn't have a driver's license, but had taken her mom's car anyway and driven it to Aynor. Davey said he liked her immediately for that, so he asked for and got her phone number. He thought she was a rebel, cute and funny, and a lot of fun to be around. They started dating, going to the movies and riding around, but agreed not to tell anyone, so as not to upset the people Crystal and Davey were also seeing at that time.

When Davey was on vacation from work, he drove to Crystal's home every morning and picked her up for school. Because Crystal would still be sleeping when he arrived, he'd knock on her bedroom window, and she would open the door and let him in. He told police he would sit on the sofa in the living room while she took a shower and got dressed.

He said one day Crystal walked into the living room dressed only in her underwear. She was carrying her clothes and told him she was going to take a shower. It was hard to resist the temptation, he told police, but he did. Crystal's momma worked at night and didn't come home until after Crystal had gone to school, and he surely didn't want her to come home and catch them in a compromising position. Crystal's mother was very strict with her, he said. When they dated on the weekends and he brought Crystal home, Bonnie Faye would cut the porch light on and off, on and off, as a signal for Crystal to come inside. Davey told police he was no fool. He was twenty years old, three years older than Crystal, and knew he could get in serious trouble with her.

When he went back to work, he called her every morning to wake her up for school and continued calling her two or three nights a week. But, he told the police, over the last couple of weeks, something had happened to Crystal. She had changed somehow.

"I called her one day and her mother answered the phone," Davey explained. "When I asked for Crystal, her mother said, 'Is this Jamie?' And I said 'No.' Then, she said, 'You sure it ain't Jamie?' And, I said, 'No, this is Davey,' to which she said,

'Oh, hey Davey, Crystal just stepped out,' or something like that, so I figured some guy named Jamie had been calling her. I heard Crystal had been going out to the airport a lot to see some guys out there. I kept calling during the week, but Crystal was always gone. I knew she didn't have a license, so she couldn't be driving nowhere. Her mom, who hadn't been home much before, now started answering the phone and saying she wasn't there. When she didn't answer, nobody answered at all, even late at night. When I did finally talk with her mom, she told me that Crystal had been going out with her girlfriend."

When the detectives asked Davey to describe Crystal, he thought for a moment and said, "She liked to party and see a lot of her friends. She liked to drink a beer, ride around, and listen to heavy metal music. I heard she had smoked pot and talked a lot about tripping on acid, but you know how rumors go. She used to tell me, 'I want to be eighteen, I want to be free to go to a Metallica concert if I want to, and I want to go where I want to when I want to.' She was the type of person that was always wanting to go, sitting on ready to go, but her mom was so protective of her she couldn't ever do the things she wanted to do."

Citizens of Horry County found out about the murder Monday morning, November 18, under a headline in the local newspaper: "Conway Teenager Stabbed." The report, which identified Crystal as a high school student and indicated she had died from "multiple stab wounds," was shocking and, predictably, sent ripples of fear through Conway. The idea that someone from the small community could actually be stabbed to death and left on a dirt road was difficult enough to comprehend. The murder of a "young, innocent" high school senior, a "personable, well-liked, bubbling, and enthusiastic" seventeen-year-old, a "very caring and special person," someone who "didn't have any enemies in the world," as the paper described her, seemed unfathomable.

That morning, the overwhelmed guidance counselors at Conway High School had to be assisted by extra volunteers and professionals as they tried to help Crystal's classmates deal with her violent death.

"All of us are having a difficult time today dealing with her death," a friend said as she wiped tears from her swollen eyes.

"We just can't understand why this had to happen to Crystal, of all people. Everybody loved her."

The police met in full force for the first time early Monday morning in a portable unit next to the Horry County Police Department and behind the county courthouse. The cramped space would become the center of operations for the case and support the large number of detectives and SLED agents assigned the top priority task of finding Crystal's murderer. Each day would begin with assignments and end with a summary of what had been accomplished.

When the meeting began, Knowles backed away from his desk, stood up, and quieted the room. He was all business as he addressed the police officers in a solemn voice. Team members were informed that the investigation would begin with a canvass of Elm Street and the Conway Middle School, where Crystal's car was found parked early Sunday morning. Someone might have seen something, but been reluctant to come forward. He reiterated the standard message of how important it was to secure solid leads in interviews with the residents. They had evidence collected at the crime scene, but they needed more. They hadn't found anything important in Crystal's car, and the results of the autopsy in Charleston wouldn't be available until late in the week. Knowles was confident the forensic analysis would produce information vital to the case, but wouldn't supplant the need for effective legwork. While they waited, they could concentrate on reconstructing the last day, and particularly the last few hours, of Crystal's life.

The long opening day for the homicide task force was the beginning of routine sixteen-hour days as the investigation unfolded and leads multiplied. On Tuesday afternoon, Chief Harris called a press conference and asked anyone who had information on the case to come forward. While refusing to answer questions concerning the murder weapon and how many times Crystal had been stabbed, he did reveal that the coroner said she had bled to death from numerous stab wounds.

"It is the most brutal crime some of my men have ever seen," Harris said. "We have questioned more than one hundred people and we are going on the theory that everyone is a suspect. Suspects are being eliminated one by one and all we can say is we believe Miss Todd was killed by someone she knew because she was not the type of person who would pick up and go off with someone she didn't know."

Bonnie Faye was at the press conference, clutching the hand of her stepson. When given an opportunity to speak, she choked back her tears. "When they killed Crystal," she said, "they took my whole life away from me."

More than 1,500 people attended the open casket visitation Tuesday night at Goldfinch Funeral Home in Conway. The flow of mourners was so heavy that doors had to be propped open and traffic directed in one way and out another. Someone remarked that every teenager from Conway High School was at the funeral home.

Over the years, Bonnie Faye, Crystal, Bonnie Faye's mother, and Crystal's aunts had been regular visitors to the funeral home, attending funerals as often as once or twice a month to pay their respects to deceased friends and neighbors. Many of the employees at Goldfinch knew and liked Bonnie Faye and were especially fond of Crystal.

"Crystal was such a lovely child," one employee remembered. "She would always come with her mother. She was so shy that when I hugged her and kissed her cheek, she would wipe the kiss off with her hand. You know, I think when she was a teenager she would still wipe my kisses off."

Friends and classmates talked about how good Crystal looked lying in her casket. Many of the teens had heard stories about how Crystal had been sliced up and beaten, possibly by a Satanic cult, and left to die in a ditch with her guts hanging out. Now, to their amazement, she looked as if she barely had a scratch.

Carla had been told that Crystal hadn't been run over by a car and left to die in a ditch, as she had previously been led to believe, and finally understood Knowles's question about Crystal's involvement with cults. But what she had heard from her friends was much worse.

"When my friends told me that night that she had been killed and cut up by a Satanic cult, I was scared to look at her," Carla recalled. "That was the hardest thing I ever had to do in my entire life. I was like in shock. I couldn't even talk when I saw the casket sitting there. I was very angry. If all of these things I'd just heard were true, then I couldn't believe they would have the top of her casket open and her body right up there for everybody to gawk at. I heard her face was skinned off, so you can imagine why I was afraid to look at her. I now know that all that stuff people were saying about her and the way she died wasn't true. But, for a while there, I didn't know what to believe."

Seeing Crystal's body displayed before them, the mourners began to believe that the many rumors about her being mutilated were untrue. She obviously hadn't been quartered or skinned. Her eyes hadn't been gouged out and her arms hadn't been ripped from her body. Her internal organs hadn't been removed by a Satanic cult.

Crystal was as pretty as ever as she lay in wake. Her sparkling blue eyes, however, were closed and sewn tight. The laughter that had brought cheer and sunshine to those around her was silenced forever. Those who knew Crystal found it incomprehensible that she could be dead.

For the police, Crystal's death remained a mystery with too few clues. Knowles was convinced that the killer was someone Crystal knew and that he would be at the funeral home to avoid arousing suspicion. The investigative team attended the visitation and quietly observed faces for signs of nervousness and guilt. But there were no further leads. No one had seen anything that seemed even remotely illuminating. Knowles left the funeral home a frustrated man.

Crystal's funeral at High Point Baptist Church was attended by more than a thousand people, requiring the use of an outdoor public address system. The loss of Crystal and the way she had died overwhelmed her family.

"I feel Crystal had the God-given right to live," cried Bonnie Faye to a reporter, "and I'm angry that that murderer took it away. There's a brutal murderer walking around and we don't know where he is. He didn't have no right to take my child's life like he did. He wouldn't have been no human being. It's a pure demon devil."

Crystal's classmates and friends had trouble expressing their pain and grief. Crystal had died without warning, with no chance for them to say good-bye, no last opportunity for them to tell her how important she was to them. It hurt them terribly to know they would never see her again.

The mourners marched from the church to the temporary green tent pitched at the gravesite. As the pallbearers lifted the large casket and slid it across the steel supports covering the empty grave, heavy sobs and uncontrolled cries of anguish rose from the throng and inundated the final prayers. Crystal's close friends locked arms with family members and joined as one swaying body as the ministers offered their concluding words and the pallbearers silently filed by to lay their white rose boutonnieres on top of the casket. The crowd lingered at the grave as the funeral director lowered the body and the hole was filled with dirt. Family and friends looked on as if the finality of the moment had come too quickly; too suddenly, it was over. Mourners held each other for comfort and slowly said their tearful good-byes. Knowles looked on and felt his resolve strengthen as each heartbroken person walked away from Crystal's grave.

Kevin James, Crystal's cousin, was one of the pallbearers. Ken Register was another. Ken had initially refused, but finally relented at Bonnie Faye's request. It only seemed appropriate, she thought, that one of Crystal's best friends saw to her last needs.

During the funeral, Bonnie Faye hugged Ken tightly several times. "If only you had been with her, things would be different, and Crystal would be alive," she told him, as she would tell him repeatedly during the investigation. Ken was a stocky, muscular young man and Bonnie Faye had always felt good when Crystal was with him. At 5'10", 190 pounds, and solid as a rock, he could protect Crystal like the brother she never had. "Ken, I feel like if you was there, you coulda saved her," she said, her eyes brimming with tears. "I just betcha the last words on her lips was your name. She probably died calling your name to save her."

Ken felt ill before, during, and after the funeral. His mother wasn't surprised when he threw up; he always got light-headed at the sight of blood. "It's probably his nerves," Shirley Register said. "He has always thrown up at times like these."

Ken made a fine pallbearer. He looked nice in his suit and Bonnie Faye smiled approvingly at him during the service. No one questioned his close ties to the family or his right to serve them by tending to the casket. At the end of the funeral, Ken dutifully performed his part in the service as he calmly waited his turn among the pallbearers. He filed past the grave and gently placed his boutonniere on top of the casket. After the funeral, he talked with Bonnie Faye and her family and told them he would come by the house.

Several people thought the funeral must have been difficult for Ken. Winnie Dale Bessant, Crystal's aunt, saw a funeral home attendant pinning a flower to Ken's coat lapel. Ken was flushed and he had a white splotch on his skin. "My Lord," she said. "The blood is about to come out of that poor boy's face."

The detectives and SLED agents assigned to the case were also at the funeral. The plainclothes detectives positioned themselves in the crowd and watched for strange behavior that might single out someone for suspicion. They also videotaped and took photographs of the ceremony. Later, they exchanged notes and reviewed the tape, but found nothing to indicate that a killer had been among them.

13

A week after the murder, Knowles took inventory of the collected evidence. A dozen officers, spending sixteen hours a day, had amassed a small mountain of information and the process of transcribing, sorting, and culling was underway. Knowles had personally selected the items from Crystal's bedroom: her diary, class composition and school notebooks, a list of phone numbers, an assortment of loose-leaf papers, and recently written letters. Technicians were busily scanning the diary and connecting phone numbers to full names and addresses. Crystal's friends were being interviewed. The canvass of the neighborhood where Crystal's car had been found was beginning to pay off.

Enough was already known to piece together a loosely organized list of where and when Crystal and her car had been seen the night of the murder. Crystal was last seen at 11:15 p.m. at the Coastal Mall. Sometime between 11:30 p.m. and nine o'clock the following morning, Crystal, her car, or both, were sighted at the Conway Middle School by twelve people. The events that took place in Crystal's life between 11:15 and 11:30 p.m. on Saturday were the key to solving the case.

"I don't think someone kidnapped her," a close friend said. "I think she saw someone she knew and got in the car and rode with them. If Crystal was meeting someone there, she sure didn't tell any of her friends about it."

Some of Crystal's family members and friends were not so certain she had been killed by someone she knew and trusted, thinking instead that she may have been coaxed or forced into a car and then taken away and murdered.

But Carla Allen's boyfriend argued, "Crystal wouldn't stop for any stranger. One time, when I was driving my work truck, I saw her and tried to get her to pull over so I could ask her something about Carla. Well, I finally had to blow the horn three times, then cut in front of her car before I could get her to stop. It wouldn't be like her to get in a car with a total stranger."

Crystal's friends were shocked that her car was found parked at Conway Middle School. Crystal and her friends often parked their cars at the Coastal Mall and rode around together, but they never left their cars in the dimly lit school parking lot.

"Crystal was very particular about her car," a friend said. "Her new Celica was an early graduation present from her mother and she always kept it spotless and shiny. She would never let anybody trash it or smoke in it, even her own mother. And she was the type of person that wanted to know for sure, when she got out of that person's car, and got into her own car, that she could see inside her car to make sure there wasn't nobody waiting in there for her. All of her friends complained that Crystal was too particular about where she parked her car and who she let ride in it."

"You looked at her car," an envious classmate said, "and it was like all nice and cleaned up, spotless. You paid a little bit more attention to it, and especially the license tag. She was proud of that, like you know, look at 'C TODD' and know she is somebody who takes care of her car. She was picky and wouldn't let anybody drive it and only certain ones ride in it. It was the car of her dreams."

Crystal's friends said that, as far as they knew, she rarely missed her curfew. Said a girlfriend: "When she was somewhere, and it would be almost time for her to be home at twelve o'clock, Crystal made it a point to leave soon enough so she was home before the time she was supposed to be there, so Miss Bonnie wouldn't get worried about her. If her mom asked her or ever told her to be home at a certain time, she was there. She just tried to be the most perfect person."

Crystal's car keys, on a golden ring with yellow wooden teddy bears, were missing. The parking lot and adjacent lots around the middle school, and even the roof of the school, were searched, but the keys were not found. When Officer Petty told the family it was OK to pick up the car, they found a spare key underneath the car in a metal box.

Knowles wondered about the significance of the missing keys. Maybe the killer needed them to get into the car to retrieve something or wipe away fingerprints. Maybe the killer kept a memento, a killer's keepsake, to help him fantasize about rekilling the victim.

It's odd, thought Knowles, *how many murderers are caught because they retain something from the crime. If they had only broken all possible links, they might have gotten away. It's understandable how it might not be possible to erase fingerprints, or get rid of DNA evidence or fibers. But to purposely keep a pocketbook, an earring, or a scarf, or a set of keys, seems stupid. But,* he thought, *I guess that's how a killer's mind works.*

More puzzling to Knowles was why a killer wanted a memento in the first place. The most emotionally charged memory of the victim would have to be the murder itself. *The memento helps the killer fantasize about killing and rekilling the victim, over and over, until . . .*

Suddenly overcome by the implication of a memento's worth to a killer, Knowles stopped short and threw his pencil onto the desk.

. . . until the fantasy is no longer enough!

Knowles slowed his car on Collins Jollie Road and pulled up short of the dirt lane where Crystal had been brutally killed. Inexplicably drawn to the scene, he sat and clutched the steering wheel. Images of police tape and cars parked at angles crowded his mind, a contrast to the quiet in front of him as the last evening shadows trickled through the bare trees.

"Go on home, Knowles," he said out loud. "What are you doing here?"

Removing his foot from the brake, the detective eased the car forward and pulled into the lane. Just ahead, the pitiful form had lain dying. The trees and the night had been the only witnesses to a savage attack that left a teenage girl heaped in a pile in a cold, wet ditch. He tightened his grip on the steering wheel and allowed the car to inch forward until he felt the gentle bump against the barricade. The dull thud refocused his attention and he switched off the engine.

The crime scene had been worked and reworked all week. Evidence technicians had scoured the road, the lane, and the woods until nothing remained except the hope that they already had the clue they were looking for. Knowles walked slowly down the lane and listened. The laughter he imagined hearing was indistinct but soft, somehow familiar. He heard overlapping sounds, perhaps conversation, in bursts and starts, mixing with night sounds. Then, a surprised voice, filled with alarm above a confusing din of cruel noises, growing frantic. Awful sounds, rushing wind, twisting, wrenching thuds, wheezes, moans. Suddenly, a staggering, guttural cry pierced the air. A staccato sound, building erratically to a numbing scream that ended abruptly with a resounding echo.

Knowles opened his eyes. Below him was the killing ground, the very spot of earth that had absorbed the life of a human being. The sand was still discolored and dark.

"I know who you are now," he said softly, as if Crystal was there. "And I'm terribly sorry."

Feeling self-conscious, he backed away and looked toward the ditch. For the next several minutes, he went over and over what he knew about the crime, allowing his thoughts to recreate the scene. *The car pulled up to there . . . for some reason you got out . . . Why would you get out? It's cold, late, you don't have a coat . . . forced out, maybe . . . trying to get away . . . a struggle . . . it happened there . . . you were dragged to there . . . you bled out there . . . and there . . . the car was there and backed out . . . you were left there.*

Knowles stared at the ditch. He thought of the pieces of jewelry lost in the attack. An earring . . . a necklace . . .

Stepping backward, he scanned the scene and said, "We haven't caught whoever did this. I guess you know that.

"But we will," he added confidently, and turned away.

14

Police departments frequently get called by worried parents who think their children are in danger. After Crystal's death, the number of calls increased dramatically in Horry County and consumed an increasing amount of police resources dedicated to the investigation.

On November 23, the local newspaper printed a story under the headline, "Witness Could Be in Danger Police Say." Chief Harris wouldn't say whether police knew who might be in danger, only that "we've got reason to believe that some other person, or persons, may have knowledge of this crime and obviously that person might be in jeopardy and may have some reason to fear for their safety."

Because she was one of Crystal's best friends and the last person to see her alive, Carla was warned by her friends that she would be the killer's next target. "I was scared to death," she later said. "I didn't have a clue who the killer might be, but I felt he knew me. I thought he might think that I know more than anyone who he might be. So I was freaking out and thinking I was going to be the next one."

Carla told the newspaper that Crystal's murder had changed her outlook on life. She was saddened that her murdered friend had missed out on her senior prom, junior-senior weekend, senior graduation, and all the other fun things they had planned for their final year in high school and in college.

"This has really hit home for me," she said. "I had been looking at life through rose-colored glasses, but this makes everything totally different now. Crystal and I were together nearly every Friday or Saturday night up until the night before her death." Carla said she hoped Crystal's murder opened her classmates' eyes to the dangers of life. "I know one thing for sure about me," she said, "that I will never drive anywhere alone at night again."

Several high school girls received death threats pieced together with words from newspapers and magazines, spelling out the message, YOU WILL BE NEXT. "I won't go out of the house by myself," exclaimed one of Crystal's frightened classmates. "My father or one of my brothers has to walk me out to my car and stay with me until I'm locked in and safe."

Whisperings around Conway were that Crystal's death was part of a Satanic ritual worship service. Friends and classmates told police they had heard all kinds of rumors about her death: She was stabbed and her pants were cut off; her arms were cut off and burned; her face was skinned; her heart and liver were missing; her eyes were plucked out; she was cut from ear to ear; her killers removed her organs and positioned them around her, along with black candles and cups filled with her blood.

One of Crystal's closest friends believed there was a Satanic cult somewhere in Conway, but could not identify any of its members. "It's not easy to identify those devil worshipers," she told police. "I don't think they are all walking around in their black costumes and drinking blood, but I believe they look just like us, wear normal clothes, and act like normal people. I don't think the majority of them you would know who they are by looking at them, so they could be any one of us. That's why it's so hard to find them. I feel like some cult group did this. Who else would be capable of such a crime?"

The police didn't consider the idea outlandish. There had been activity in the county linked to a satanic group. In 1988, two Conway teenagers had been caught digging up graves so they could use the skulls for rituals.

Chief Harris said there were no signs that the killing was related to satanic rituals. "I'm not going to get into whether it was satanic or ritualistic," Harris said. "We have nothing at this point in time to lead us to that conclusion. These rumors of a Satanic killing are most likely the result of someone's inability to understand how a person could commit such a brutal murder, and any time you have a brutal murder, people try to relate it to that type of crime."

15

Knowles answered the phone as it rang for the umpteenth time that morning.

"Bill, this is Bonnie Faye." She sounded as if she had been crying.

"Oh, hello, Mrs. Todd," he replied, "you're just the person I wanted to talk to." His attempt to sound cheery was unsuccessful.

Knowles had daily conversations with Bonnie Faye throughout the investigation. She was distraught and needed to know everything was being done to find her daughter's killer. Her frequent calls became part of the daily routine which he worked hard to accept. Her agony was unimaginable and he felt she deserved his attention and respect for what she was enduring.

"We all were inspired by Bonnie Faye to work hard," Knowles later recalled. "It was her continuous phone calls that drove us on. I remember she once called at eleven o'clock at night, and when I said, 'Hello,' she simply said, 'Good. I just wanted to see if you are working.' At eight o'clock the next morning, she called me again and said the same thing."

Knowles hated being unable to answer Bonnie Faye's direct questions about her daughter's death. There were things no one could know, even the victim's mother. Instead, he often tried to direct their conversations toward potential suspects. He scoured Bonnie Faye's memory of Crystal's friends, old boyfriends, and enemies.

"She didn't have no enemies," Bonnie Faye said angrily to Knowles' inquiry. "I told you that."

"Yes, ma'am, I remember," he replied. Knowles reexamined the list gleaned from Crystal's papers and address book. Crystal seemingly knew everyone in town. Dozens of the names were close friends. More were just regular friends and acquaintances. Most of the people on the list had been interviewed, but nothing had panned out. "I'm just making sure we didn't miss anything," Knowles said.

"Well, you must be," she replied sharply. "Did you check on that mean one in Aynor? I think he called the house again."

"Yes, ma'am," he responded as his eyes scanned back to the top of the page, where Crystal's closest friends and family members were listed. "Here's one that we've talked to, but haven't formally interviewed," Knowles said, thinking out loud.

"Who's that?" Bonnie Faye's voice brightened.

"Ken Register."

"Ken?" Her voice dropped again. "Well, Ken ain't the one," she said disgustedly. "Why are you wasting time? Ken's our best friend. He's just like family. Why don't you look for the ones that coulda done something like this?"

"We're doing our best, Bonnie Faye, not to overlook something."

"I know," she replied. Her voice cracked and Knowles knew the conversation was about over. "I'm sorry, Bill, I know you're doing everything you can, I just can't . . . I just miss her so bad." Bonnie Faye coughed deeply. Her raspy voice strained as she spoke. "Ken's been the most help. I don't know what I'd do without him. He calls and comes over and he's always asking what you found out."

Knowles always felt terrible after Bonnie Faye's calls, yet he knew they provided him with strength and focus. After saying goodbye and hanging up, he continued scanning the list, all the while thinking, *Just what are we missing?*

16

The day Crystal's body was found, a Michael Jordan baseball cap was removed from her car and sent to the SLED forensics laboratory for analysis. The hat was solid black with "23" and "Flight by JORDAN" written across the front. A preliminary investigation produced two black, curly hairs and suggested the owner was an African-American male. Many of Crystal's friends were shown pictures of the hat and asked if they knew whom it might have belonged to. Carla Allen's boyfriend laughed and told the detectives he didn't know anyone that wore a hat like that.

"Nothing to do with Michael Jordan," he added, "but what white boy would wear a hat like that? Everybody I know wears a Browning, Remington, Buck, or Budweiser hat, something like that. They definitely don't wear no Michael Jordan hat."

Working under the assumption that the killer knew the victim, the homicide team assumed the cap belonged to a black male friend of Crystal's. They wanted to know whether Crystal associated with or dated African-American males. The detectives knew their inquiries would not be well received. Race mixing was sensitive territory for the small southern town. But then, so was murder.

In another era, the detectives admitted, they might not have asked questions about interracial interactions. In 1991, however, interracial dating was far more prevalent than it had been before school integration in the 1960s. Still, the homicide team correctly concluded that Crystal's family and friends would not be receptive to questions about Crystal having interacted with black males.

Crystal's people were west Horry County folk who were not emotionally prepared to deal with questions about race mixing. Among the first settlers in Horry County were black colonists, who arrived as slaves to work the rice fields and timber forests of the southern coastal fringe. Most early settlers, black and white, lived on small farms and worked side by side in the fields, sharing the fruits of their long, hot labor. That blacks labored under discriminatory laws and customs was understood and endured in Horry. Life was hard and tenuous for blacks and whites. Peace was maintained by white supremacist groups, most notably the Ku Klux Klan, which ruled with an iron fist and, for many decades, obstructed the appearance of racial tension. Apart from work-related activities, black and white interactions were limited and strained. The white majority preferred not to think of tension existing. The black minority quietly endured the oppression.

Martin Luther King's famous cry in 1964, "Free at last, free at last, thank God Almighty, I'm free at last," served as a rallying cry for Congress to officially replace America's "separate but equal" schools with race-integrated schools.

The forced intermingling of the races through integration received, at best, a cold reception from many people in the south and, at worst, a defiance that heightened racial tension. In some communities, the federal government's intrusion into private lives and the established order was deeply resented. Thirty years later, forced integration still serves as a major organizing point for white groups intent on resisting intermingling of the races.

West Horry County had adapted slowly to the concept of racial equality.

Although most white people from west Horry readily tolerate and accept blacks as neighbors and classmates for their children, most interactions remain at the polite, work level. For many, the notion of black-white pairings isn't even considered.

In August 1989, racial tension in Horry reached a high when black Conway High School football players boycotted the team after a coach's decision to replace a black quarterback with a white player. The walkout was the second racial incident involving athletics at Conway High School. Two years earlier, a handful of black football players had walked off the team during spring drills in protest of a school policy allowing more white than black cheerleaders. In the boycott of August 1989, the county's NAACP director represented the players. Flanked by thirty-six black team members at a press conference, the local civil rights leader accused Conway High's football coach, Chuck Jordan, of racial discrimination. Jordan denied the charge and warned the players against walking out. Team rules stated that any player missing three consecutive practices without an excuse could be dropped from the team.

The NAACP representative saw the tension on the team as indicative of racial tension throughout the nation. But one African-American school leader, the chairman of the school's advisory board of trustees, said he was upset that the students and parents had taken their complaint to the local NAACP director, who took the matter to the media before talking to school officials.

"Our school is in good shape, and I hate to see this thing blown out of proportion," the advisory board chairman said to the newspaper. "I'm a black man, but I don't look at this as a black and white thing. We've worked hard to make Conway High School number one in the state, and to see somebody try to create a racial problem that's not there angers me."

The dispute was a hot topic in the media for months and demonstrated that race relations needed improvement in Horry County. Coach Jordan was found innocent of wrongdoing, but that didn't satisfactorily resolve the issue for many citizens. Some African-Americans in the county felt that years of oppression and institutional racism had come to bear in this issue, so they were resentful when Jordan was simply excused. After all, Conway High had lost thirty-six African-American football players that year and lost all ten of its games. Some whites in the county were angry at the perceived political motives of the NAACP director and felt he should have been censured for the advice he gave the students, some of whom lost college scholarship opportunities. Most people in the community, however, were simply glad when it was over.

Following the death of Crystal Todd a year and a half after the walkout at Conway High, the homicide detectives knew that asking Crystal's family and friends race-related questions was a delicate issue. They were dealing with age-old stereotypes by suggesting that Crystal had been involved with a black male.

Bonnie Faye resented the implication and said so, dismissing it as "pure gossip." She was adamant that her daughter would never have been involved with a black man. "I ain't never believed in black and white mixin', and my daughter felt the same way," she said. "I don't know who told you this trash, but whoever did it told you a pack of lies."

In response to police questions about blacks and whites dating, Crystal's friends said flatly that it happened, but they didn't approve of race mixing.

"Now, I'm not saying I'm a racist or anything, 'cause I know, I mean, I've just been raised in the south," said a friend of Crystal's when asked if Crystal would have dated a black person. "And my family isn't prejudiced, but that's just how I've been raised. It's not like I think I'm any better than them, but I just don't associate with 'em. There is a difference, you know. Around my house, at least, there is a difference, and that's how I was raised. I think Crystal was raised the same, to some extent, because Crystal didn't mess with, like, she didn't date, black guys. I think someone asked Crystal to go out with a black guy one time, and Crystal didn't want to go out with him. When she told her friend Carla, Carla said, 'Well, if you're gonna start doing that, girl, I'm not going to haul you around with me anymore.' Crystal had lost her license, you know. And, I didn't blame her because that just makes my skin crawl. I'm not a racist or anything, but like the rest of us, I was raised in the south and there is a difference between blacks and whites."

Crystal had at least one African-American male friend: The young man who owned the baseball cap. One of Crystal's girlfriends had somehow acquired the cap and given it to Crystal to return. The cap, which turned out to be insignificant in the murder case, had remained in Crystal's car while her license was suspended and was ultimately returned to its owner after her death.

The autopsy report confirmed what was apparent from evidence at the crime scene: Most of Crystal's blood had flowed out of her body and into the surrounding area.

Her outer skin was first examined for cuts, bruises, wounds, and puncture marks. There were thirty-five separate cuts and stab wounds, seven bruises, and three abrasions. Some of the wounds were made before she died, some while she died, and some after she died. Crystal's face had been cut on her left cheek, on her right eyebrow, below the right eye, and below the inside corner of the right eye. She had bruises on the left temple, upper and lower lip, right eyebrow, right upper eyelid, and in the right temporal area. There were three knife wounds to the neck, any one of which would have been fatal. All three of the throat-slashing cuts had moved from behind her right ear, down across the middle of the front of her neck, and up on the left side of her neck to meet behind and below the left ear. Measuring the depth of the three cuts was impossible. After the sweeping motion of the first cut from ear to ear, the knife had been inserted into the cut for a second slashing motion from ear to ear, and reinserted for yet a third slashing cut. The knife cuts slashed through all of Crystal's tissues, including her windpipe, and resulted in nearly total decapitation. The medical examiner reported that the spinal column and bones of the neck were all that had kept Crystal's head attached to her body. So much force was used in making the cuts that the killer actually sliced into the bones of her spinal column.

There were six more stab wounds in Crystal's chest measuring slightly more than a half inch long and approximately two and a quarter inches deep. One of the wounds penetrated the right lung. One knife cut was made through the middle of the stomach and under the breastbone into the liver while Crystal was dying. Twice she had been stabbed in the back with such force, the knife stuck into the bone of the spinal column. Another three-inch deep wound was made between the ribs and penetrated the aorta. Most of the additional knife plunges into Crystal's abdomen were made after she had died and penetrated the liver and small bowel. Two wounds had opened the abdominal wall. Crystal's intestines protruded through the hole.

A sample of blood was taken from the body for typing. Urine in the bladder was analyzed and tested positive for caffeine. Drug screens were negative.

Numerous bloodstains found at the crime scene were matched against Crystal's blood. The medical examiners found three wounds on the underside of Crystal's left hand (one to her thumb, one to her middle finger, and one to her ring finger) that they and the police believed resulted from her attempts to defend herself.

The examination of the head showed three stab wounds on

the left side that penetrated the skull and passed into her brain. One of the medical examiners said that he had never in the four hundred–plus autopsies he had performed seen knife stabs so deeply penetrate the brain. "It was extraordinary that so much power was used to actually penetrate the skull not once, but three times," he said.

Crystal's clothing was examined. The police and medical examiners noted that the knife holes in her bloodied shirt aligned with the knife wounds in her back. The alignment of holes in clothing gives investigators an idea about the posture of the body when it was stabbed. Clothing rides differently on a body when the person is standing, sitting, kneeling, or lying down. The failure of the holes to align properly can be an indication that the body was re-dressed or moved after a murder.

The medical examiners ruled the cause of death for Crystal Todd as exsanguination: bleeding due to cuts and stab wounds. They concluded that she was conscious during the several minutes it took for her to die and that she was cut and stabbed repeatedly as she lay bleeding.

The medical examiners also discovered significant bruising around the vaginal and rectal areas from blunt force. Because the openings of the vagina and anus were dilated and the muscles from both areas were stretched, she had almost certainly been raped. Spermatozoa were found by microscopic examination of the vaginal and anal areas.

Despite the apparent frenzy of the injuries inflicted on the helpless girl, the pathologists determined that it had been "a very controlled and deliberate attack." The investigative team assembled the data and concluded it was certainly possible that more than one person had been involved in the attack.

On November 25, 1991, the homicide task force announced to the public through the newspaper, "This has become the biggest murder investigation in the police department's history. It is also one of the most terrifying killings we have ever investigated."

17

During the second week of the investigation, the police stressed that someone with knowledge of the murder could be in danger. Crystal's classmates and friends were more terrified than ever, certain the killer would go after them.

The local newspaper was in close contact with Bonnie Faye throughout the early weeks of the investigation and knew she'd always give them something interesting to write. An article in the November 25th issue of the *Sun News* read:

> Bonnie Faye Todd said Sunday that classmates of Crystal's continue to visit her as she mourns her daughter's death. "I tell everyone to be careful because there's a maniac still out there. We don't know who that devil is ... If they don't catch him, he is liable to get somebody else."

The police were concerned when they read Bonnie Faye's statement. Her words were sure to promote fear in the community.

Three days later, on Thanksgiving Day, the newspaper ran a four-page holiday spread that pictured several families celebrating with their friends. The homicide investigative team, however, found little time for Thanksgiving celebrations.

During the last three weeks of her life, Crystal had the ominous suspicion that someone was following her and wanted to kill her. After her death, the police diligently searched for the person that might have been stalking Crystal. A witness had seen Crystal's car parked at the school and remembered a slender man and an older, gray-haired woman with Crystal late that night. Under hypnosis induced by a SLED hypnotist, the witness described the man as of medium build with an olive complexion and salt-and-pepper hair. He wore a dark tan jacket and a plaid shirt, and drove a dark gray Ford Granada or a similar Mercury car. The witness was sure he had seen the man leaning into the driver's-side door. The gray-haired woman was sitting in the passenger seat talking to the young, dark-haired woman seated behind the steering wheel. Both the man and the older woman appeared to be calmly talking with the young woman. Because the witness was positive he could identify the man if he saw him again, SLED brought in a profile artist to draw a composite sketch of the man.

The first composite appeared on TV and in newspapers on November 28. The police received more than twenty calls with names and descriptions of people resembling the man in the composite drawing. Many callers identified the man in the composite as Eugene, Bonnie Faye Todd's boyfriend.

Police hadn't targeted the man in the composite as a suspect. He was someone they wanted to talk to as a possible witness. "It's not an unusual profile, it could be one of a hundred guys," Chief Harris said. "And we're not saying this person participated in the murder, but we think he knows something about Crystal. He may even have seen what vehicle she entered before she was driven to her death. We just want to talk to him."

Eugene and Bonnie Faye had been dating for more than four years. He knew Crystal well and said she was a "good girl." Eugene told police that he didn't remember any problems she might have had with anyone. He said that on the day of Crystal's murder, he, Bonnie Faye, and Bonnie Faye's mother had gone to a birthday party in Marion at around 5:30 p.m. Crystal had followed them to the party in her car and left at around seven o'clock. He and Bonnie Faye arrived back at her house around midnight, and then he went home.

Shortly afterwards, at about one o'clock, Bonnie Faye called Eugene to say that Crystal hadn't come home. At 1:30 a.m., he and Bonnie Faye rode in his car around the Coastal Mall, stopped for gas at the Texaco station adjacent to the mall, and then continued their search in and around Conway. They returned to her house at approximately 3:30 a.m. He stayed until 4:15, then told Bonnie Faye he had to go back to his house, but to call if she needed him. Eugene called her at eight o'clock in the morning. Bonnie Fay said she still hadn't heard from Crystal. He advised her to call the county police. He started getting ready for church, then called Bonnie Faye and told her he would come back over to her house.

He arrived back at the Todd house sometime before nine a.m. Officer Wade Petty was there completing a missing persons report. Eugene stayed for just a few minutes before returning home. After he got home, Bonnie Faye called and said that the police had found Crystal, and that she was dead. So he went back over to Bonnie Faye's.

The police decided to ask him about Crystal's relationship with her mother.

"Did you ever hear Crystal discussing any problems she might have had?" they asked.

"No sir, if she had a problem, she kept it to herself. I mean, she didn't bring it home with her," Eugene said.

"Well, did her mother ever tell you that Crystal had discussed with her any problems she might have been having?" probed the detective.

"She . . . ah . . . one night . . . I'm gonna tell you the truth," Eugene said slowly. "One night she went out to a party. She went down there and she come in drinking a little bit that one time. But her mama talked to her about that and she promised she wouldn't do it no more. But she did it one more time and she, she wrecked the car down there at the light pole and totaled it. And I don't think after that she ever drank and I don't think she had nothing to do with no drugs. I mean, as far as I know."

Eugene said that he and Crystal had always been friends. She was like a daughter to him. "I used to give her money sometimes, five or ten dollars, 'cause when we was going out, her mama and I, she didn't cook. She wouldn't have no dinner, so I'd give her money so she could get her something to eat, too."

"Have you heard anything about Crystal receiving any kinds of threats from anyone?" asked the investigators.

"No sir, I have not."

"No harassing phone calls or anything of that nature?"

"No sir."

The detectives asked Eugene what he thought would have happened to Crystal if she didn't come home on time. Someone close to the family had told police that upon returning home one night after her curfew, Crystal got into a terrible fight with her mother. Crystal had been to a party where she drank and got home nearly two hours late. "It began as an argument," the friend recalled, "which got out of hand and ended up a real nasty, ugly incident." Bonnie Faye was furious that Crystal hadn't at least called.

"She was careful about when she come in," Eugene told police. "Most of the time she come in by 12:30, but if she was late, she knew to call Bonnie Faye and let her know. 'Cause if she didn't, Bonnie Faye would start walking the floor. She'd get nervous to death if Crystal didn't come in on time. She was always looking for somebody to grab her or something. I don't know why, but she was always afraid for that to happen."

"Have you ever been out and around and seen Crystal out anywhere?" the detective queried.

"Most of the time if I seen her car at the mall, I'd never pull in and talk with her while any of her friends were around. I didn't hardly ever do that, but Bonnie did it a lot."

"Would Crystal have told her mother if she was having any trouble with anybody, or if anybody was threatening her?"

"No, I don't believe she would," Eugene insisted. "But that's the way Crystal was. She never complained about nothin'. I remember once her shoes hurt her feet and she wouldn't even tell her mama."

Although the homicide team at headquarters had heard from Bonnie Faye almost every day since Crystal's death, they were uncomfortable asking her about certain things. Perhaps now, the detectives thought, was the right time to ask those questions.

Every murder investigation begins with the immediate family. Most murders are committed by someone close to the victim. The process of elimination begins, often indelicately, with the immediate family and friends of the murdered individual. No one is more aware than the police of how cruel and indecent this can seem. When the detectives ferret out and catch a killer in an immediate family, it's good police work. When the same process doesn't produce a killer, an incensed public criticizes the ethics of police procedure and rushes to comfort the aggrieved individuals who have been victimized again, this time by a cold, ruthless system.

Bonnie Faye was never considered a suspect. After the police spoke with Eugene, however, pieces of the puzzle no longer fit. Maybe Bonnie Faye hadn't told the investigators everything she knew about her daughter's behavior over the last months of her life.

Detective Knowles thought Crystal might have been killed because of something she was involved in or something she knew. The homicide investigative team had heard stories about Crystal being involved in drugs and wild sex. They had heard that Crystal was a paid informant for the police department. They had heard she was involved with cult-related activities. They had heard she was a sweet girl who was a joy to be around, just a typical teenager. Knowles knew how easily rumors got started and desperately wanted to track down every angle, no matter how bizarre. Many of the most promising leads had been played out. Had Crystal been involved with something or someone that she shouldn't have been involved with? Had Crystal been murdered for what she knew and might reveal? Was Bonnie Faye withholding vital information from the police to protect Crystal's reputation?

Knowles decided that perhaps only two people could best answer those questions. One had been buried almost two weeks earlier at High Point Baptist Church. The other was alive, but not so well, at her home on Juniper Bay Road.

18

Knowles was confused. Although he had told himself it was beyond reason to think Bonnie Faye would purposely withhold information relevant to her daughter's murder, the evidence implied otherwise. If she was holding anything back, he had assured his fellow officers, it was because she was protective of her daughter and had a desperate need to cling to all she had left—her memories. "Since when is it a crime to love your child too much?" he had asked.

Knowles breathed deeply and looked out of his car window at Juniper Bay Road. "Maybe I've gotten too close to her. Maybe I do feel sorry for her," he thought out loud. "Even if I could ask her, would she be able to tell me that she has been completely honest with me about her relationship with Crystal?"

He could no longer pretend to be ignorant and allow Bonnie Faye to continue a deception if, in fact, the evidence led in another direction. As a police officer, the people had entrusted him to carry out his sworn duty. He knew he would do the right thing. Now if someone would just remind him what the right thing was …

"I had a feeling you was coming to see me," Bonnie Faye said sharply as she opened the door. "Gene told me you was askin' questions about me and Crystal, so I figured you'd be comin' to see me next. Might as well come on in."

Bonnie Faye seemed to look older than when they'd last met. *Was it just a few days ago?* he thought as he entered the trailer. The long hours he was working were distorting time. The bags under Bonnie Faye's eyes were more pronounced. The dark circles looked like permanent half moons. Knowles was aware that she had been through a lot in the past few weeks and felt sorry for her. She told him that since Crystal's death, her nights were so long that day and night ran together. She sometimes didn't know if she was awake or dreaming. Knowles thought she looked sullen. She seemed thinner than before. She was very fragile, he thought, like glass, and if he wasn't careful, what he was about to do might shatter her. He needed just the right words at the precise moment to prevent that from happening.

The time had come for Bonnie Faye to tell him if something about Crystal wasn't as she had always hoped it would be. The investigative task force had to consider the possibility that the sex and drugs Crystal was reportedly involved with might have contributed to her murder. Bonnie Faye had to be confronted and encouraged to tell the whole truth if she expected the police to ever find her daughter's killer.

Knowles knew he needed a subtle, gentle lead-in. Reaching into his pocket, he produced a small bag.

"Miss Bonnie, thank you for seeing me again this morning." He sounded apologetic in a southern, genteel way. "Detective Chestnut gave me these things and asked me to return them to you. I knew you would want to have 'em."

Her swollen eyes fixed on the brown paper sack as he extended his arm. Puzzled, Bonnie Faye took the bag and sat down at the kitchen table.

"Oh, my word," she said, peering into the top of the sack. Her eyes brimmed with tears.

Knowles cleared his throat. "This is all the jewelry that Crystal was wearing the night she was killed. The boys at headquarters thought you might like to have it."

"I sure would," she answered softly.

One by one, Bonnie Faye examined the fourteen pieces of jewelry that had been worn by her daughter the night she was murdered, then placed them side by side on the table. Each piece was shiny and in perfect condition.

Knowles stood quietly and watched. The last piece of jewelry was a herringbone necklace with a bend in the chain links because of the attack. Knowles winced when he saw Bonnie Faye's expression change. As she held up the necklace to examine it, her chest heaved. Unaware of why, but knowing something wasn't right with her daughter's necklace, she fought to retain her composure.

What strength, the detective thought. *With all she's been through.*

Knowles suddenly felt his spirit, sagging from the weight of the investigation, lift to match the compassion he felt for Bonnie Faye. His vision of why he was there was clear again, his mission restored. He was there to help her. She would understand if he had to delve into unpleasant areas. He was confident the interview would go well.

"Bill, why do you think somebody would wanna kill my youngun?" she asked.

He pulled back a chair and sat down. "I don't know, Miss Bonnie," he said, looking straight into her eyes. "That's why I'm here. I'm hoping you will tell me something that will help us figure that out."

After several seconds, he leaned up to the table and said softly, "Miss Bonnie, I hope this doesn't offend you. I know you've been through an awful lot, but I need to ask you something important. Did you ever know of Crystal being involved in any trouble of any kind?" She looked puzzled. "Like for instance, had somebody, anybody threatened her recently, or called to say she was in any kind of trouble?"

The second Knowles sat down, Bonnie Faye had sensed the detective didn't want to forge ahead with the interview. She mistakenly concluded, though, that he was going to comfort and console her. He was on her side, after all, and would protect her from the rumors and insinuations. She had no way of knowing that the investigation had suddenly shifted to spotlight the secrets of her and her daughter's life. When the detective hinted that he had heard talk from Crystal's friends of her promiscuous behavior and drinking and drug use, Bonnie Faye became still. Knowles watched as her face changed, this time into an expressionless mask.

Bonnie Faye would not, or could not, talk to Knowles about Crystal being anything other than the sweet loving child she so missed. She appeared confused and stammered that she had put so much out of her mind. There was so much she couldn't remember.

So, thought Knowles, *this is how she's been dealing with her daughter's murder. She's in such a state of shock that memories of her daughter's life are frozen in her mind. Bottling up the bad memories in favor of the good ones allows her to cope with her loss.* The homicide investigator had seen this before with individuals who had gone through extreme amounts of emotional stress. How would Bonnie Faye cope, he wondered, when she learned the truth about the horrible way her daughter had died?

"So, tell me, Miss Bonnie," he prodded cautiously. "Was she involved with anything that she shouldn't have been?"

"No, not that I knowed of," she answered calmly. "Oh, you hear a lot about what's goin' on, but that's just people running their mouths, just talking about something they don't know nothin' about." Bonnie Faye shifted in her seat.

"What you're saying to me, Miss Bonnie," he continued, "is that you have never received any knowledge of any kind that she was in any type of trouble with the law? Or maybe she knew someone who sold drugs?"

Bonnie Faye's disposition turned sour and she stared at Knowles. She gritted her teeth, sucked in her bottom lip, and replied acidly, "I know what you're asking."

Knowles watched her fury build and thought of the eerie, primal noises she had emitted on first learning her daughter was dead. He didn't know whether to move forward to comfort her or move back out of her reach. He sat still.

"I know people's been talkin'," she said sharply, her voice rising, "but they ain't got no business talking 'bout a dead girl like that. She weren't no different than any of these other younguns which live around here. She was just like 'em and she did the same things any of 'em do. If you ask the ones that's runnin' their mouths, you'd find their younguns are doin' stuff way worse than what Crystal ever done."

Knowles immediately felt an overwhelming desire to take his words back and start over. As Bonnie Faye ranted, he thought of his children and how he might respond in similar circumstances.

"And Crystal weren't no bad girl! She was a good girl!" Bonnie Faye, who had risen from her seat, slumped back. Knowles tried to look into her eyes, but he couldn't. Bonnie

Faye had lost the one thing in life that had meant anything to her, had nothing left but her memories, and now he had threatened to destroy those memories. Knowles wondered if she was reevaluating him as no better than the animal that had killed Crystal.

Knowles tried to ease the tension by diverting Bonnie Faye. "That was a pretty cat on the porch out there," he said abruptly, but he felt foolish for being so obvious. He was grateful when Bonnie Faye let him off the hook by allowing the distraction.

"Yeah, there's two of 'em," she commented evenly. "They belonged to Crystal. One is named Church, and the other is Snuggles. Crystal used to diaper them cats and push 'em around in a baby carriage. She weren't no more than a baby herself. You know, before Crystal died, them two wouldn't come in the house, but now I can't hardly keep 'em out. Rubbin' on me and purrin' and all, I figure they miss Crystal just like I do. They might be tryin' to comfort me."

Knowles understood what Bonnie Faye was trying to tell him. More than anything else, she needed to be comforted. She needed him to understand her, to be sympathetic toward her. She couldn't take another tragedy in her life. Any more pain would probably destroy her, might even kill her. She couldn't afford to lose her memories.

"Miss Bonnie, I thought Crystal looked fine at the funeral," Knowles said in another obvious attempt to reestablish ground.

"Yeah, I wished I'd seen what she looked like before she was fixed up," she replied, "but Mike Hill said I didn't want to see her."

Knowles didn't want to leave Bonnie Faye with that image in her mind, but he was at a loss for words. He desperately needed to know the truth about Crystal's life, but he wasn't going to get any further with Bonnie Faye, at least not then. Her version of the truth was as she remembered it, and that was that. The real truth might lay hidden forever. She might never be able to tell all she knew.

But how could he find Crystal's killer without her help? Maybe she would ultimately find peace with her memories and be able to face the bad as well as the good. He couldn't wait for that to happen.

"I'll be in touch, Miss Bonnie," he said as he got up and walked across the small living room. "I'll let you know the moment we have anything significant on the case."

"Please do," Bonnie Faye responded. She abruptly shut the door behind him.

Knowles stood on the porch for a moment.

I wonder if her not saying good-bye means she's mad at me? he thought. *Maybe she thinks I'm . . . Oh, Jeez, what are you doing, Knowles?* The detective walked to his car and got in. *Have I been working too hard, or what?*

He felt miserable about what he had just done. He had baited the mother of a murdered child.

Rolling down the window, he let in the crisp December air. He breathed deeply for a minute, but didn't feel any better. He cranked the engine, switched the heater fan to high, and rolled up the window. A sudden chill overtook him and forced his body forward. Drawing his elbows tight to his sides, he tried to take slow breaths. Cold air blew from the heater. He put the car in gear and backed out.

He had repeatedly found himself drawn back to Collins Jollie and the blood-soaked dirt lane. Recreating murder scenes in his mind helped him focus and provided him with insights into possibilities he wouldn't have otherwise seen. He liked to create dialogues and movement and watch as the actors went through the motions, predator and prey, killer and victim. He imagined scenarios of last thoughts and last actions.

Knowles shivered and thought of the last warmth Crystal had felt. She hadn't taken her coat on the ride to her death, so she probably felt comfortable enough with her assailant to adjust his car heater. He had heard she was a fiddler, always messing with the radio or the mirror, even in someone else's car. She shivered and tried to stick her cold nose on the killer's cheek. Perhaps the killer told her to stop playing with the heater, so she rolled down her window, laughing.

That was probably the last time she rolled down a window, Knowles thought.

It may have been the last time she laughed.

It wasn't the last time she felt cold.

As he drove down Juniper Bay Road, oblivious to the lingering colors of a late fall, Knowles shivered again. *Why is the heater taking so long?* he wondered.

He didn't question why he was so cold. He knew why. After what he had been through the last couple of weeks, he felt like he might not be warm again for a long time.

19

Profiling, often seen in movies and on television, involves developing a demographic and behavioral profile of a person who committed a crime, based on known characteristics of criminals, victims, and, most importantly, on evidence available after the crime is committed. David Caldwell, a behavioral analyst from SLED, was brought in to develop a profile of the person responsible for Crystal's death. This was one of ninety criminal cases David Caldwell worked in 1991. He would more than earn his keep as an integral part of the Todd homicide team.

"What I try to do," said Caldwell, "is paint a picture of possible suspects that will give investigators a starting point." Many investigations proceed, as did the Crystal Todd murder case, by systematically eliminating those with no involvement in the crime. Given that investigators have to start somewhere, profiles can shorten the list of persons to contact. "The profile is not," continued Caldwell, "a substitute for an investigation. Interviewing people, knocking on doors and looking at physical evidence is what solves crimes."

The extensive profile produced by Caldwell was used by the detectives in the Todd case, but was not released to the general public. The profile read as follows:

PREDICTED CHARACTERISTICS
OF CRYSTAL FAYE TODD'S KILLER

These characteristics are probable; however, the investigators are cautioned not to rule out any good suspect because he does not fit this description.

White male, between 20 and 25 YOA

Recklessness is probably a noticed characteristic.

He has some social skills; can smile; can converse. He is not too scary.

The murder is not suggestive of a lot of forethought or planning.

We would expect that he transferred blood to his automobile after the crime.

He is an angry man with generalized anger towards most people. Many people have noticed that something is not quite right with him.

He is probably episodically employed; he is not a businessman or a professional person. He probably has trouble with policies and coworkers and consequently has not had long-term employment. His performance, generally, at work, would be cyclical. He may work well one week and not so well the next. We would expect cyclical social performance as well; he may be nice one day, ornery the next. People that know him may say that one never knows what to expect from him.

He has no tremendous need for money. He is not chronically unemployed. He is not worried about where he is going to get his next meal. He is able to make ends meet. There is probably another person, perhaps a family member, on whom he is partially financially dependent.

He is not a cocaine addict who steals money or valuables thinking about his next fix.

He is not the product of a wholesome, nurturing family environment. In his formative years he had no solid male role model. He probably had a missing father; almost certainly an emotionally missing father (perhaps divorced, father worked all the time, traveled a lot, was dead, was an alcoholic).

He probably is a local person from Horry County familiar with the site of the body recovery (either he lives near there or a family member lives near there, or perhaps he hunts, fishes or works in that area). At any rate, he has been there before.

He is impulsive and is angry at the world. He has a large chip on his shoulder. Life has not been easy for him and deep down he feels someone must pay for the way his life has gone.

The 11:30 p.m. rendezvous with the victim could be the

result of having gotten off a second shift or perhaps a result of having left a party earlier that evening.

He feels fairly confident that he will not be a suspect. He does not believe he will be associated with her that night. He would probably best be described as, not an intimate acquaintance, but a peripheral acquaintance.

He sees himself as a social outcast and probably rightly so. He probably is not widely accepted by his peers.

He is unable to sustain a warm, nurturing relationship. If he was ever married, there were lots of problems.

Whether or not he had a specific plan to kill that night is equivocal.

One hallmark of his life would be frustration. The stress of every day life is tough on him. He projects his problems ("I'm not the problem, they are."). When he was in school he was not the type to say, "Whoa, yeah, the teacher is right, I should have . . ." He is the type to say, "*They* are full of it!"

He does not enjoy the reputation of being particularly smart.

He regularly carries a knife, shows it off, considers it to be part of his image. He likes to think of himself as macho and tries to pose himself as macho. He probably drinks the long neck Buds and Jack Daniels.

He probably cannot take protracted pressure; however, he probably handles acute, immediate pressure very well.

He probably does not have a lot to make him attractive to peer females. For the most part, females from his peer group do not have a lot to do with him. He is not witty. He is not charming. He would probably be attractive to younger girls simply because he is older. Perhaps what he could offer peer females would be drugs or maybe money (though it is not expected that he would have much money).

He has come to the attention of law enforcement before; perhaps when he was 12 or 13 he was torturing animals, starting fires, committing random acts of vandalism.

He is probably not doing much dating. He is not a ladies' man. He may have some date rapes in his history; maybe raped a cousin, but he is not doing stranger/kidnap rapes, he is not doing burglary/rapes.

Alcohol intoxication on the night of the murder is a good bet.

It is possible that two perpetrators were involved.

After the commission of the murder this perpetrator probably would have gone straight to a safe haven, either to his home or to a relative's house as opposed to going out and setting up an alibi somewhere. It should be considered that this safe haven might be in the same direction from the crime scene as the crime scene is from her abandoned car.

It should be considered that after staying in town for a few weeks he will leave for an ostensibly good reason, such as to visit or live with a relative or for some employment opportunity in another town.

Sophia couldn't help but notice the young man who came into the store every morning, always at the crack of dawn. He seemed so friendly and he sometimes chatted with her about the weather. He always had to ask her for help with his purchases. The items he wanted to buy were kept behind the counter, away from children.

Sophia had worked the night shift until December 13, when she became day manager of the convenience store in downtown Conway. From then until sometime in February, Ken Register stopped by the store each morning on his way to work and purchased adult magazines. Sophia noticed that he bought all of the new editions of over two dozen different magazines.

One morning, when curiosity overcame her, Sophia casually asked Ken what he was doing with all those magazines. He said he was buying them for his boss, who reimbursed him at work. Sophia didn't know, although she might have suspected, that he was buying them for himself.

The Christmas season was a time of grief and depression for Bonnie Faye.

Sitting at home, she stared at the collection of Crystal's jewelry. She had planned to give Crystal a pink ice ring and bracelet for Christmas. Crystal had picked out the items early in November on a weekend trip she and her mother had taken to a department store at the beach. After Crystal's death, Bonnie Faye went back to the store and took the items off layaway. Her daughter would not be getting any new jewelry for Christmas that year. In 1991, the only gift she had for Crystal was a Christmas tree for her grave.

"It's awful," she said ruefully. "You can't buy your young'un nothing but a Christmas tree. She's got no business being dead. She's supposed to be here with me. Crystal didn't have any enemies that I know of. It was somebody the devil sent down here to kill her. I just hope they'll catch him. I'd rather have her back than anything I've got."

The investigators placed a hidden camera near Crystal's grave, knowing killers frequently visit the final resting places of their victims. When the film was viewed later, the detectives watched in silence. The only person they saw was a grieving mother bent and weeping over the grave of her only child.

On January 6, 1992, Officer Dale Long and SLED Agent Campbell Streater rode out to Kenny and Shirley Register's home to talk with their son, Ken. Nobody was home, so Long left his card in the door jamb with a note asking Ken to call headquarters.

Two days later, Shirley called the police department and asked what the police wanted with her son. Long explained to the concerned mother that Ken wasn't a suspect, but he was needed to help develop leads in the Todd case. Shirley Register said she would contact Ken and pass along the message.

The police had spoken briefly with Ken early in the investigation, but saw no reason to conduct a detailed interview. He apparently had a solid alibi and, as a friend of the family and a pallbearer at Crystal's funeral, had presented no reason for suspicion. He had even talked with the victim's mother the night Crystal was missing. The second interview was being arranged as standard procedure to produce and develop information that might have been missed, and to request samples of hair and blood for forensic analysis. Two days after Shirley spoke with the police, Ken called and agreed to the interview.

That evening, Ken went to Bonnie Faye's house and expressed concern over the upcoming interview.

"Well, why do you think it's gonna be so terrible, Ken?" asked Bonnie Faye. "And sit down, won't ya? You're making me nervous."

"I'm just worried 'cause they haven't found anybody yet to blame it on," he said, anxiously pacing in the small living room. "Everybody says they're looking to blame it on somebody and I don't want it to be me."

"Lord, it ain't gonna be you, Ken," replied Bonnie Faye. "You didn't do it, did you?"

Ken lit a cigarette as he mashed out another in the ashtray. "It don't matter now," he said, frowning. "They can't find anybody, so they pull your blood and rig it to make it look like you did."

"What?" said Bonnie Faye, her voice rising with surprise. "Well, I never heard of such . . ."

"It's true," he blurted out. "Everybody's talking about it, how now ain't the time to be giving blood, 'cause they're getting desperate."

"Well," scoffed Bonnie Faye, "how do you even know they're gonna pull your blood? They probably just want to ask you things about Crystal, like who the ones are that coulda done this to her."

"They told me on the phone. They're getting it from everybody now." He flicked his cigarette repeatedly. "Everybody I know, practically, has give blood."

"I told Bill Knowles the whole time, honey, that you ain't the one," she replied, lighting another cigarette for herself. "Use the ashtray, Ken," she added, noticing Ken's irritating finger tic.

"Those tests ain't perfect, you know." Ken stopped and looked at the end of his cigarette.

"Lord, don't burn up the house," Bonnie Faye said, looking at the floor. She got up. "Let me get you something, Ken. I hate to see you like this."

"I don't want nothing now," he replied, following Bonnie Faye into the kitchen.

"I just think you're all worked up over nothing," she said, turning to her friend and taking his hand. "You've been my source of support, Ken. I don't know what I'd a done without you. Now let me get ya some tea."

Ken sulked. "No, ma'am. I just want 'em to get the one that done it and leave me alone."

"Ken," she said impatiently, "you're acting like they're picking on you."

"Well, don't be surprised when they arrest the wrong one," he replied defiantly, following Bonnie Faye back into the living room where she plopped back onto the couch.

"You've got to calm down." She noticed he wasn't going to sit. "Nobody's gonna be arresting you."

"I wanted to see 'em tomorrow, but now I've got to worry all weekend over this," he said.

"You're making me nervous. I wish you'd sit down."

"I can't, Miss Bonnie, I got to figure this out."

"Figure what out? I don't see there's anything to figure out."

"The blood pull," he replied excitedly.

"Oh, that, you don't . . ."

"It can be beat, you know."

She paused and looked at Ken, but then dismissed what he had said. "You're talking crazy now."

"I'm not. It can be done, you know. You could fake 'em out."

"Fake 'em out?" she said, shaking her head. "Well, you have gone crazy now, boy."

"I haven't either. I have to think on this."

"Why's that?" Bonnie Faye asked. "Why are you even worried over that?"

"You could take somebody else's blood to give 'em."

Bonnie Faye snickered. "What if you took the real murderer's? Then where'd you be?"

"This ain't no joke!"

"Oh, come on, Ken, you're the one supposed to be cheering me up." Bonnie Faye looked out the front window and saw her niece, Deena, arriving. "Thank the Lord," she said, rising again from the couch. "Deena's here. Maybe she can talk some sense into you."

"I got to go anyway," said Ken.

"No, you need to wait a few minutes and talk with Deena."

"No," responded Ken as he moved toward the door. "I'm sorry, Miss Bonnie, I got things to do."

"You ain't got nothing to do, you know," she said in a motherly way.

"Yes, ma'am, it's Friday night, and I got a date."

"Well, don't be talking that crazy talk to her or she'll drop you," Bonnie Faye said. She hugged Ken's waist as Deena entered the house.

"What crazy talk?" Deena asked as she stepped into the room. "Are you leaving, Ken?"

"Yes, ma'am."

"Tell her," said Bonnie Faye.

"Aw . . ."

"Tell her," Bonnie Fay insisted.

"All right. They're getting ready to put it on the wrong man now so they can get somebody arrested for this case," Ken replied.

"What? Who?" said Deena, looking at Bonnie Faye as she slipped off her coat.

"Oh, Ken's got this crazy idea that the police are after him," Bonnie Faye said.

"I told you, it ain't no joke!" he said quickly.

"For what?" asked Deena.

"He thinks the police are gonna get him for Crystal's murder," said Bonnie Faye.

"What?" Deena studied the look on Ken's face. "That is crazy talk. Why would they be after you, son?"

"I got to go in Monday," Ken said bitterly, his voice lowering. "I know they're gonna pull my blood and if it comes out to be me, they're framing the wrong one."

"You're serious, aren't you?"

"He's been talking like that ever since he got here," said Bonnie Faye. "About to drive me crazy."

"Son, why do you think the police are after you? They're not after you," Deena said comfortingly.

"I told him that, but he don't want to listen," said Bonnie Faye.

"They can't get anybody and everybody says they're gonna pull a frame job on somebody," Ken said.

"Well, bless your heart, we won't let 'em get you, honey," Deena said, smiling and wrapping her arm around him.

"It ain't funny," he replied sullenly.

"Well, you're serious!" she said. "I can't believe it!" Deena's expression changed. Placing her hands on his shoulders, she said calmly, "Well, Ken, let's look at it. You ain't done nothing wrong, have you?"

He looked down and shook his head.

"No, you haven't," agreed Deena. "We know you wouldn't do that. You're just too close. You're like family."

"It don't do no good to tell him that," Bonnie Faye snapped.

"That's not gonna matter to them," he answered, turning toward the door.

"Ken, it does, too. I've been sitting right here when Bonnie

Faye told Detective Knowles that you're our best friend. You got yourself all worked up over nothing. Why don't you stay and I'll get you something to drink? We'll help you calm down."

"He don't want nothing," said Bonnie Faye.

"No, ma'am, I got to go." Ken stood quietly for a moment, looked at the two women, and then stepped out the door.

Deena watched him cross the yard. "Well, what do ya reckon that was about?" she said, thinking out loud.

"I told you, he's been like that the whole time," Bonnie Faye said. "Him talking about beating the blood test . . . taking somebody else's blood."

"For what?" asked Deena.

"Says to fool the police."

"Fool 'em? That doesn't make sense. Why does he think they need fooling?"

"I don't know," Bonnie Faye said, lighting another cigarette and drawing deeply a couple of times before speaking again. "Sounds mighty suspicious to me."

On Monday morning, Bill Knowles pulled Officer Long aside.

"Dale, aren't you going to interview Ken Register today?" Knowles asked.

Long checked his calendar. "Yeah," he said, "at around 3:30, after he gets off work."

"I got a strange call over the weekend," said Knowles. "Seems Bonnie Faye is now suspicious of him."

"Suspicious? How so?"

"Register's nervous about coming in. According to Bonnie Faye, he was acting, as she says, real suspicious, and she wants us to check it out."

"Most of 'em are nervous," responded Long. "He's been close to the family, hasn't he?"

"Yeah, seems he told her that he was worried about the blood test. Something about it's possible to beat it."

"Beat it?" Long said.

"Yeah, that's what I thought," agreed Knowles. "How did he sound on the phone the other day?"

Long thought a moment. "Nothing unusual. Are you suggesting anything else?"

"No, I don't think so," Knowles said. "He's been there all this time, comforting Bonnie Faye. They regard him as family. I'm sure it's nothing. It's not the first time Bonnie Faye has called in suspicious of somebody."

"What do you want us to do?" Long asked.

"Just what you were doing. I knew you were going to see him today, so I thought I'd say something."

"You want we should mention it to him?" asked Long.

"Yeah, why not? That's a good idea. Ask him if he said those things. Bonnie Faye said he went on and on about how somebody else's blood could be used to fool us."

"He doesn't know anything about how it works, does he?"

"Apparently not. It's probably nothing, but you might as well throw it in."

"Sure thing," replied Long.

22

Ken showed up at the police department Monday morning several hours before his scheduled appointment. He sat calmly in the interrogation room and eyed the detectives sitting across the table. The detectives casually examined Ken for signs of nervousness. Long and Streater knew that many of the teens they'd interviewed had limited experience with the police, so nervousness was normal. By that definition, Ken appeared normal.

"OK, Ken, as I'm sure you know, the reason we asked you to come in again today is to try and help us with the murder investigation of Crystal Todd," Long said. "I understand you knew the victim, Crystal, and she was a good friend of yours."

"Yeah, she was," Ken answered. "I've known Crystal and her family all my life. Her cousin, Kevin, is my best friend. Crystal and I used to hang out together some, just friends."

"Did you and Crystal ever date?" asked Long.

"For about a month, two and a half years ago. About a month in 1988."

"Did you ever have sex with her during that time or any other time?" Long asked. Long and Streater watched Ken as he answered.

"No," Ken responded matter-of-factly. "I never had sex with Crystal Todd."

"At any time?" Long continued.

Ken shook his head and was reminded to speak up. He cleared his throat. "No," he said.

"Do you know who Crystal might have been involved with at the time of her murder?"

"I think she was seeing some guy named Tony."

"Tony," repeated the detective. "Anyone else you know of?" continued Long.

"Crystal once dated a boy from Aynor named Todd, but I don't know his last name," Ken said in a strong voice.

"Did you know any of her close friends?"

Ken named nine girls he remembered being close to Crystal.

"Did she ever mention using drugs?" Long asked.

"One time, when Crystal was drinking she told me about the time she was with her friend and they smoked some dope. I don't know if this was true or not because I never actually saw her use any type of drugs. I did hear about the time she got drunk and ended up shitting all over things. That's how she got the name Shitter." The joke broke the tension a little for Ken and he sat back in his chair.

"How would you describe her personal reputation among your friends? You know, what did the guys say about her?"

"I guess I would have to describe her reputation as loose. That's what all my friends said, but I don't really think she did as much as the guys said she did. People like to brag about stuff that never happens."

"Ken, when was the last time you saw Crystal?"

"I saw her only two or three times in the past six months," he said.

Long rephrased the question. "How close to the night she was killed had you seen her?"

"I saw her about three or fours days before the . . ." Register said. "She wanted me to take her to the Department of Motor Vehicles to get her driver's license back, but I couldn't."

The detective counted back from Saturday, the day of the murder. "So, the last time you saw Crystal was on, what, Wednesday?" asked Long.

"Yeah, and then her mother called me Saturday night to go help look for her."

"Why do you think Mrs. Todd called you, Ken, and not any of her other friends?"

"I think she did call some of the others, but I had helped her find Crystal once before when she was late coming home from a party."

"Did you go out and help Mrs. Todd look for her?" Long asked.

"No, I had a cold and my mama said I shouldn't go out in the night air. I had already been out at the go-cart track that night with my girlfriend. That's how I got the cold."

"Ken, what time did you leave the go-cart track that night?"

"Around 11:30."

"Where did you go from there?"

"I drove straight home."

"Did you talk to anyone when you got home, maybe your girlfriend on the phone?"

"My mama was in the kitchen when I got home. We talked before I went to bed."

"What time would you say you arrived home that night?"

"A little after midnight, because Bonnie Faye called me at 1:15."

All things considered, Ken handled himself remarkably well. He was forthright, pausing appropriately before answering, and ostensibly eager to help.

"Before you go, Ken," Agent Streater said, speaking for the first time, "what, in your opinion, should happen to the person who killed Crystal Todd?"

"I'm not sure," replied Ken. "Jail, I guess."

The interview lasted almost forty-five minutes. Long and Streater had no reason to think Ken had anything to do with the murder. Then they asked him to take a blood test and Ken hesitated for the first time in the interview.

"What do you want my blood for?" he asked.

"For DNA comparisons," said Streater. "It's standard. We're asking a lot of people for blood."

"What is DNA?" Ken asked cautiously.

"It's a genetic fingerprint that we'll use to compare to other evidence taken at the crime scene. No two people have the same DNA. We're using it with a lot of other white males that were associated with Crystal Todd."

Long and Streater finally asked Ken if he had said anything to Bonnie Faye about beating the test. Ken suddenly became wary and hesitated, but he admitted he had said something to Bonnie Faye. When asked how he could beat the blood test, he said, "All you have to do is to just carry someone else's blood with you and give that as the sample."

"That's not the way it works," Long replied. "You would go personally to the hospital, accompanied by a police officer. At the hospital, a doctor or nurse would take the samples and it's all supervised. There's no way anyone could fake the tests."

"Will you submit to a blood test?" asked Streater.

"Can I talk to my mother about it first?"

"Sure. You can talk to anybody you want. Your mother, your father, a lawyer, anybody," said Streater.

"You're an adult," added Long. "You're eighteen years old, and if you want to consent, you can go ahead and do that now, or you can leave and talk to whoever you want to and come back."

"It's a voluntary thing," continued Streater, "and it's up to you. You'll be the one signing the form. A lot of other people have been asked to do the same thing."

"What did they do?" Ken asked.

"Everybody that's been asked to this date has consented," Streater answered.

"Well, then I guess I will, too," replied Ken.

Horry County officer J. J. Costello immediately transported Ken to the Conway Hospital.

"You know I don't have to do this," Ken said to Costello on the way to the hospital. "In fact, I shouldn't be doing this at all. My mama warned me and told me not to say anything or do anything until she talked to a lawyer first."

"You can talk to anyone you want to," Costello said. "It doesn't matter to us."

To Costello, Ken seemed very nervous and asked a lot of questions about DNA. He wondered how the test could lead to the arrest of someone for murder, and how long it took to get back the results. Costello explained that DNA was like fingerprints. No two people had the same pattern.

"Son, we have an expensive piece of equipment for blood samples," Costello said, "and whatever's in the blood will show up."

At Conway Hospital, under the watchful eye of the police officer, a phlebotomist drew three vials of Ken's blood. The vials were sealed and signed by both the phlebotomist and Ken. An emergency physician at Conway Hospital took the head, pubic hair, and saliva samples. The doctor had to tell Ken to relax so that he could get the samples.

The physician sealed the samples in the Suspect Evidence

Kit and handed the package to Costello, who drove to the police department. Officer Kim West entered into evidence the blood, hair, and saliva samples of Johnnie Kenneth Register II. Register's sample, along with forty-seven others, was sent to SLED headquarters in Columbia, South Carolina, where the DNA testing was being conducted.

Ken left the hospital and drove directly to James' Tires, where Kevin James worked.

"Kevin, the police were awful," Ken told him. "They were just awful."

"What did they do to you?" Kevin asked.

"Well, they told me Bonnie Faye had called and told them I said something about rigging the test. Then they took me to the hospital and took my blood. They made me feel like a criminal. They talked to me something awful, treated me like a dawg!"

"Man, that does sounds awful. What'd ya do?" asked Kevin.

"Weren't nothing I could do," Ken answered. "All I could think about was I wanted my mama."

Ken had always been a frequent visitor to the Todd home, but after the murder he visited and called more often than before.

"He was the person most interested in what was going on in Crystal's investigation," said Winnie Dale, Bonnie Faye's cousin. "He was real interested in helping Crystal's mom. He would hug her neck and tell her, 'They will soon find the person that killed her.' He would pat her on the back and assure her that things would be OK."

Once, Winnie Dale recalled, when Bonnie Faye was very upset, Ken "stood there for approximately two minutes and just held his arms around her, and she was crying and said, 'Ken, I just don't think I can live without her.' Ken kept rubbing her up and down her back and patting her and saying, 'Yes, yes.'"

Two days after he gave blood, Ken again visited Bonnie Faye. He paced agitatedly around the house, nervously flicking his cigarette ashes. He wouldn't sit, even when offered a seat.

"They treated me terrible," he complained to Bonnie Faye. "They kept asking me, 'If you could find who killed Crystal, what would you do for her, what would you do to the person?'"

"What'd you say?"

"I said, 'I guess put them in jail,'" Ken replied.

"They deserve a heap worse than that," said Bonnie Faye.

"When I got to the hospital, all I could think about was I wanted my mama," he said. "They're fixing to arrest the wrong one now. I know if they say I did it, they have rigged my blood."

With that, Ken left Bonnie Faye's house. He never again called or went back.

23

No one was sure exactly when Randy arrived in Horry County or where he came from or why he came at all. He was there, though, and a string of scared women and former employers, reluctant to answer the police's questions, added to the mystery. Just who was this guy? About the only thing immediately apparent was that he wasn't the type of person you could just walk up to and ask.

Among the many names of Crystal's friends and associates garnered early in the investigation was Randall Lew Vaughn (not his real name). The name was doodled across the cover of a notebook taken from her school locker. Knowles ran the name through the National Crime Information Center (NCIC), a registry of wanted persons in the United States. The investigative team was ecstatic when the NCIC identified Randy as a fugitive from Alabama and indicated that further information regarding a criminal record was available. This was exactly the break they had been looking for.

Randy had an extensive arrest record under fifteen known aliases and six Social Security numbers. In 1984, he was sentenced to the Mobile County, Alabama, prison for ten years on a theft conviction, culminating a series of arrests across the southeast that began in 1979. He was released in April 1986 for good behavior, but less than two months later, he was ordered to appear before the State Pardons and Parole Board at the Alabama penitentiary to answer charges of parole violation. When the Alabama police went to arrest Randy and return him to prison, they found that he had jumped parole and disappeared.

The homicide investigative team thought it had hit pay dirt. After determining that Randy was still in Horry County, work-

Crystal Todd was 17 years old when she was brutally raped and murdered by her friend Ken Register. DALE HUDSON

"Driving quickly down the the road and over a little bridge, he pulled into a small opening to the right. The dirt lane amounted to little more than a path, with a grass strip running between two bare treads . . ." The murder was committed in a secluded portion of the countryside. DALE HUDSON

Tragically, Crystal never made it back to her home on Collins Jollie Road
DALE HUDSON

Detective Bill Knowles worked long hours trying to solve a case that, for months, seemed almost impossible to solve.
COURTESY BILL KNOWLES

When DNA testing pointed to Ken Register as the most likely suspect, Knowles and the community were shocked.
HORRY INDEPENDENT

The trial took its toll on the families of both the victim and the accused. Bonnie Faye Todd (left) phoned police headquarters at all hours of the night and day to make sure investigators were trying to find the person who killed her daughter. But to this day, Shirley and Kenny Register (below) refuse to believe that their son murdered Crystal Todd.

BOTH *HORRY INDEPENDENT*

Statement of Johnnie Kenneth Register, II
February 18, 1992

On the night Crystal Todd disappeared, I left the go kart track and drove to Conway. I saw Crystal in her car at the red light close to the Middle School. I tooted the horn to get her attention. She couldn't leave her car right there so I followed her to the Middle School and she got in my car to go riding around.

We ended up parked on the dirt road. We started kissing and one thing lead to another and we started having sex. I didn't have a rubber. She said, "Don't shoot off in me.", but I couldn't help it. She started screaming and hit me in the chest and she said if I got her pregnant, she'd say I raped her. I was scared. I didn't know what to do. My knife was between the seats. She got out of my car and started getting dressed and was still screaming.

I stabbed her outside of the car and threw the knife as far as I could. ~~I left~~ I left Crystal there and headed home.

On my way home I cut through Coastal Mall and waved at Raymond Conners and Bret Davis. I then went straight home as fast as I could.

Johnnie Kenneth Register II
Johnnie Kenneth Register, II

WITNESSES:

David M. Caldwell

W. Brooks

SWORN TO AND SUBSCRIBED BEFORE ME
THIS 18th DAY OF Feb , 1992.

William A. Knowles
NOTARY PUBLIC FOR SOUTH CAROLINA
10-17-99

Ken Register signed his name to a confession that was the key piece of evidence at the trial.

Defense attorney Morgan Martin was concerned that extensive pretrial publicity would make it impossible for his client to get a fair trial.
HORRY INDEPENDENT

Solicitor Ralph Wilson, on the other hand, was concerned that he wouldn't be allowed to enter some of his key evidence.
HORRY INDEPENDENT

The Horry County Courthouse was packed with spectators throughout the trial, which one person described as "the best show in town."
DALE HUDSON

The spectators were silent when Ken Register took the stand in his own defense and claimed he was under duress when he confessed to the murder.
TOMMY BRITTAIN

From the time of Register's arrest, famous crime writer Mickey Spillane was convinced police had the wrong man, so he had his wife, Jane Spillane, attend the trial. Jane Spillane proclaimed Register's innocence on several radio and TV shows and became suspicious of a police conspiracy.
BOTH *HORRY INDEPENDENT*

ing for a local cable company, the detectives put him under surveillance while they found out all they could about him. When
the time came, he could at least be picked up for parole violation. The first order of business, though, was to find the answers
to some important questions. How had the name of this 30-
year-old felon made its way to the cover of Crystal's notebook?
Crystal must have known him. Just what was their relationship?
And what did he know about her murder? Thus began the examination of the first real suspect in the long investigation.

SLED Agent Virginia Jacobs conducted one of several interviews about Randy with Amy, one of Crystal's close friends.
Crystal had written the pretty, 17-year-old high school senior's
name on her notebook, close to Randy's name.

Amy said she had met Randy at the Bi-Lo Grocery, where
she worked as a cashier. He had checked out in her line, and
they had exchanged small talk. Several hours later, Amy received a note with a phone number and a message to call State
Farm Insurance and ask for Randy. She hoped she didn't have
an insurance problem. Her father took care of that stuff. When
Amy later called the number, which was really a home phone
number, Randy answered.

"I told him how old I was and I went to school, and that I
worked mainly on weekends and on Wednesday nights," Amy
said to Agent Jacobs. "He told me that he was twenty-three or
twenty-four. I can't recall which one."

"Did he ask you out that night?" Jacobs asked.

"No ma'am. We just kind of talked on the phone and he told
me he'd call me back the next day."

"What was the conversation this time?" Jacobs asked.

"He told me that he was gonna be honest with me because,
you know, if we did start seeing each other, it'll come up anyway. He told me that he was divorced, but he did have a child."

"Did he ask you out?" Jacobs asked.

"He wanted me to do something with him, like go out to eat
or something that Friday night, and I told him I was going out
with my friend, Crystal, and he said he would just call me back
Friday afternoon and just see if I was still doing something with
her 'cause he wanted to go out. When he called me Friday, he
said, 'Why don't you just stop by,' and I didn't want him to feel
bad, so we stopped by his house."

"How long were you there?"

"We didn't stay but about fifteen minutes. I introduced him to Crystal, told him that she was my friend, and I told him we were going to a football game and a dance."

"When was the next time that he called you and you met him?"

"That was either Monday or Tuesday. He wanted me to meet him at Taco Bell after I got out of school. So I told him I got out at two o'clock and I met him up there. I pulled up beside him and I went over there and I told him I had to go home and he's like, 'Well, I never get to see you or do anything with you cause you're always doing something else.' I said, 'Well, my momma wants me to go home right now, right after school.' And he said, 'Well, I want me a smooch,' and I said, 'No, I don't even know you.' And I just kind of blew it off and went to my car and then I left."

The interview with Amy added to the picture the police were putting together of the 30-year-old fugitive with an extensive criminal history. Randy was apparently a persistent man who could lie convincingly about his age. He also had a taste for high school girls.

"Did you ever have a conversation with Crystal about him?" Jacobs asked.

"After we left his house that Friday, she said that she thought he was cute," Amy answered.

"When was the next time you had a conversation with Randy after the Taco Bell?" Jacobs asked.

"I talked to him, I think, that Friday night and I probably talked to him a couple of nights during that week, too. I told him I had to go to work the next day at Bi-Lo, and he said, 'Well, why don't I meet you out there before you have to go in?' And I made sure to meet him thirty minutes before I went in and we just sat in the parking lot and talked. I mean we both sat in our own cars. The cars were facing each other."

"What would you talk about?"

"He talked about this girl from McDonald's. He said, 'Well, you're going to work. You don't have time for me. I'll just go talk to Miss McDonald's.' She was on that McDonald's commercial and he said that he was going to talk to her, just playing around. He's going to flirt with her or something."

"So you think he was doing that just to sort of make you jealous?"

"Uh-huh," the teenager responded.

Add manipulation to his bag of tricks, thought Agent Jacobs. Randy had seen Amy once more during October, and then quit calling her until the early part of January, a month and a half after Crystal's murder. Amy had spoken with him about ten times and seen him three times during two weeks in October of 1991. In January, she said she wasn't going to have anything to do with him, particularly in light of what was being said about him.

"You stated to me earlier," said Agent Jacobs, "about a conversation that you had with a girl that you go to school with."

"Yes ma'am."

"Tell me about that conversation," Jacobs said.

"A friend said that her cousin had made a date with him and he tried to rape her," Amy said. "She also said, 'He's tried to rape about two girls before my cousin,' but she said her cousin was gonna file a report on him 'cause he tried to rape her."

"Did she tell you how she knew this?"

"She said that she was at her cousin's house when he called to make the date and then her cousin told her that."

"Yeah, but how did she say she knew that he'd tried to rape several other girls?"

"Um, I'm not really sure," Amy said. "She just told me that."

The investigators had the important link between Randy and Crystal, but they knew they needed more. Many people were linked to Crystal, and Randy had never been arrested for a violent crime. They needed motive.

The detectives went to businesses where Randy had worked, and received consistent reports about his attitude and work behavior. Randy often lied to get jobs, had poor work performance, and was frequently fired. Randy was clearly a charming, efficient conman, who could lie his way out of a lie. But how could such a person be so well received, at least initially, by those with whom he had contact?

Randy was a frequent visitor to health clubs and the softball field. He had the physique of a body builder and was once likened to a Greek god as he swaggered around in his stretch pants. At 5'11", 220 pounds of steroid-produced muscle, he mesmerized women with his white teeth and curly brown hair.

His slow southern drawl and tanned good looks provided easy access to both working-class circles and society gatherings, where almost anyone would stop to hear what he had to say. Many, particularly the young, were taken by his initially polite and gentlemanly ways. It usually didn't take too much exposure to him, the investigators found, to see a totally different side.

Randy was the kind of guy that you liked until you got to know him. Then you worried about whether you could get away from him without being too seriously harmed. Randy had the most dangerous of antisocial qualities: He was a person who did what he wanted when he wanted.

Randy had married a local woman in June 1988 and settled down. They had one child during three years of a rocky marriage and divorced in December 1991, one month after Crystal's murder. An affidavit from Randy's wife, filed in August 1991, told the story.

She knew of at least three separate adulterous affairs by her husband during their marriage. The first relationship occurred eight months after they married and two months after she became pregnant. She found out when the woman called her and asked if she knew Randy Vaughn. Randy had apparently told the woman that he and his wife were getting a divorce, that his wife was pregnant when they were married, and that she had trapped him into marriage.

Randy's wife forgave him again and again. She was concerned for their unborn child and fought to make the marriage work, despite his best efforts to end it. Randy's second affair began through softball, four months after the first affair ended, when his wife was six and a half months pregnant.

"He fell head over heels for her and showed little concern for me or the baby," his wife said. "I was devastated over this. The other woman and I confronted him and requested that he make a choice. Shockingly, he chose her over me and moved to Sumter to live with her and her parents. I filed for divorce, but he begged and cried and lost his job. Somehow, he convinced me to take him back and give him one more chance for the baby's sake. I was then eight to eight-and-a-half months pregnant and in no emotional state to go through with the divorce. I allowed him to come back home and he promised that he would go into counseling. The counseling never took place."

Randy's third affair occurred late in the spring of 1991. He met a woman at the softball games, which he had refused to allow his wife and child to attend. Randy's wife said, "On July 21st at 7:30 a.m., I went to our house to confront him, knowing the woman would be there. It took ten minutes to open the door and he put the woman in the shower stall to try to hide her. However, I found her jewelry, clothes, and shoes by my bedside and I waited until she came out. When she did, my husband introduced me to her. I understand now that she has been seeing my husband for two months."

An uncontested divorce on the grounds of adultery was granted on December 16, 1991, one month after Crystal Todd's murder. On the morning of December 17, Randy called his wife and, sounding upset, said he was going to kill himself. Still under his influence, she went to his apartment and found him in bed, apparently unconscious. An empty syringe was by his side. She called EMS and Randy was transported to Conway Hospital to be treated for a possible drug overdose. En route to the hospital, Randy was given Narcan, a drug to counteract the effects of narcotics, but he remained unresponsive. He immediately perked up, though, when the EMTs put a couple of ammonia inhalants in his nostrils, and he answered their questions about what he had done.

Randy's behavior got the attention of his ex-wife-of-one-day and let her know that he wasn't going to just go away. Indeed, in an interview a month later, in mid-January, while her husband was under twenty-four-hour surveillance, she reported to the investigative unit that Randy had called her every day since the divorce, sometimes several times a day, and that he stopped by the house every couple of days. She was afraid to date for fear of what Randy would do if he found out.

Interestingly, she didn't know important facts about her partner of several years that people ordinarily know about their mates. She didn't know where Randy had graduated from high school. She didn't know if he had gone to college. Randy was very good at keeping secrets about himself, even from those who knew him best.

Randy's wife was unaware of his troubles with the law. This might be understandable, thought the detectives, if his troubles had simply included an overnight in the drunk tank. But Randy had an extensive history of arrests and close encounters with the criminal justice system, dating back a dozen years to high school. They were also hearing about Randy's involvement with sex-related crimes against women who were afraid to report him. Every interview, every new tip, every piece of information that came in supported their conclusion that the long investigation into the murder of Crystal Todd was about to end. The homicide team thought it had its man.

Randy had a habit of trying to force himself sexually on women. Some of the women were new acquaintances, unaware of his predatory nature until the first time they found themselves alone with him. A couple of other women had known Randy for a while and made the mistake of thinking of him as a friend. Another victim was seven months pregnant when she opened the door of her home for Randy when he arrived to install her cable TV. All of the women were scared to talk about Randy to the police.

"You think he's dangerous?" Agent Streater asked one of the women.

"Yes," she replied. "After that night he attacked me, I was fearful for my life. Not only did I think he was going to rape me, but I thought he was going to kill me. I've never had that feeling before."

"Do you think that he would hurt a female?" Streater asked.

"Yeah," she said quietly. "He hurt me. He was very demanding, very forceful and scary. I just can't explain how scared I was. I feel like if I hadn't told him that my brother lives right next door, and the houses are real close, and if I hadn't told him that I thought my daddy was on his way, and my son hadn't been there, I think yes, he would have raped me."

"What kind of expression did he have on his face at this time?" Streater asked.

"Blank," she replied. "Just like he had nothing, he just went blank. I'd look at him but he wasn't looking at me. He was in another world."

"When was the last time you talked with Randy?"

"Last night," she said.

"Has he ever apologized to you in any way for what he did?"

"No, he hasn't. He keeps saying, 'I want to come over,' and I'll say, 'No, especially not after what you done to me last time.' And he goes, 'Well, if you hadn't jumped me like you did.'"

"It's almost like he's reversing the situation," Knowles said.

"He's totally reversing the situation and he laughs. He thought it was funny."

"Do you think this is the first time this has ever happened to him?"

"No, no, I don't," the young woman said.

Another woman, who had fled to another state to get away from Randy, said she would not return to testify against him unless she was forced to. She had dated Randy for several weeks during the summer of 1991, despite warnings from friends and family. She admitted she and Randy had a sexual relationship that began one night on a blanket at the beach. Randy simply reached under her skirt and pulled down her panties, pulled out his penis, and climbed on top of her.

She said Randy was very nice and seemed to be a gentleman for the first couple of weeks of the relationship. He then became insanely jealous, calling her whore and bitch in public, and accused her of having sex with other guys. When he got angry one night and threw her against a car, she knew she had to get away.

She told Detective Knowles that Randy was very forceful while they were having sex. He enjoyed rolling her onto her stomach and getting on her back. He sometimes pinned her arms and hands above her head so tightly that he left bruises on her wrists. His repeated attempts to force anal sex on her furthered her desire to get away.

Knowles asked her if she would be surprised to find out that Randy had raped other women. She said no. In fact, she thought that sexual assault was normal behavior for Randy. Knowles then asked the young woman if she thought Randy was capable of killing someone. She said yes. "The more that I resisted him and the more I would ask him or plead with him to stop, the more insistent he became and the more he was turned on by that activity," she said.

* * *

On January 17, 1992, following a phone call from Randy, Collie (not his real name) went to the Food Lion in Conway, where Randy had worked for a couple of weeks. Randy said he couldn't talk there, but would come by Collie's house that evening. When Randy never showed up, Collie drove to Randy's to see what was up.

The day before, Collie had spoken briefly with Agent Streater and Officer Long and told them he sometimes worked with Randy out of town. Collie confirmed that Randy owned and used a three- to three-and-a-half-inch lock blade knife, was unpredictable and a compulsive liar, and that he had seen Randy do "out-of-the-ordinary things to pick up women."

Collie thought of his conversation with the police as he knocked on the door of Randy's apartment. The interior was dark and everything seemed quiet. Suddenly, Randy opened the door and walked out toward the parking lot. He told Collie that he might need a place to sleep later. Collie said OK and got back in his car. As Randy sped off in his truck, Collie sat for a minute and thought again about his decision to not tell Randy that the police had been asking a lot of questions about him. Something was definitely going on, and Collie got the distinct impression from the police that he did not want to be part of it. He had decided that Randy was the kind of guy who could handle his own business. But then Randy had called him that morning and he worried all day. Collie knew better than to mess with the police, but he absolutely didn't want to tangle with Randy, either.

Collie sat in the dark and went over what he had told the police. He convinced himself he hadn't said anything wrong. *He is a liar,* he thought, *and he does bird-dog the women. Maybe I shouldn't have told them about the steroids. Hell, Randy had an ad in the newspaper once, "If you want steroids, Call Big Randy." Nah, I didn't tell them anything. He ain't selling no more. Not since he got busted.*

Collie drove home and waited, but Randy never showed up. Around midnight, the phone rang. It was Randy, who said that someone at one of the cable companies said SLED was asking questions about him. Collie said nothing. Randy then asked if he knew whether SLED investigated homicides. Collie said he didn't think so. SLED was probably only interested in him because of steroids. Randy didn't sound convinced, and Collie again decided not to say anything about his conversation with the police. Randy hung up after telling Collie he didn't need a place to stay. He would just see him later. Good, thought Collie, much later. He never again heard from Randy.

Over the next three days, Randy's movements were erratic as he drove around Conway, often inexplicably and quickly turning around, doubling back, and taking side and dirt roads. Although he had always burned things in his yard, he now did so more often. A neighbor saw him use a hose to control a raging fire.

Randy had figured out that the police were watching him and he didn't like it. The detectives knew Randy did not like rules and hated it when someone was in a position of authority over him. He was a stalker who didn't like being stalked. Randy probably knew he was being pursued as a suspect in the Crystal Todd case. The police would later discover, however, that Randy had a couple of other secrets in his life.

On January 21, at a little after nine p.m., Randy returned to his ex-wife's house to pick up his truck. Two unmarked cars followed him when he left. Randy began driving erratically and managed to lose both of the unmarked cars. He doubled back one too many times, though, and passed one of the officers, who had pulled his cruiser down a side road to wait and watch. The unmarked car pursued Randy again, this time with its headlights off. Randy and the officer passed a South Carolina Highway Patrol officer, who, seeing a car speeding by without its headlights on, quickly pulled out and turned on his blue light. Randy was unaware of the unmarked car and mistakenly thought the blue light flashing suddenly in his rearview mirror was intended for him. Instead of pulling over, though, Randy took off.

As the Highway Patrol Officer rolled to a stop, the officer in the unmarked car jumped out with his badge in his hand and shouted that he had a vehicle under surveillance. The state trooper, however, would not let the officer go, and detained him long enough to verify his identification. Finally, the officer jumped back into his car and continued the chase. He saw Randy's taillights in the distance. Randy drove around a curve, pulled off, and went down another road. The officer drove to the exit point, slowed, and looked for signs of the vehicle. It seemed to have vanished. Additional officers were dispatched to the area and, after a street-by-street search, the parked truck was found about an hour later.

Randy, however, was gone. He had fled by foot into the woods. His break marked the beginning of a manhunt that would last all night and involve bloodhounds and a helicopter on loan from SLED. Randy traveled all the way from Highway 90 to the Intracoastal Waterway, near Myrtle Beach, and then back to Coastal Carolina University, a distance of close to twenty miles, over eight-and-a-half hours.

At approximately four a.m., four members of the homicide investigative team went to the home of Randy's ex-wife, not too far where the manhunt had started. Knowles and SLED Agents Ben Thomas, David Caldwell, and Campbell Streater woke up the woman and searched her home. Randy wasn't there. Knowles and Caldwell went back to headquarters in Conway. Streater and Thomas remained at the house. Randy never showed.

At 7:45 a.m., Randy's ex-wife called the command post and said she had spoken with Randy and that he was ready to give himself up. Agent Streater asked her where Randy was. She said she didn't know, but had a phone number where he could be reached. Streater immediately dialed the number and Randy answered.

"I asked him if he was all right and he said he was tired of running," Streater recalled. "He said, 'I want to end it all, kill myself.' I told him, 'Randy, that's not the answer. That will not accomplish anything.' I said, 'Let me come out there and pick you up. I'll bring you in here where it's dry and it's warm, get you something to eat, make you comfortable.' I said, 'There's a lot of police officers out there looking for you.' I said, 'You'd be better off letting me come pick you up.' And he hesitated, but at approximately 7:46 a.m. he told me that he was at a pay phone at the Coastal Carolina baseball field."

Agents Streater and Caldwell immediately drove to the baseball field, where they saw Randy talking on the pay phone. "As I pulled up, he hung up the phone and walked over toward my car," Streater said. "I was dressed in my SLED greens and was easily identifiable as a police officer. I told Randy that I was the SLED agent that he talked with on the telephone and that I was there to pick him up and I wanted to help him."

Randy, dirty and wet from his ordeal, started crying. "I talked to him for about thirty seconds or so," Streater continued, "telling him to calm down, trying to put him at ease, put the cuffs on him, and put him in the back seat of my car, where David Caldwell, at 8:02 a.m., advised him of his Miranda warnings."

The interrogation back at headquarters began at approximately 8:30 a.m. and lasted until 1:30 p.m. Surveillance pictures of Randy were posted on the walls and his name was written in big letters on a board in front of the chair where he was seated. Files and papers with his name were strategically placed about the room so he would see them and realize he was the focus of the Crystal Todd investigation.

Randy, however, maintained his innocence. He consistently made statements to clarify the record, such as, "That's what you say I did, I never said that," and, "I have never raped a woman," and, "I did not kill Crystal Todd." After five hours, the interview ended without producing a confession or any new information about the rape and murder of Crystal Todd.

Randy admitted having met Crystal once, corroborating Amy's story, but maintained that he had not seen her or talked to her after that. He said he didn't remember saying anything to her at all, and told the detectives that Amy could verify that.

Caldwell, who had accidentally come across evidence linking Randy to a rape in 1978, introduced an interesting aspect of the interview. When he was in tenth grade in Irmo, South Carolina, Randy had allegedly raped a girl in his class. The young girl had told her best friend, Laurie Varnadoe, about the rape, and Laurie had confronted Randy and told him that the girl's parents were considering pressing charges. Varnadoe grew up to become a SLED agent who worked on the Crystal Todd case. She eventually married Agent Caldwell. During the investigation, Caldwell had mentioned Randy's name to his wife, who recounted the story of her friend from high school. A little checking showed that Randy was the person her friend had accused of rape.

When Caldwell first mentioned the girl's name during the

interrogation, Randy said, "Where did you dig her up from? What, are you going out finding girls I've dated before?"

"So you know her," Caldwell said.

"No, I don't know her," Randy answered.

"You sure you didn't rape her?" Caldwell asked.

"Yeah, I'm sure," Randy said. "You got the wrong man. You're barking up the wrong tree."

Agent Varnadoe had contacted the alleged rape victim, who gave a voluntary statement about the incident just five days prior to the interrogation. David Caldwell read the statement, word for word, to Randy, and continually asked, "You don't remember that?"

"No," Randy said. "That wasn't me. I told you. You're barking up the wrong tree. I ain't never raped nobody."

Randy voluntarily consented to a search of his home and his two vehicles. Several items were seized, but Crystal's key ring and keys were not among them. A burned shotgun and an assortment of burned wires, cables, and electrical parts were recovered from the yard. Randy had apparently stolen cable and other things from an employer. When he found out about the police inquiries, he had tried to burn the evidence.

Randy voluntarily submitted blood and pubic hair for typing and DNA analysis. After the interrogation, he was escorted to the Conway Hospital to submit the samples, and then back to the J. Reuben Long Detention Center, where he remained until the analysis was complete.

Randy's samples were sent as a top priority to SLED for immediate analysis. Anything from Horry County was automatically sent to SLED Agents Lori Johnson and Emily Bishop. The two serologists initiated the DNA analysis process and typed the blood sample, a much quicker process to determine if further analysis is needed. Blood typing can eliminate the need for additional analysis, which is exactly what happened in this case. Randy's blood type did not match the samples taken from Crystal Todd. Subsequent DNA analysis confirmed the blood analysis report.

Knowles received the bad news from SLED on January 23. All of the hours spent tracking down and confirming the possibility of Randy's guilt in the Crystal Todd case were now for naught. Knowles called the Alabama police to tell them that

Randy was being sent back as a parole violator. He was stunned, however, by the response. "We don't want him back," he was told. "He's your problem now."

On January 25, 1992, as Bill Knowles and the members of the homicide investigative team watched, Randy walked out of the Horry County Jail, and went back to his home in Conway, South Carolina, a free man. Two years later, Randy successfully sued Horry County for harassment and was awarded $10,000.

24

In early February, several days after almost fifty blood samples were sent to SLED for DNA testing, Special Agent Lori Johnson phoned Detective Knowles with encouraging news.

"Bill, we think we may have something interesting for you with those last samples you sent us," Johnson said. "Nothing to get excited over yet, but we got a serology match. We're proceeding with the DNA and we'll have something for you soon." The serology, or blood typing, was the first step of the process.

There was a long pause on the other end of the phone line, followed by a sigh of relief.

"Thank Goodness," Knowles said. "I knew we'd get something."

"Well, we can't say for sure yet," Johnson cautioned. "You just keep sending 'em along and we'll keep working on this one."

The new science of DNA fingerprinting had become a godsend in tough cases. In 1991, few people had even heard of DNA, let alone considered the possibility of precisely identifying a killer from a single bit of hair or body tissue. This was a learning period for the police, as it would soon be for people in Horry County as the mysteries of DNA took center stage in the investigation.

Every nucleus-containing cell of a person's body has the genetic blueprint for that individual, called DNA (deoxyribonucleic acid). This blueprint is so specific for each person that it can establish identity far more reliably than fingerprinting. DNA is most often extracted from hair, saliva, semen, bone, and blood, and all of it from the same person is identical. For example, DNA taken from a person's hair will be identical to DNA taken from his saliva or semen.

DNA can be used to identify criminals because people committing crimes often leave behind traces of themselves, which is all that's needed to provide a sample of the genetic material. Even a single hair, or a drop of blood or semen, or a few skin cells, can be analyzed and traced to the criminal. In a murder case where a woman is raped, minute amounts of semen can be found inside of the woman and processed to reliably identify the DNA structure of the rapist. Then blood or hair samples can be collected from suspects and systematically matched to the DNA in the semen. The police investigating Crystal's rape and murder hoped to find a match for the DNA extracted from semen found in her body. The next task was to connect the rapist to the crime scene.

On Saturday, February 15, their hopes paid off. Agent Johnson phoned Knowles with an updated report on the DNA analysis.

"Bill, we got it! We got a match," Johnson said. "It's the sample we suspected earlier. The additional tests we ran, though, confirm it. We're more than certain we have a positive match for the semen sample!"

Knowles was overcome with anticipation as he waited, seemingly forever, for Johnson to go on.

"Which sample was it?" Knowles blurted out when he could wait no longer.

"According to our analysis," Johnson responded, "the DNA profiles from individual number 137.4 visually match the DNA profiles from items 41.8 and 41.11, the vaginal and rectal swabs. This individual, 137.4, definitely cannot be excluded, or in other words, is to definitely be considered the donor of the biological evidence found on both the items, that is 41.8 and 41.11. It is his blood and, I might add, the only blood we've seen so far that comes anywhere close to matching the victim's samples."

Knowles fought to control himself. After all the waiting, he felt giddy and had an almost uncontrollable urge to laugh.

"And who is individual 137.4?" he asked, his heart racing.

"The sample 137.4 is identified as one Johnnie Kenneth Register II," Johnson said. "Register has a type O positive blood and he is a secretor. He has a PGM subtype of one minus-two plus."

"What?" Knowles asked.

"That means he's rare," replied Johnson.

"No, did you say Ken Register?"

"Sure did. Johnnie Kenneth Register II," she repeated. "Well, actually, the type O is common, but the PGM subtype is rare. Only five percent of people have that. Combine that with the frequency of the type O in the population, forty-five percent, and you have between two and three percent of the population with that combination. Then you can eliminate females, because we're working with a semen stain."

"Ken Register?" Knowles asked again. He was dumbfounded.

"Yep, he's our boy," continued Johnson. "We'll send everything explaining what we did with the DNA analysis, too. That's even more impressive. We are convinced the semen in Todd's body came from one source and only one source, Johnnie Kenneth Register II."

"Right under our noses," Knowles muttered. "Crystal's best friend. Bonnie Faye's source of strength."

"Congratulations, Bill," Johnson said, "I know you have a ways to go, but it looks real strong from this end."

"Yeah, uh, thanks, Lori."

Knowles hung up. He suddenly had some urgent business.

Knowles sat quietly at his desk and gathered his thoughts. *So, it's not a drifter, or even a stranger. It's a local boy.* Reaching for the phone, he anticipated the community's shock when word of this leaked out. He knew he had to keep a tight lid on the news.

He immediately phoned Chief Harris and began formulating a strategy for arresting Register. The arrest had to be clean and supported by as much evidence as possible. As much as they trusted the information provided by SLED and knew the crime lab's standards to be second to none, even the FBI's, this new evidence would be considered circumstantial and probable, not absolute, by higher authorities and a court. A confession would be needed for a jury to feel sure of Register's guilt beyond a reasonable doubt.

Two days later, on Monday, a team of fifteen officers met to plan the arrest. At exactly 9:30 the following morning, the teams of officers would go into motion. The first team would make the arrest in Garden City, where Ken worked. Two teams would simultaneously alert Bonnie Faye where she worked, and Shirley Register, the mother of the suspect, where she worked, that the arrest was taking place. The fourth team, carrying search warrants, would search the Register home and property.

Knowles felt good about the plan. Almost three months earlier, he had gazed at the dead girl in the ditch and reaffirmed his commitment to finding her killer. Three long months of sacrifice for his family, his officers, and the community. But now wasn't the time to consider the sacrifice.

Knowles put down his pencil on his paper-strewn desk and focused his eyes on a distant point outside the window. Now was the moment to draw down on his prey. The heavily breathing animal had momentarily stepped from the woods, giving away his position and direction of movement. Knowles held the image of his pursuit in sight and felt himself stealthily creeping forward, eyes fixed, stopping and starting in bursts, for the one shot. Raising his weapon, he felt the rhythm of his body and readied for the moment when his quarry would pass for an instant through the crosshairs. As his finger tightened on the trigger in anticipation, the power of the moment locked in. The months of tracking and stalking were about to be fulfilled. He and his cohorts had withstood criticism, ridicule, and self-doubt, but were about to emerge victorious. They had labored under misperceptions and misdirected blame, but that was all about to end. He was so near the supreme feeling of the consummation of the hunt, he could smell it.

He exchanged glances with officers in the small room that had practically served as home for the long investigation. He felt a shared rhythm. They would all join together in that ultimate moment when they saw the surprised look on the quarry's face, the instant of recognition that the promise of capture had been fulfilled.

Satisfied that every detail was accounted for, Knowles closed the folder on his desk. Breathing deeply, he rose from his seat, turned off his desk lamp, and strode confidently out of the building.

* * *

Knowles turned the cruiser into the mouth of the lane off of Collins Jollie Road and got out. He had big news and wanted to deliver it right away.

As he moved toward the spot, he braced himself for the sounds of the murder. As he had hoped, a new element appeared in his imagination.

The laughing, soft, familiar voice was accompanied by a lone male voice, deeper, abrupt, and insistent. OK, now, he thought, turning his head slightly to listen carefully. When the expected cry came, though, it was muffled, garbled, not nearly as distinct as he thought it would be.

How can this be? he thought. *Am I missing something?*

He added Ken Register's blue Plymouth Sundance to the picture. *Two occupants, movement inside, tussling? Is that fighting? What are they saying? Why isn't the door opening?*

Knowles breathed heavily. Forcing his mind to refocus, he again saw the car pulling up and stopping just before the spot. The interior was dark, the faces washed out. Was there movement inside?

"Well," he said aloud. "I came to tell you that we're gonna make an arrest tomorrow. We've got our fingers crossed."

Knowles felt foolish when he thought about whether to tell Crystal that her killer was Ken Register. He shook his head slowly and added, "We'll see, I guess."

Halfway back down the lane, he stopped, turned, and scanned the scene. *Why won't it materialize?* he thought. Knowles had been on his way home when he realized the pending arrest offered an opportunity for a new insight. *Perhaps this was premature?*

He took another deep breath, his signal for changing focus, and inhaled sharply through his mouth. As he exhaled slowly through his nose, he noticed some of the trees, and particularly the bushes, were budding. The absence of bugs made him reconsider what he momentarily regarded as a sign of spring.

That might be premature, too, he thought, making the comparison between the changing seasons and the evolving investigation. *There could still be some cold winter left.*

PART III
THE ARREST

25

The morning of February 18 found Knowles and the members of the homicide investigative team full of optimism. The long-awaited arrest was officially on schedule as detectives rechecked assignments and prepared to leave headquarters. The ordinary task of picking up a suspect was anything but routine this morning and had been carefully choreographed around the minute of Ken's arrest.

Headquarters was abuzz with teams of detectives going over their parts in the day's events. If all went well, by evening the suspect would be in custody and they would have a confession.

The first three teams left at nine o'clock. At 9:30, Detectives Russell Jordan and David Avant, along with Detectives Vic Neal and Tommy Flowers, arrived at the Santee Cooper Building to make the arrest. Jordan and Avant entered the main office while Neal and Flowers stayed out front in the parking lot.

Jordan introduced himself and Avant to the receptionist and asked to speak to Jimmy Long, Ken's supervisor. The secretary led the detectives to a warehouse behind the main building.

"You can find Mr. Long here," she said uneasily before hurrying back to the front, looking over her shoulder several times.

Long had been contacted earlier and asked to call Ken back from a job site. He knew of Ken's friendship with Crystal and that the police had spoken with him. Upon entering the warehouse, the detectives found five or six people standing around talking and immediately recognized one of them as Ken Register.

"Where can I find Mr. Long?" Jordan asked the group, which became quiet and looked at the plain-clothed officers.

One man stepped forward and extended his hand.

"I'm Jimmy Long. How can I help you?" he asked.

"Mr. Long, I'm Detective Jordan of the Horry County Police

Department and this is my partner, Detective Avant. We need to speak to one of your employees about a police matter."

Several of the men were uneasy with the detectives' presence.

"And who would that be, officer?" Long asked.

All eyes followed the detectives' gaze to Ken. "That would be Mr. Register," said Jordan, alert for movement.

"Certainly. Ken, would you go with these gentlemen to the break room?" Long shifted his gaze to Register and back to the detectives. Jordan nodded to Long that the break room would be fine.

Ken stiffened. His face flushed. He was suddenly all alone as his coworkers backed away, leaving a space between him and the detectives.

"What is this?" he inquired as they moved toward the break room. "I thought I was done with y'all when you took my blood."

Once inside the room, Ken was visibly nervous and had to steady himself. He placed his hand on the table as he stood and faced the officers. He started to hyperventilate as Jordan pulled what appeared to be legal papers from his inside coat pocket.

"Mr. Register, we have a statement which you've given to Law Enforcement that we need you to read and sign if the statement as worded is true."

This was a distraction to put Ken at ease and make him easier to contain. The young man was very strong and, by definition of the crime for which he was a suspect, capable of anything.

"I don't understand," said Ken, looking down at the offered papers. "What do you mean papers? What kind of papers?"

"Do you remember the statement you gave us on January 13 about the Crystal Todd investigation?" asked Jordan. "About Crystal's behavior and where you were the night of the murder?"

"I think so. Is that what this is about?" Ken looked puzzled, but he took the papers.

"Well, let's see if you'll recognize what you said."

Ken looked at the detectives and placed the papers on the table. Leaning forward on his arms to support his wobbly legs, he read the document. Jordan and Avant, following the arrest plan, positioned themselves on either side of Ken as if they were reading over his shoulders.

"We need to check for accurate wording," said Avant as Ken alternately looked at the officers and the papers.

Ken relaxed as he read and laughed when he saw the wording of one portion of the interview. When he finished, he looked at Jordan, who held out a pen and said, "If that's true, would you sign there on the bottom where we've indicated?"

"Yeah, that is true," said Ken as he took the pen. As he finished signing and straightened his body, his hands dropped to his sides long enough for the detectives to execute a well-practiced movement. Avant and Jordan each grabbed a wrist and, with a strong, swift motion, twisted Ken's arms behind his back and cuffed them.

"What are you doing?" exclaimed Ken in surprise. "Let go of me!"

"Johnnie Kenneth Register, you are under arrest for the murder and rape of Crystal Faye Todd."

"What? You've got the wrong person!" he protested.

Taking a card out of his shirt pocket, Jordan positioned himself in front of Ken and said, "Mr. Register, I'm going to read you your rights now, so you need to listen very carefully. Do you understand that?"

Ken's face turned beet-red.

"Mr. Register, do you understand? I'm going to read you your rights."

"Yes," he said. "I understand."

The detectives held Ken's arms and felt his body shaking. Jordan read from his Miranda card. "You have the right to remain silent. Anything you say can and will be used against you . . ."

Avant felt Ken's taut arm muscles through his shirt as he pulled against the restraint of the cuffs.

"What is this?" Ken said loudly. "You don't understand, I wasn't even around that night. I couldn't have done it."

When Jordan finished, he asked, "Mr. Register, you've been informed of your rights. Do you understand what you've been told?"

"Yes, but there's been a mistake! You'll see. My mama can clear it up. I want to call my mama."

* * *

At 9:30, two officers pulled into the parking lot of the building in which Shirley Register worked.

"Mrs. Register, I am Detective Winburn of the Horry County Police Department, and this is SLED Agent Anderson."

She nodded at the men and noted their badges.

"We'd like to ask you a few questions if we could," Windburn said.

Shirley Register's first thought, she later recalled, was that there had been an accident and that someone she knew was hurt or dead. But when she saw a folder in the detective's hand with a picture of Crystal clipped to the outside, she was relieved and realized the interview was "only about the investigation."

"Sure, I don't mind a few questions," she said. "I don't know much, but I'll be glad to help you in any way I can." She seemed sincere. She was friends with the Todds and had known Crystal for years.

The detectives first asked about Bonnie Faye's call to the Registers' on the night of the murder.

"So, she called your house?" Winburn asked.

"About one o'clock, uh huh."

"Was your son home at that time?"

"Yes, he was," she answered, then recounted for the detectives her and her son's actions from the time he got home until the phone call from Bonnie Faye. Ken had called the hospital for Bonnie Faye, but Shirley didn't want him to help Bonnie Faye look for Crystal.

"I'd rather you not go. You're about sick like it is," Shirley said she had told Ken. "If Miss Bonnie Faye's going and Gene's going, she won't be by herself. Now, if Gene's not going with her, I don't mind you going with her. But if Gene's going, I'd rather you didn't go."

Shirley described her son's car and what he had been wearing. She reconstructed Ken's day and evening for the detectives, apparently not realizing that all of the questions were about her son.

Following an abrupt end to the questioning, Winburn said, "We, ah . . . we wanted to talk with you about something. We've got some bad news we've got to share with you."

Shirley seemed surprised and stared at the detectives.

"We've got warrants for Ken," said the officer.

"For what?"

"For the murder and rape of Crystal Todd."

"Well," she said matter-of-factly, "I'll tell you this: Ken didn't do that."

"We're not here to discuss that with you," said Anderson. "We're just letting you know and I guess you need to call your husband. There's a team headed out to your house with a search warrant to search your property."

"Are y'all really telling the truth?" asked the incredulous woman.

"Ma'am, I'm not here playing with this," said Anderson.

Winburn spoke up, too. "We're not lying."

"No ma'am, this is no joke," Anderson said again, seeing the disbelief on her face.

"Could you call your husband and let him know what's going on? If not, we're gonna have to go locate him. There are officers out at your house waiting on him to unlock the doors. We can't tell you right now what evidence we have on your son for obvious reasons. You'll hear everything at a later time, but we've got good evidence. We're sure that it's him. We wouldn't have warrants on him for this crime if we didn't. I know you've got a lot of questions and it's a big load dropped on you right now, but it's something that we can't talk about right now."

"Y'all, I can't believe this," Shirley said. She heard the detectives, but found it difficult to grasp the meaning of the words. Her loving son, a fine Christian boy, was being arrested for the brutal murder of his long-time friend. Certainly she, as a mother, would have known if her son had done something like this. Some kind of terrible mistake was being made.

At 10:05 a.m., Detective Jordan turned from the front seat of the unmarked car that was on its way to Conway. He looked at Ken, whose face was red. His eyes were swollen. Jordan read the charges from the two arrest warrants.

"You are being charged with the murder of Crystal Faye Todd. You are being charged with criminal sexual conduct in the first degree committed against Crystal Todd."

Ken interrupted the detective. "Who are you?" he asked through gritted teeth, glaring at the detective.

"I'm Detective Jordan, Special Investigator with the Horry County Police Department."

"Let me ask you something," said Ken. "If I killed her, why would I have given blood?"

"You tell us, Mr. Register," the detective fired back.

Ken whimpered as the car sped to headquarters in Conway. By now, he realized he was not only the prime suspect, but was actually being charged with murder in one of the biggest investigations in Horry County history. The police would later discover that Ken had fantasized over and over about getting caught and going to jail. His nightmare was coming true.

"I want my mama," Ken said again. He would say it repeatedly all day.

Jordan continued reading the charges. "You are also being charged with the kidnapping of Crystal Faye Todd. And you are being charged with the sodomizing of Crystal Faye Todd."

Detective Flowers leaned across the seat and placed folded copies of the signed interview statement and the arrest warrants in Ken's shirt pocket. Ken remained silent, sniffing occasionally, and bowed his head the rest of the way to Conway.

Shirley contacted her husband and told him about the detectives' visit and the search warrant. Kenny Register immediately left work. Upon arriving at home, he was greeted by a team of police officers and SLED agents. At 10:40, as the members of the homicide investigative team were about to enter his home, Kenny screeched his pick-up truck to a halt and jumped from the cab.

"Mr. Register, we have a warrant to search this property for evidence that we believe is connected to the Todd murder case," Jordan said. "We want to go into your house, please." Jordan saw a confused and angry man in front of him.

"No, hell, you ain't. You tell me what you're going in for," said a belligerent Register.

Jordan repeated his statement and reaffirmed that they had the legal right to enter and search.

"Well, I'll sure as hell go in with you and see what you find."

"No, I'm sorry, you can't go in," Jordan said.

"What? Who in hell's going to keep me out of my own God-damned house?" argued the angry father.

"We're saying it would be better if you allowed us to go in to take care of our business," continued the detective, trying to remain calm.

Kenny and Shirley engaged in a futile, albeit brief, effort to explain that on the night of the murder, Ken was at his girlfriend's house and then home with them.

"Don't you think a mother would know if her son did something like that?" Shirley asked. "I saw him right after he got home and there was nothing wrong. I know my son!"

The detectives allowed Kenny to follow them as they prepared to search the house.

"Mr. Register, is there one room in the house where your son keeps most or all of his things?" Jordan asked.

Kenny led the detectives to a bedroom at the front of the house. As they passed the den, he said sharply, "If anyone goes into my gun case, I want to be there."

The search began in Ken's bedroom, where the detectives went through everything. They dismantled furniture to look for hidden compartments and cracks. An empty knife box, which would later have relevance in the case, was noticed, but passed over.

The search then moved to the room next to Ken's, his sister's. When the police asked her to leave, she acted like her father had. "You see what that says on the door? Kim's room!" she said. "And I'm Kim. This is my room, and I'll not move for you."

The police searched Kim's room while the teenager sat defiantly on the bed with her arms crossed.

Bonnie Faye was at work when the police told her about Ken's arrest. The grieving mother had been holding up under the strain for three long months, hoping and praying she'd see the day Crystal's killer was identified. But when she finally heard the killer's name, the expression on her face went completely blank.

Ken Register? How could that be? He was Crystal's best friend, she thought.

Bonnie Faye looked closely at the officers for a sign that they weren't telling the truth. She saw none. Noting the seriousness in their manner, she sat down hard, numb from the shock, and, with shaking hands, lit a cigarette. As she smoked and thought, her expression turned bitter. What would have been a satisfying moment was complicated by her relationship with the arrested suspect. The detectives kept quiet as she abruptly stood and walked aimlessly around the room.

"Ken's behavior since the murder doesn't make sense," she thought aloud. "Unless . . ."

"Didn't he come over to see me to comfort me? Or was that just to find out if there was anything new in the investigation?"

"He cried and hugged my neck, or was that because he felt guilty?"

"He helped me when I told him I needed it, or was that because he felt like he owed me something?"

The more she smoked and paced and thought, the angrier she got. Her daughter, her precious and only child, had been murdered by a friend, who then only pretended to be concerned, sympathetic, and loving.

"And to think I felt sorry for him because he lost his good friend," she said disgustedly.

Bonnie Faye's expression turned hard.

"I shoulda knowed," she said bitterly.

The detectives stood in awkward silence and listened.

"I called him that night," she continued. "He said he had the flu. I bet he didn't call the hospitals like he said, 'cause he knew where she was.

"He didn't act one bit different than he always did. He was not nervous one bit. The only time I saw him nervous was when he had to have his blood pulled. Guess he called to see if we knew who the killer was so it would be safe to come. When he did come, he was so nervous he couldn't sit down. He said they talked awful to him."

Bonnie Faye stared into space. "That's the last time he came to see me at all," she said. "Guess he was too scared to come back." She tipped her cigarette into the ashtray. "Now I know why. And dumb me still trusting him."

Bonnie Faye's bitterness turned to anger as she reflected upon the past three months of her life. She believed in and trusted Bill Knowles. If Ken had been arrested, he must have killed Crystal. His behavior since that awful, sleepless night when she paced the floor, crying in worry, only to have her nightmare come to life, made Ken the worst person she could imagine. "He is the most cold-hearted, no-conscience, no-feeling killer I've ever known," she said. "I hate him with all my heart and more. I want to kill him."

26

"I didn't have anything to do with it!" Ken Register shouted. "Will you talk to me? What do I have to say to you to get you to understand?"

The handcuffed suspect was hustled down the sidewalk by detectives. The entrance to the homicide office appeared quiet, as planned. The door abruptly swung open, though, and Ken found himself standing before Bill Knowles and two other men in civilian clothes. The arresting officers were suddenly nowhere in sight.

"Mr. Knowles, Mr. Knowles, you know I couldn't have done this!" Ken said. "There's a mistake being made!" He looked frantically at the men. His swollen eyes darted from one to the other and into the room to which he was being led.

Knowles ignored Ken's pleas and removed his handcuffs. Agents Caldwell and Streater remained on the porch of the modular unit and stood at the entrance. Two other uniformed officers stood quietly in the distance.

"Ken, we're here to ask you some questions, and it may take a while," Knowles said.

"There's no questions!" Ken blurted. "I ain't done nothing. I want to call my mama!"

The sparsely furnished room had several chairs positioned around a center seat, the obvious focus of attention, to allow access to its occupant from all sides. A small table with a tape recorder was behind the chair, close to the door.

"Mr. Knowles, I'm trying to tell ya, this is a mistake!" Ken pleaded. He shifted his weight nervously to keep his legs from buckling. Taking his arm, Knowles said calmly, "Sit down, Ken. Do you understand me?"

Ken resisted being led toward the middle seat by stopping

and starting in baby steps. Then he slowly sank into the chair. "We don't need to do this," he said.

"Do you understand me?" Knowles asked, pulling a chair forward. "We'll take a break if you need to."

Ken was on the verge of tears. "Yeah, I understand you," he said impatiently. "You're not listening to me, either. I tried to tell them others."

"We're gonna listen to you." Knowles replied. "We want to hear all about it." The detective watched as Ken began to hyperventilate. His face flushed bright red. His shoulders and hands trembled. "Have you been told what your rights are here this morning?"

Ken appeared confused. His eyes momentarily glazed over. His pupils dilated quickly, then he squinted, a glare that the detectives would see often as the day wore on.

Knowles repeated the question. "Ken, have you been instructed concerning your rights? Do you understand what I'm saying?"

As he slowly nodded his head, Ken responded, "Yeah, yeah, I understand. I'm telling ya, if you'd just call my mama, she could clear this up."

"You have been told your rights?"

"Yeah."

"Are you willing to talk to us this morning?"

Ken hesitated, then slowly nodded his head. "Yes," he said softly before bursting into tears. He bowed his head. His sobs shook his body and tears streamed down his face.

Knowles walked outside the room and conferred with Agents Caldwell and Streater on the porch.

"Is he ready?" asked Caldwell. "He's ready," he added, answering his own question. "Says he'll talk to us."

"Yeah," Knowles said, barely above a whisper, while glancing back into the small room. Ken's cries could be heard outside. "Let's give him a minute, though. It's after ten o'clock already, but let's let him calm down some."

"He doesn't look so cocky now," said Caldwell. "He's scared."

Knowles motioned for the uniformed officers, who quickly moved to the platform steps. "We're clear, now? Nobody comes in. Absolutely nobody. Right? Not his mama, not some volunteer lawyer, nobody."

Nods all around confirmed the plan. The interrogation had been carefully orchestrated to have Knowles and Caldwell working on Ken, with Streater operating as the third man. They wanted to make Register feel completely isolated and cut off from his normal sources of support.

"Ken," began Caldwell, "we want to be clear with you from the start today. We know that you killed Crystal Todd and we're here to listen to your side of it. We're sure you've got something you want to say to us." Caldwell sat to Ken's right as Ken faced Knowles.

"What?" Ken said anxiously, his face clearly reflecting the alarm he felt. "I didn't do it! I'm tryin' to tell ya." He had to turn his head to see both detectives at once.

"Wait, we'd like to record this, Ken," said Knowles, getting up and walking to the door. "Do you mind if we turn on the tape recorder?"

"Record it?" Ken asked, turning in his chair and looking at the small cassette recorder.

"We got a tape recorder here, see?" Knowles lifted the corner of the machine. "I could just push that button. We'd like to turn it on."

Ken shook his head. "I don't want no recorder on."

"If we tape it, we'll have a record of everything. We'd like to turn it on, Ken, but we won't if you don't want us to."

"No, there ain't nothin' to tell anyway. I don't want no recorder on, though."

"All right, then, we won't turn it on," Knowles said, sitting back down. "You can go ahead, then, and tell us what you did. We want to work with you. You can see that. We're not turning the machine on, but you have to work with us. We can't help you unless you work with us."

Ken eyed Knowles cautiously, suspicious of his seemingly friendly manner.

"All right, now," continued Caldwell, "tell us why you did it."

"Wait, wait, now listen to me carefully," Ken said deliberately. "I didn't do this, I'm telling ya. I didn't kill the girl. Just ask my mama."

"We're asking you," replied Caldwell. "Your mama wants you to tell us what you did."

"I didn't kill nobody!"

"Why did you kill her, Ken? We know you did it. We've got a witness that saw you with her that night."

Ken flushed. He was on the verge of tears again. "I didn't do it! I didn't do it! What's wrong with you? Why don't you listen?"

"Did you have to kill her? Was that it? You had to kill her for some reason?"

"Do I get a phone call?"

"Tell us why you killed her, Ken. That's all you have to do."

"Don't I get a call? I want to call my mama."

"You're not going to get out of here, call anyone, see anyone, until you tell us why you killed Crystal," Caldwell said, sliding his chair forward and moving his face within inches of Ken's. "We know you did it, there's no use to deny it. We're here to hear your side of it and that's what's going to happen."

"What about you?" Ken said to Knowles, who sat back with his legs crossed. "You know I couldn't have done this. Tell him! Tell him about me and Bonnie Faye. How we're friends and all."

Knowles didn't say a word.

"He can't help you, son," Caldwell said softly in his deep voice. "Only you can help yourself."

Ken leaned away from the large man. "Tell him!" he exhorted Knowles.

"There's nothing I can say, Ken," Knowles responded. "He told you how it is. You've got to tell him what happened."

Ken exhaled forcefully through his nose. His voice quavered. "I didn't do anything. You're not listening. I didn't do anything." He began to cry again.

Caldwell backed off momentarily. After letting Ken compose himself, Knowles took over. Moving forward a little, he said, "Ken, I'd like to help you, I really would, but there's not a lot I can do for you unless you help us."

Ken looked at the detective.

"We got the DNA, Ken," he continued, "and it says you did it."

"That's a lie," he exclaimed.

"No, sir, we got it. We wouldn't have arrested you if we didn't have the proof. The DNA don't lie."

Both detectives leaned in, cornering Ken against the desk.

"That's not all we have," Knowles said.

"We've got everything," Caldwell added. "We got your tire prints, son. Match your car."

Ken's eyes widened. "That's . . . That's a lie, too. You can't have that, 'cause I wasn't there."

"No use to deny it, son, we got 'em, and we got a lot more than that. Tell us why you killed her. That's really what we want to know."

Caldwell shook his head and said disgustedly, "We're wasting time here, Ken. Tell us why you killed Crystal."

"I didn't kill nobody!"

"We know you did!"

"I didn't, I'm telling you!"

"And we know you did!" Caldwell shot back, his voice hard and insistent.

"I didn't!"

"Don't deny it, son!"

Ken shut his eyes as he felt the force of Caldwell's voice. Small bits of saliva splattered against his cheek.

"I want my mama! She'll clear this up."

"There's no mama, no daddy, there's nobody but you, boy. Tell us why you killed the girl!"

Knowles nodded to Caldwell and leaned back. "Wait, now, this is getting out of hand. David, why don't you take a break? It's not gonna help us to get upset here."

Caldwell abruptly slid back his chair and stood up. "When I come back, I want some answers," he said dryly.

After Caldwell left the room, Knowles said calmly, "OK, Ken, I know this is hard on you, but it doesn't have to be. Let's just take a little break, too, right here, me and you. Do you need something? Can I get you something?"

Ken rocked back and forth with his arms crossed and shook his head.

"OK, let's just rest," Knowles said. "We don't have to talk."

Knowles, Caldwell, and Streater systematically tore holes in Ken's version of what took place on the night of the murder. When asked to explain his whereabouts that night, Ken said,

"There was no way I could have killed Crystal because I was at the Dodge City Race Track until 11:45 and drove straight home, got home near 12:15, spoke with my mother, then Bonnie Faye called."

Ken said he didn't drink or do drugs, had never hurt anyone in his life, had a job, played guitar in his church, had a nice girlfriend, and that everything was going his way. He maintained his story that he had last seen Crystal three or four days prior to her death when she asked him to take her for her driver's license. In response to the detectives' accusations, he repeatedly asked, "Why would I have killed her?"

The morning was getting long. The interrogation had already lasted close to two hours. Ken was alternately angry, upset, and defiant as he repeatedly denied having been anywhere near Crystal on the night she was murdered. Caldwell and Knowles, with Streater moving in and out, continued with the plan that they knew from experience might take a long time to work.

Ken glanced at Caldwell when the detective sat back down, but averted his eyes when the big man looked in his direction.

"Ready again?" Knowles asked Caldwell.

"All right," Caldwell said, sitting back in his chair. "Ken, we believe that you killed Crystal, but let's let that go for a minute. We have to try to look at this thing in terms of what a man will and won't do."

Ken sat with his arms crossed and avoided looking at Caldwell.

"Sometimes," continued Caldwell, "a man will do something and it's because he's just a mean person. You know what I mean, Ken? There's just mean people in the world. There's no accounting for them, they're just born mean, I guess. And they'll do things out of meanness, even kill someone, just because. You with me, Ken?"

Ken listened and said nothing.

"Sometimes, though, a man will do something, even kill somebody, 'cause he makes a mistake. He didn't want to, maybe didn't even mean to, but it happens. It's a mistake, and he's sorry."

Caldwell looked at Knowles.

"What he's trying to say, Ken," said Knowles, "is that Crystal could have been killed out of meanness, or it could've just been a mistake. A terrible mistake. You understand?"

Ken nodded.

Caldwell continued. "The reason we're telling you this, Ken, is because it's important for a man to know the truth about himself. About whether he's a mean man or whether he's not. And the reason that matters is because of the difference between guilt and shame. Shame is when you've done something wrong and you feel bad that someone knows it. Shame is a terrible feeling. On the other hand, guilt is when you've done something wrong and you feel bad about it inside, and that can feel terrible, too.

"Which is the worse feeling depends on whether you're a mean person or not. You see, the mean man will feel shame anytime somebody knows he did something wrong, and he'll always live with that. He won't always feel the shame, but he can't get rid of it. As long as somebody knows about what he did wrong, he'll feel shame and feel bad.

"But a good man who makes a mistake is in a better position. He'll feel guilty and feel bad about something he's done, inside of him, where it'll eat at him, but he doesn't have to feel bad. He can tell somebody about what he's done and get rid of the guilt. He doesn't have to live with it. But he has to confess it to somebody or it'll just keep eating him and eating him and eating at him until he's just a hollow man.

"So, you see," said Caldwell, "a good man needs to own up to his mistakes, no matter how bad they are. That's the only way he'll ever be able to live with what he's done."

The detectives sat quietly and let Ken absorb the information.

After a couple of minutes, Caldwell asked, in an even tone, "Which are you, Ken? Are you a mean man?"

Ken shook his head. "I ain't no mean man."

"You're not a mean man, Ken?"

"No," he said quietly.

"How are we supposed to believe you?" asked Caldwell. "You make it hard for us to believe you."

Ken said nothing.

"Sometimes people make mistakes in the world, Ken.

Everybody makes mistakes. There's no perfect man. But a real man owns up to his mistakes."

Ken kept quiet, so Caldwell continued.

"Of course, there's different kinds of mistakes, too, some not as bad as others. And sometimes we can't help it. Something else influences whether we do something. Isn't that right, Ken?"

Ken nodded.

"Like when somebody's drunk. You ever seen anybody do something when they're drunk, Ken, something you just know they wouldn't have done otherwise? I bet you have."

"Yeah," Ken replied, "I seen that before."

"Sure you have. We all have. And how about when somebody makes you mad? Remember earlier, Ken? When you bowed up on me? I said something to make you mad, didn't I? And I don't blame you for getting mad at me."

Ken's eyes narrowed. He remembered. At Caldwell's repeated insistence that he had killed Crystal, Ken had angrily risen from his seat. He controlled himself, however, and sat back down. Knowles had said, "Well, Ken, I think you've got a temper."

"I wasn't angry," Ken said.

"Sure you were," said Caldwell, "and it was all right, Ken. I made you angry!"

"You shouldn't have done it."

"You might be right, maybe I shouldn't have," said Caldwell, moving his seat forward slightly. "But it happened. And it's OK to say it did."

"You just shouldn't have, is all."

"Maybe that's what happened to you that night, Ken."

The words hung in the air.

"Is that what happened, Ken? Did Crystal do something or say something that made you mad?"

"No. I told you. We've been through that. Why would I have killed her?"

"Well, Ken, let's see what you told us," said Knowles. "You told us that you were at the go-cart track with your girl, and then you went straight home. And I thought you said you didn't go to Conway. That's what you told us, isn't it?"

"That's right. I went straight home."

"Well, does your straight home take you through Conway, Ken? Because we know you were in Conway. We got a witness that saw you in Conway. So don't tell us you didn't drive to Conway because we know you did."

"Well, see, there's different ways I can get home," Ken said. "There's four or five ways I can drive."

"And you took one of the routes that took you through Conway, didn't you?" asked Knowles. "We got a witness says you did."

"I had some time so I drove the long way, and . . . uh, and I circled through the mall. That's all I did, though."

"You made the loop around the mall?"

"No, I drove around behind the mall and then out the side on 501. I didn't make the loop."

"Well," Knowles said. "OK, that makes more sense, then, 'cause I was confused. I mean, we've got this witness that says they saw you, but now I understand. They must have seen you when you drove through the mall parking lot."

"Can you show us which way you drove, Ken?" asked Caldwell. "I'm not as familiar with the mall as y'all are."

Ken took the pad and pencil and drew the route around the back of the mall, adding that he had waved to a couple of friends as he drove by.

"You talked to a couple of friends?" asked Caldwell.

"No, we just waved at each other as I drove by."

"You saw 'em wave at you?"

Ken hesitated. "Yeah . . . maybe they did."

"That's easy enough to check. But you know what, Ken? Our witness didn't say they saw you at the mall. They said they saw you on Elm Street."

"I wasn't on Elm Street," Ken said, his voice cracking. He began trembling again.

"You don't seem to know where you were," said Caldwell, pulling in his chair again. "First you're not in Conway and then you are. And then you're at the mall, saying hello to your friends, which, by the way, we're gonna check on right now."

"I didn't say I saw 'em!"

"Yes, you did, you said you waved to them!"

"I meant I don't know if they saw me."

"Well, that's just another lie, isn't it! That's all we've heard is lies, Ken. You've done nothing but lie to us for close to three hours now!"

"I'm tired!" Ken shouted.

"We're tired, too! We're tired of the lies, we're tired of hearing you keep changing your story every time we catch you in another lie. Tell us the truth, Ken! We want the truth! We know you killed Crystal and we want to hear your side of it!"

"I want to talk to my mama!"

"We told you, Ken. There's no mama until you cooperate with us and tell us what we want to hear."

Ken sat quiet and thought for several seconds. When he finally spoke again, he said, "I am not going to tell you about it until I talk to my mama."

Knowles and Caldwell looked at each other.

"Let's take a break, Ken," said Knowles.

Ken had repeatedly asked for his mother, but Knowles and Caldwell thought this new wrinkle was worth considering. The detectives felt he was on the verge of confessing and decided to pay a quick visit to the Registers' house to elicit support from his parents. They knew they couldn't let Ken see his mother, but they had something else in mind.

The team of officers searching the Register home was finishing their work when Knowles and Caldwell arrived. They found Mr. and Mrs. Register, along with Mr. Johnny, Kenny's father, standing under the carport.

"Please, take us to see our son," Kenny Register begged the detectives.

"I'm sorry, sir, that's just not possible now," Knowles replied. "He has been asking for his mother, though, we can tell you that."

"I'm sure we could straighten this out," Shirley Register said.

"You take us to see him and you can go in the room with us," Kenny said. "Just let us talk to him. You got the wrong person!"

"No," Knowles replied, "but there is something you can do."

Caldwell asked Shirley if she would write her son a note telling him to cooperate, something like, "Go ahead and tell the truth."

Shirley insisted that the truth was that Ken didn't kill Crystal. Knowles said that that couldn't be the truth because the police were sure that he had killed her. This angered Kenny, who got in Knowles' face and told him not to call his wife a liar. The hotheaded father had already had a day of perceived attacks on his family and he wasn't going to take any more.

Shirley quickly intervened and said she would send Ken a message, but not the one the detectives wanted. The note she actually wrote read: "Ken, I love you, I know where you were at. We know when you left the racetrack and I know when you got home. I'll stand by you. I love you! Mama." This was not the note the detectives had in mind.

"Well, he doesn't get to see the note," Caldwell said to Knowles on the ride back to the station.

"No, we can't show him that," Knowles agreed.

The detectives believed Ken had left the go-cart track in time to hook up with Crystal between 11:15, when she left Carla at the mall, and 11:30, when her car was first sighted in the middle school parking lot. This would have given him about an hour, less travel time, to drive to the parking spot five miles away on Collins Jollie Road and from there to his home, another few miles. He might have had an extra fifteen or thirty minutes on the back edge of the time window because reports of when he had arrived home varied by that much.

Knowles and Caldwell knew the key to the case was keeping the window open. The sighting of Crystal's car had set the early edge of the window. Ken had tried to push up the time of his arrival home by as much as he could, but the detectives knew, from interviews conducted before Ken became a suspect, that he had arrived home after midnight and as late as one o'clock.

Satisfied that they were doing the right thing, the detectives looked at each other and exchanged nervous smiles. They knew they needed a confession quickly. Time was getting short. They couldn't interrogate the boy forever, and they wouldn't get another chance before a lawyer got to him. The public defender had already tried to intervene by presenting himself at the steps of the trailer where the interrogation was taking place. He had been turned away.

One of the friends Ken claimed to have seen at the mall came to the police station while the detectives were away and denied seeing him on the Saturday of Crystal's murder. He hadn't seen Ken since the previous summer and had left the mall that night no later than 9:30. Here was proof that Ken was lying. With the boy still at the station, the detectives went back into the interrogation room ready for a confrontation. Once inside, both men moved in closely.

"Ken, we've got Raymond inside," Knowles said matter-of-factly. "He says he didn't see you at the mall that night."

"What? Did you talk to my mama?"

"We talked to your mama, Ken," Knowles replied. "She said for you to go ahead and tell the truth."

"What do you mean? Where is she? I want to see her."

"You can't see her. She doesn't want to see you right now, anyway. Now why did you lie about going to the mall?"

Ken appeared confused. "What do you mean she doesn't want to see me?"

"Forget that, Ken. You're not seeing her. Now tell us why you lied about the mall."

"I didn't lie! You said I could talk to my mama," Ken protested.

"No we didn't. We said we'd talk to her. Your father made it difficult to get a word in, but the gist of it is, she wants you to cooperate with us and just tell the truth."

"You talked to Daddy, too?"

"Yes, you could call it that," Knowles said. "He was there, all right, talking nonstop. They don't want to see you right now. They want you to go ahead and tell the truth."

Ken shuddered. The detectives thought he was ready to fall apart.

"Now tell us why you lied about the mall."

"I didn't," Ken stammered.

"You did! We got the boy right here. You want us to bring him in here to call you a liar?"

"No . . . maybe he just didn't see me, I don't know. I thought he did."

"Your story's falling apart," Knowles continued. "Our witness that saw you in Conway didn't say you were at the mall. We know you're lying about that, Ken."

"They said they saw you on Elm Street, with Crystal," Caldwell added. "That's where you were!"

"I was not on Elm Street."

"Give it up, Ken," Caldwell said. "We've got the whole story now and we're all you've got."

"You're confusing me. You're trying to trick me again!"

"If you don't come clean with us," added Knowles, "there's no way we can help you later. We can't speak on your behalf if we don't have cooperation."

"Plenty of people have been sitting right where you are now, and they're always better off if they cooperate," Caldwell added.

"How are we going to go to the judge and say, 'Yes, Judge, he did cooperate,' if you don't?" asked Knowles. "There are people who've confessed to crimes that are out leading productive lives right now. Do you hear what we're saying, Ken? Do you hear us?"

Ken nodded, but maintained his resistance.

At approximately three o'clock, Knowles thought of a new and, perhaps, final approach. If this didn't work, he didn't know what would.

Ken was a religious young man who went to church and played music during church services. Leaning in close and speaking softly, Knowles said, "Ken, have you asked God to forgive you for what you've done?"

Ken broke down and sobbed. He gasped for air. Several minutes later, as Ken composed himself, Knowles, maintaining an even, calm voice, asked the question again.

"Ken, have you asked God to forgive you for what you've done?"

Several more minutes ticked by as Ken's anguished cries filled the room. Finally, with red cheeks and swollen eyes, his hands shaking violently, Ken slowly nodded his head.

"Yes," he said.

"Tell us about it," said Knowles, glancing at Caldwell. "Do you mind if we turn on the recorder now?" They didn't want to push their luck if Ken was truly going to confess.

"No, don't turn it on," Ken said.

Ken said he had driven back from the go-cart track and seen Crystal in her car at the Ninth Avenue stoplight on Elm Street.

They had driven from there to the middle school, where Crystal parked her car, and, taking only her keys, got in with him. They rode out to a spot in the country to park. They started kissing. One thing led to another. He maintained they had consensual sex without protection, and Crystal got mad after he ejaculated inside of her. She began to hit him in the chest. In a fury, she got out of the car to put her clothes back on, all the while screaming at him that if she got pregnant, she was going to say that he had raped her. Ken said he was confused and angry and wanted her to stop screaming. So, he got out of the car and, using a knife that he kept in the compartment between the seats, started stabbing her.

The detectives probed for details, but Ken simply said he was frantic and couldn't remember everything that had happened. He remembered being very frightened when he realized what he had done. He then dragged Crystal's body from beside the car to a ditch close by, threw the knife as far as he could, and drove home as fast as his car would take him.

"I didn't get very bloody," Ken said.

When he arrived home at about 12:15, his mother greeted him in the kitchen and commented on him being home early. Ken talked with her for a few minutes. Then Bonnie Faye called.

Knowles and Caldwell had their confession. Now they had to get his signature, in front of witnesses. Caldwell took out his handwritten notes, hurriedly wrote a summary confession, had it typed, and took it back into the room for Ken's signature.

As he proofread the confession, Ken noted that Caldwell had incorrectly written that the knife had been a gift from his girlfriend's father. "What's that?" he said. "I didn't say anything about him."

"Well, if that's incorrect," said Caldwell, "just mark through it and then initial it."

Ken did as he was told, unaware that his simple act had demonstrated presence of mind after a long grueling day. The detectives knew exactly what they were doing.

While Knowles and Caldwell were out of the room making copies of the forms, Ken said to Agent Streater that he felt better and was glad it was finally over. Every time he saw a police car, he said, he had become frightened and thought about going to jail.

"I would think about getting locked up and stuff," said Ken. Maybe Caldwell had been right. Confessing did alleviate guilt. Now that the confession was over, Ken felt better.

When Knowles and Caldwell got back, Ken asked what kind of sentence he might get for his crime.

Caldwell replied, "The police don't make those decisions."

"I had a good job," Ken said. "I was about to get the boat I always wanted, and I'm probably going to lose my girlfriend."

The officers stared at him in amazement. There was no mention of Crystal in his reflection.

"You said I could see my mama when it was all over. Can I see her now?" Ken asked.

"Sure you can, Ken. You can see your mama, just as soon as we get you to jail."

At 4:30 p.m. on February 18, 1992, Knowles and Streater escorted the confessed murderer of Crystal Faye Todd to the J. Reuben Long Detention Center. During the ride, Ken seemed nonchalant. He talked about weightlifting and football.

27

Ken looked terrible when his first day in custody ended. Shirley was the only family member who could visit him in jail. Tim Johnson, the Registers' attorney, anticipated her arrival and met her outside. Trying to soften the blow of seeing her son in such a pitiful state, Johnson told Shirley that Ken looked better than he had when he first arrived. Ken's mental condition, however, was like he had been "beat to hell and back," Johnson said.

Dressed in the tan jumpsuit given to him when he was admitted to jail, Ken appeared stuporous. He mumbled to himself and was barely able to keep his head up. When he saw his mother, Ken wept. His body convulsed uncontrollably as he repeatedly said, "Mama, they say I killed Crystal. They say I killed Crystal." She lovingly comforted him.

Shirley was crushed to see her strong son in such a state and seemingly unaware of what was going on around him. His eyes were glazed over and his head bobbed forward and from one side to the other.

"Mama, they said it was me," he mumbled over and over. "They said it was me." His teeth chattered and he was unable to keep his hands and knees from shaking.

"Son, don't you remember where you were at that night?" she asked.

Ken was placed on suicide watch and received priority attention from the jail nurse. He had not eaten all day, having had only the soda given to him during the interrogation. Johnson had earlier given him five dollars, which he spent on the cigarettes that he chain-smoked as he slumped against the block wall of the holding cell.

"Mama," Ken slurred, "they said you and Daddy told them to tell me, 'The hell with you, go ahead and tell them, confess and get it over with.' That you knew that I wasn't with Tammy that night. They told me I had nobody, that it was the only way I could get out of there. To confess to Crystal's murder. That if I would confess, I could get out of there. They would then talk to the solicitor and the judge. They would go easy on me, maybe probation or a suspended sentence. But if I didn't, I would get the electric chair. Mama, all I thought about was if I could get out of there and get to you, I could straighten everything out."

On her way home, Shirley had the feeling that the situation had somehow been contrived to make her son appear guilty. Her husband had always kidded her about being so naive and innocent, always seeing the good in people, trusting too much. Maybe it was true. What if the DNA had been rigged to show Ken had killed Crystal? Who could do such a thing? Was such a thing possible?

She pulled into a church parking lot, sat for a few minutes, and tried to pray. "I wanted to go to Bonnie Faye's house to straighten it all out with her," she later said, "to let her know that my son did not kill her daughter. She would know, she knew Ken, she would understand. But I was afraid. I didn't know what to say. What do you say to a woman when your son has been arrested for killing her only child? What do you tell her to comfort her? If she was as confused as I was . . . I had no idea."

Upon arriving home, Shirley found her house crowded with family and friends.

"It was like a death," she recalled. "Everyone was stunned, confused, hurt. I have gone through deaths before. I lost my mom when I was twenty-four, my dad when I was thirteen, but this was worse."

Shirley believed none of the charges against her son. She was shocked. She had never detected the slightest hint of deviant behavior in her son. She and his father had always been his staunchest supporters. And now this? How could Ken do all this: rape, stab, and kill, and then act as if nothing had happened?

Two days after Ken confessed, the police returned to the Register home, armed with another search warrant, to search for a knife box they believed was important. The visit didn't go well.

"You are not all coming into my house!" Kenny Register defiantly told the officers. He had fumed about the first search for two days, thinking he should have done something to prevent it. Now here they were back at his house again, as if they were calling his bluff.

"We can come in your house," Agent Streater responded, "and do anything we damn well please, and there isn't a thing you can do about it."

"Let me tell you something, Streater," Kenny said angrily. "You might can tell me you're coming in this house, and you might think you can, but who's gonna guarantee Heyward Goldfinch won't be the next one to wipe your ass?"

Heyward Goldfinch was the funeral director.

Detective Jordan intervened and suggested that he go into the house by himself to retrieve the box. Kenny reluctantly agreed, and Jordan entered the home and found the knife box in a dresser drawer.

"Mr. Register," Jordan said. "You need to calm down. Please don't do anything to produce more problems for your family."

"Son," Kenny replied, "I have been and still am living in hell over everything that's happened."

"Yes sir," Jordan said, "I can well imagine that you are."

Kenny apologized for his emotional outbursts and shook hands with the officers, including Streater.

"I'll tell you what though," Kenny suddenly said. "This is my cut-off date. There'll be no more searching of my home. Y'all are pulling a frame job on my boy, anyway. So don't be coming around here acting like you're looking for something. I know where my boy was at that night. You just say the word, Jordan, and I'll bring a hundred people down to the station to jack off in a cup. Then let's see y'all tell who is who."

With her son's arrest, Shirley entered the bleakest period of her spiritual life. She went eight days without praying. She felt like her prayers were "bouncing off of the ceiling," she said. "My body was fighting my soul. God was just not there for me at that time. I had never done anything to hurt anybody. I was so naive that I couldn't tell you what most people even talked about when they used sexual references."

Prior to her son's arrest, Shirley would have described herself as trusting, loyal, family-oriented, and conservative. Now, she was discovering, "it was all different. We were treated differently. We were all treated like killers." She was the object of derision and scorn, ridicule and pity. She felt emotions that were new to her. She felt rage and hatred for the first time. She hated her life, she hated what was happening to her family, and she hated what was happening to her faith. Confused by the tragic turn of events, she was angry at her god for deserting her.

Eight nights after Ken's arrest, Shirley locked herself in the bathroom. Carrying a pocketbook that contained her husband's pistol, she sat on the floor, pulled her knees to her chest, and rocked back and forth in a state of delirium.

"Nobody's going to bother me anymore!" she screamed in despair. "I can't take it!"

Where had she gone wrong? If something had been happening in her life, she would have done something. How could she not have known if something was going on in her son's life? Ken's emotions were always so transparent. She could always tell when he was happy or sad or afraid. Had she missed something? Had she done all she could? Had she somehow put him at risk by not being more in touch with . . . reality? Is that what it was? Was she so naive, so out of touch with her son's reality that she didn't notice something wrong? Without realizing it, had she led him to do this terrible thing of which he was now accused?

A little while later, Kenny came home and looked for his wife. "Shirley, where are you?" he called through the house. He couldn't find her in the backyard. She wasn't on the porch. She wasn't in the kitchen.

"I saw the bathroom door closed," Kenny recalled, "but I thought she would have answered me as I called, so I didn't think to look in there. I didn't like the terrible feeling I had creeping up on me. I knew Shirley was home. Maybe she walked over to the neighbors.

"And then I heard a whimpering sound, like a small frightened dog. As I walked through the house, I realized it was coming from the bathroom and, in a panic, I turned the knob and found the door locked. I called to Shirley, but she didn't answer. I beat on the door, calling for her to answer me, and tell me she was all right, but she didn't. 'Shirley, open the door!' I hollered. God, I didn't know what happened. But I knew right then that I was scared. I mean, as bad as I thought things were, I knew right then that they could get worse. A whole lot worse."

As he told the story, Kenny paused, took a deep breath, and took his wife's hand. She continued the story.

"Kenny had to kick the door down. I remember I was laying on my side and the feeling of the floor on my face. Then I heard Kenny's voice, and then a sound like an explosion. He sat down beside me and put his arms around me and we cried together, right there on the bathroom floor. I guess it sounds silly now, but he was so sweet. He was just what I needed. He said, 'Honey, I need you. If everybody in the world turns against us, if you stand by me and I stand by you, we'll make it. Together we can make it, but I can't make it without you.' I had been so ready to give up, so ready for this to be over. I wasn't taking care of my home, I wasn't cooking, I wasn't doing anything. Kenny was drinking too much, and he needed me, but I wasn't there. My daughter needed me, my grandchild needed me, my church needed me. I knew then that I had to be strong for my family, very strong for those who needed me.

"Something still wasn't right, though," she continued. "I had my reason to live renewed, but I still lacked the purpose to make it all worthwhile. I've always had a strong faith and I just knew that God hadn't deserted me. I just hadn't looked hard enough to find out his purpose for me. So I got on my knees in the walk-in closet in the bedroom. I don't know why I picked the closet, but I did, and I started to pray. I said, 'Show it to me, Lord, show me your purpose.' I just began to pour my heart out to him. 'Lord, I've been so naive, so trusting in others, I don't know what to believe. So, you show me the truth. Show me what to believe.' And it was at that moment that I was sure that He heard me and would answer my prayers.

"I wasn't the same person after that. I began to speak positively about Ken's situation. I knew he wasn't guilty. Somehow, all of the doubts are now gone. No matter how long it will take, the truth will come out. He will be vindicated. That was when I decided to put yellow ribbons on the tree out front. They're still up there now and will be until my son comes home. And slowly I've become a whole person again."

PART IV

THE WAIT

28

The talk in Conway over the morning coffee and paper was of nothing but the arrest. The *Sun News* carried a couple of articles under the headline, "Todd Murder Suspect Held." The sub-headlines, "Friends shocked by suspect's arrest," and, "Register a family friend and pallbearer at funeral," struck at the heart of the community's sensibilities. Businessmen, students, church leaders, and friends of the Todd and Register families were stunned by the arrest of a popular, well-known local boy from a nice family.

Many people contacted by the police didn't think Ken had committed the crime. "Who can believe it's Ken?" they asked. "He's such a nice, Christian boy, always willing to help out. And he was a pallbearer at her funeral. Why, who's ever heard of such a thing?"

Ken had a reputation in the community as a hard worker. His grades in school had been average and his teachers said they couldn't remember any problems with him at Conway High. His peers liked him. Being a varsity football player made him and his family highly visible with the small town, Friday night high school football crowd.

Ken had occasionally accompanied his minister and done chores for some of the older church members. Many people in the rural Bible-belt communities considered Ken's church attendance and participation evidence of his moral upbringing and good character. He had, in fact, spent the morning of the day Crystal was murdered scrubbing the floors of the new church that he and his father had helped construct. Ken had arrived early at the church the next morning, after visiting Bonnie Faye, and had made last minute preparations for the ten a.m. service. During the service, he played his guitar and led the music. The small church counted on its members to become actively involved and depended upon Ken for music. On that particular day, as he had for several months, Ken attended Sunday school and church services at his church and then drove to Aynor to attend a church function with his girlfriend. He was a family-oriented, well-mannered Christian boy. Ken certainly had a good side that ran contrary to his new image as a cold-blooded murderer.

On the day Ken was arrested, the police interviewed his girlfriend and her parents. Her father couldn't say when Ken left the go-cart track on November 16, because he was busy in the flag stand. He wasn't sure, but thought Ken was at his house when he heard the news that Crystal had been killed.

"He acted like he was shocked, like he was just shocked to death," he said. "Ken said he can't hardly believe it, anybody do her like that."

When Detective Long asked what Ken had meant by "do her like that," Tammy's father responded that he didn't think Ken meant anything specific. He said that he and Ken had heard "a hundred different things about it all around the county."

Long asked, "Have you seen any changes in him since Crystal was killed?"

"No," he responded, "that's why I don't believe it, because the boy is just a good, Christian-hearted acting kid. I mean he's not a high-strung or high-tempered boy. He's just easygoing good, you know."

Tammy's mother had been home all night on November 16 and had a better recollection of Ken's comings and goings, although she couldn't say precisely what time he had left the go-cart track. Asked if she wanted to add anything to her statement, she said, "I'm just being honest with you, I don't think Ken could kill anybody. I just don't think he could."

Tammy also said she wasn't sure when Ken had left the races. "It was between 11:30 and twelve o'clock," she said. "The best I can remember it was 11:30 something, I mean, it weren't a lot after 11:30, but it weren't real close to twelve you know."

"Did you talk to him the rest of the night?" Long asked.

"No sir," she responded.

"When was the last time you heard from him?"

"Sunday morning," she replied.

She explained that Ken had gone to her church in the early afternoon for a pot luck dinner to celebrate Harvest Day. Her brother showed up with a message from Shirley that she relayed to Ken.

"I asked Ken had he heard about Crystal and he said, 'Yes,' and I said, 'You did?' and he says, 'Yes.' He goes, 'They found her car but they haven't found her.' I said, 'No, they found her, she's dead.'"

"Did he act surprised when you told him that Crystal was dead?" asked Long.

"Yeah, he was hurt," she said.

"Did he act pretty upset?"

"Yes, he was very upset."

"Did Ken drink?"

"He had parties and stuff before he met me, but I don't date anyone who drinks or is real wild, 'cause I'm not. He started coming over and we went to his church and everything. And he started liking me and we didn't go to parties. I have never seen Ken drink or do dope or anything like that."

Ralph Wilson, the solicitor of Horry County and the lead prosecutor, was concerned when he first saw the case because he wasn't sure Ken Register was guilty. The odds were against it. He was a pallbearer in the funeral. He was a family friend and he had an alibi. He was a local boy. Wilson was concerned. He would have much rather prosecuted Randall Lew Vaughn. He would've been a great defendant, Wilson thought. He had a criminal record and was a fugitive from justice from Alabama. He wasn't a local person.

"I'd have had a field day over there trying to convict him," Wilson said. "I'd have had to fight the jury off to keep them from giving him the electric chair."

Everywhere the police turned, they found strong support for Ken and hard questions about DNA. These were fair questions in early 1992. The use of DNA in court was relatively new in South Carolina, having been used only since the late 1980s. In 1987, DNA evidence was successfully used in Georgetown County to convict a rapist who had disguised himself so well that the victim couldn't identify him. The accused subsequently appealed. One criticism of DNA is that it was used in courts before being universally accepted by science. The Supreme Court of South Carolina upheld the Georgetown rape conviction in May 1990, just two years before DNA evidence was used to identify Ken as Crystal Todd's killer.

In 1987, prosecutors in the Georgetown case had the DNA tests performed by a private lab because SLED didn't have a DNA lab to handle the analyses. In 1992, however, utilizing a new multimillion-dollar facility, SLED had three specialists who worked full time performing DNA analyses for police departments throughout the state. This was similar to what was happening across the country, but information about the new forensic tests was only slowly becoming available to the general public. *National Geographic* magazine didn't publish an informational story on DNA until May 1992. No wonder, then, that before February 1992, the average person in Conway had never heard of DNA analysis. People wanted to know why someone as unlikely as Ken had been arrested for Crystal's murder. The investigative team knew it had to come up with something or the DNA evidence linking Ken to Crystal would be its only evidence. Detective Knowles and the rest of the homicide team knew of the Richland County jury that, in 1989, ignored DNA evidence and set a suspect free.

The local community wouldn't find out about Ken's confession for more than two months, when the indictments for murder and rape were handed down by the grand jury. Solicitor Wilson knew that important issues of motive, means, and opportunity would have to be more fully developed before the state of South Carolina would be ready to battle with Ken Register's defense team.

29

Two months prior to Crystal's murder, Ken was on his way to a class at the technical education school located next door to Coastal Carolina University. Driving through the university campus, he pulled up his car next to two female students and asked for directions to the library. One of the young women had noticed Ken unfastening his pants and said so to her friend. Ken pulled forward and passed the young women, then abruptly swung his car around. He drove back past them and said, "Excuse me," to the women, who turned to look again. Ken pushed up his body, arched his back, and shook his exposed genitals at the women.

"Come and get it," he said.

As Ken drove away, one of the females remembered something her mother had once told her. "Wait!" she shouted. Ken hit the brakes and slowed down long enough for the woman to run behind the car and get his license number. The women reported the incident to campus police and gave a detailed description of Ken.

The tag number was checked by the campus police and traced to Shirley Register. When later questioned, Shirley—unaware of the officers' intent—admitted that Ken had been driving her car that afternoon. When told about the incident, Shirley questioned whether Ken could have been the person seen committing the lewd act. Ken told the police, in front of his mother, that he had not been on campus that afternoon and certainly hadn't exposed himself to any female students.

Based on the description the students gave to the police, a photographic lineup was arranged and the women were asked to identify the person they had seen. Within thirty seconds, one of the students picked Ken out of the lineup. But, after approximately five minutes, the other student picked someone else. Ken was arrested and released on bond.

When Ralph Wilson heard about the pending indecent exposure charge following Ken's arrest for murder, he had Ken's name pulled off the pretrial intervention program list. Pretrial intervention allowed youthful offenders to avoid indictment and keep their records clean by performing public service and attending classes. Wilson saw the charge as relevant to the murder investigation and decided to try Ken on the indecent exposure charge before trying him for Crystal's rape and murder. A conviction on indecent exposure could be used to establish Ken's character for the jury in the murder trial.

An interview with Ken's football coach, conducted by Knowles, Caldwell, and Streater, introduced another element of Ken's personality. Coach Chuck Jordan believed he saw his players under conditions of extreme stress that provided insights into the extremes of a young man's personality. He saw himself as a coach, but also as a friend, and sometimes, when a player had a problem which affected his game, as a counselor.

Jordan said he had seen Ken's temper during a game. Ken had been called for a personal foul and became upset, first because of the foul, and then with Jordan, who sided with the official. Ken had difficulty letting the perceived injustice pass. When he was benched for the infraction, he got in Jordan's face to explain himself. Jordan was busy with the game and didn't have time for Ken. Ken was persistent and glared at Jordan in the nose-to-nose confrontation. After several failed attempts to calm Ken, Jordan told Ken to shut his mouth and listen to what he had to say. Ken was infuriated.

"I really haven't seen that degree of a lack of control out of a kid in all my coaching years," Jordan told the police. "There was no question in my mind he was totally out of control." Ken continued his verbal aggression on the bench. After unsuccessful intervention by two other coaches, Ken eventually calmed down.

Ken was suspended from the team for a week and had to meet with his parents, the principal, and Coach Jordan. Jordan said that despite Ken's behavior on the field, the meeting focused on how he had cursed at Ken during the incident. Agent Streater, in his analysis of the interview, wrote, "Register had convinced his parents he had done nothing and that Jordan was wrong, so they attempted to cause trouble for Coach Jordan."

"I wanted to make sure his parents understood that Ken

cussed too, and I very vividly remember their reaction was, 'No, not Ken,'" Jordan recalled. "His dad made the comment to me that they had never heard him cuss before."

When the detectives asked if he had anything else to say, Jordan replied: "Ken always wore his feelings on his shirt sleeve. You knew where he was coming from. If he walked into my office I knew what kind of mood he was in and I knew whether he was sad or happy or whatever. I find it hard to believe that Ken could go that length of time from when the murder happened until the time of his arrest concealing his emotions and his feelings and not have his personality change in such a way that it would be observable by somebody close to him."

As Ken's hot temper became more apparent, Wilson was convinced that the profile developed by the forensic experts of Crystal's killer was very close to the mark. Without revealing their real motive for asking pointed and direct questions about Ken, the police, following the arrest, conducted interviews with several of his coworkers.

A coworker told police that Ken had once lost his temper on the job with "one of the big guys." Ken was temporary help and the temporary guys got all of the dirty jobs. The other fellows often kidded the temps, and Ken usually took the ribbing in stride.

"One of the boys, T.R., was really getting on his case, must have been a bad day for him," the coworker said. "Ken picked him right up and slammed him on the ground 'cause he had edged him too far, you know, he bugged him, and bugged him, and bugged him until finally he lost his temper and picked him up and threw him down."

T.R. confirmed the incident, but insisted that he and Ken were only roughhousing. He discounted the idea that Ken had been mad at him. It was just a case of boys having fun. "For his size," T.R. admitted, "Ken was a fairly strong guy."

For three months, T.R. and Ken rode together in the work truck as they went from one job site to another. He also commuted to work with Ken every morning, beginning the twenty-one-mile one-way trips around November 15, just before the murder, and ending in early January. He and Ken got to know each other and became friends.

Ken had driven his mother's car to work for a week after the murder. Ken had told T.R. that his car was in the shop because of a computer problem that was difficult to fix. Ken followed the murder investigation closely, and sometimes had T.R. read the newspaper to him as he drove in the predawn.

The detectives also learned from T.R. of Ken's interest in pornographic magazines. Ken hadn't brought magazines to work until early January, according to T.R. "He started bringing magazines, I'd say every other day, or two or three times a week. He said he was getting them from a friend of his."

Ken never took the magazines home. He kept them in his truck, according to R.W., another coworker. After Ken's arrest, his supervisor found out that Ken had claimed that he was buying the magazines for him.

"I thought Ken was all right, he was certainly a good worker, but when I was told he said he purchased the magazines for me, well, I knew that was a lie," the supervisor said. "And that lie made me rethink everything I knew about him."

The picture of Ken's character was changing. The churchgoing, hard-working young man was starting to look like a troubled young man who exposed himself to women, had a hot temper, and was fascinated by pornography. Ralph Wilson knew much of the evidence didn't seem to be too damning, but when piled up, a pattern would emerge for the jury. Of course, Wilson didn't know how much of the evidence would be admitted in court.

In early March, Ken Register sat in jail and watched as the CBS television show *Hard Copy* aired a segment on Crystal's murder. The segment, entitled "The Pallbearer," featured interviews with several local people, including Bonnie Faye and Bill Knowles.

This was the first, but not the last, nor the most controversial, of the national attention Ken and the town of Conway would attract during the investigation, the trial, and the aftermath. The notoriety wasn't well received. Several years later, local folks still smarted from the unflattering coverage of their small town and simple way of life, which suddenly wasn't so simple.

For Ken, his simple life had suddenly become overwhelmingly complicated.

30

The Horry County courthouse sits majestically on an entire city block of unfenced grass and is the centerpiece of Conway's historic downtown area. Framed on its front by massive columns and a widow's walk, the two-story red-brick building has survived hurricanes, tornadoes, and almost one hundred years as the nerve center for the county's business. Although the courthouse is too small to meet all the needs of the rapidly expanding coastal county, it remains home to the sheriff's and solicitor's offices and is the site of the criminal court activities for the area.

In April, eleven days after celebrating his nineteenth birthday in jail, Ken was shackled and led into the courthouse for the first time since being arrested. People at the courthouse stepped back and stared as Ken, flanked by armed guards, was paraded through the hallways. Dressed in a prison-issue jumpsuit, he was noticeably thinner than when he had been arrested and had dark circles outlining his eyes.

Ralph Wilson announced that he would seek the death penalty. He provided to the press a lengthy list outlining the hundreds of items of evidence being turned over to the defense. Included on the list was the first mention of Ken's confession.

The court appearance was the first time Ken had been in Bonnie Faye's presence since he had his blood samples taken. During the brief proceeding, he looked directly at the judge and avoided looking into the eyes of the distraught mother, who clutched hands with family members and glared at him from her front row seat.

After the hearing, reporters asked Bonnie Faye how the day went.

"It was awful," she said through tear-filled eyes. Having

dreaded this day for months, she simply added, "I made it through it."

For Shirley Register, the weeks and months after Ken's arrest and indictment were frustrating and exhausting. She knew she had to be strong, if not for herself then for her son and family, and her worn eyes revealed that she wasn't sleeping well.

Her new cynicism and bitterness toward the police for mistreating her son broadened as she watched her family fall prey to innuendo and vicious remarks from people she met on the street.

"You don't know what it's like to go to the store and have someone stare, as if to say, 'That's Ken Register's mother,'" she said. Conversations ceased when she entered rooms. People sensed that small talk was no longer appropriate. Shirley felt in her heart that she needed to respond, that it was somehow important for her to speak up. But what was there to say? What words would let others know what she and her family were going through? What would convince someone of Ken's innocence with all that was being said against him?

The upcoming trial was both her greatest fear and her hope for Ken's salvation. Though at times she felt utterly alone, she knew her loved ones needed her and she assured them that their faith would carry them through their ordeal. The Lord would never put more on them than He knew they could withstand. They would stand together as a family and place their confidence in God, each other, and Ken's lawyers.

What would have been Crystal's high school graduation took place in June. Her friends and classmates honored her with two white roses placed on her empty chair. A moving rendition of the song played at her funeral, *It's Hard to Say Good-bye,* was sung by a soloist and Conway High School's *a cappella* choir as the tearful crowd stood and cheered.

Earlier that week, four of Crystal's best friends had presented Bonnie Faye with a floral wreath that had a mortarboard and tassel attached to the top. A banner across the wreath read, "Class of '92." Crystal's friends had worked and saved more than two hundred dollars to buy Crystal the wreath, a cap and gown, and a yearbook. Leftover money was donated to buy a headstone for their friend.

"They loved Crystal so much they want to do this for her," said Bonnie Faye. "It just tickled me so much."

"Nothing's ever enough," said one of the friends. "She did so much for us while she was alive. You just feel like there's no way you can ever repay her."

Two other tributes in memory of Crystal, one by her mother and one by her friends, appeared the same day in the *Sun News* along with her picture. Bonnie Faye's tribute read:

IN MEMORY OF CRYSTAL FAYE TODD
Conway High School

Your seat will be empty tonight because you have taken a seat in heaven. You won't physically be in your chair but I know your presence will fill it. I'll look at the chair, through my tears, and know that your face would be radiant if only you could have lived to graduate. All of our hopes and dreams on this earth have been shattered. When I see you again in heaven we will continue our dream. You will always live in my heart because you are my heart.

I will always love you,
Mama

31

"**H**ello, Mr. Register? This is Bill Knowles. Did you want me to call you?"

"Yeah, Bill," Kenny Register responded. "I'd like for me and you to sit down and talk a little bit." He and Knowles hadn't seen each other since Ken was arrested several months earlier.

"OK, when did you . . ."

"It's at your convenience," Kenny cut in, "probably tomorrow."

"OK, let me check." The detective looked at his calendar. "Is Monday too late?"

"Well, what time Monday?"

"Whatever time you need it to be."

"OK. How about Slater?" asked Kenny.

"You want me to bring who to the meeting?" Knowles asked.

"Slater," Kenny said again.

"Streater?" Knowles asked. "Streater, with SLED?"

"Yeah."

Knowles hesitated. Agent Streater was no longer in the area every day. "I don't know what his schedule will be," he said. "I'll have to sit down and talk with him."

"Well, let's change it," Kenny continued. "We need to be seriously talking."

Knowles was confused. He didn't know what to say. "OK, we'll . . . I'll do it. I'll . . ."

"I'll have Tim and Morgan with us," Kenny added. "And we'll talk." Tim Johnson and Morgan Martin were Ken Register's lawyers.

"OK," the detective said tentatively, "you want me to call

Morgan's office and set it up? Or do you want to take care of that?"

"No," Kenny said. "Let's me and you and Slater talk by ourselves."

"Mr. Register, why don't you come by here when you get off?" Knowles suggested, thinking Kenny just needed someone to talk to. "What time do you get off Monday?"

"5:30."

"OK, why don't you just come by Monday and . . ."

"No, I don't want to go to no office," Kenny said flatly. "I want to . . . let's go on the outside."

"Tell me where you want to go, Mr. Register."

"Anywhere you say, Bill. Just tell me where to meet you after 5:30."

"How about Coastal Mall in Conway, right in front of Belk's?"

"I know exactly where you're talking about."

"Can you tell me what it's about?" Knowles inquired. "Do I need to bring anything?"

"No, the onliest thing you got to do is bring your tape recorder and I'll bring mine."

"Well . . . I'm . . . OK . . ."

" 'Cause I'm gonna tell you what I think of y'all. Y'all framed my young'un, and that's it."

"Well," said Knowles, "if that's what we're going to talk about, there ain't no sense in going to talk."

"Well, you better," Kenny blurted out.

"I thought you had something to talk about. I'm not going to meet you if you're going to criticize me, Mr. Register."

"I'm not going to criticize you, Bill, but what we need to do is sit down and talk about some shit."

"OK, why don't you do this. You say you don't want Morgan there?"

"No, Bill, I'd rather for us to meet face to face."

"Well, you've already told me what you think of me, Mr. Register."

"Bill, you've got my young'un in there on a frame charge to start with," Kenny said caustically. "And you know that as well as I do. And I just want to see you face to face." His tone of voice changed. "And hey, look a here, it's no arguments, it's no this, it's no that."

Knowles thought it over. "I don't see any reason to meet if that's all you want to do, Mr. Register."

"Well, I wanna talk with you face to face and tell you where my young'un was at."

"You've already done that, Mr. Register," Knowles said patiently. "Remember, we talked in your front yard?"

"Well, I'm gonna tell you again, because y'all has framed an innocent young'un."

"I would respectfully disagree with you," Knowles added. Kenny wasn't easily dissuaded.

"That's your damn place, 'cause you was gonna lose your job if you hadn't arrested somebody. And I'm gonna bring that up in court. But I just wanna see you face to face and look you dead in the damn eye and tell you what I think of you."

"You'll have an opportunity to do that, Mr. Register, but it will be in court."

"No, no, I'm serious, Bill, I'd like to speak with you and there won't be no arguments." Kenny was rambling.

"Well, I don't see where it would accomplish anything," replied the frustrated detective, "but if you want to speak to me, you can come down to my office. How about that?"

"No," snapped Kenny, "I don't want to go to your office. I'd like for me and you to meet face to face, just get out and talk man to man."

"Well, you call me Monday, if you want to do that and we'll set it up." Knowles knew that any meeting with the emotional man would have to take place at the police station.

"Bill, look a here," Kenny said. "What's so bad about it? I know where my young'un was at."

"I understand that, Mr. Register. I can't say I understand what you're going through."

"No, Bill, you've put me through more hell than if I'd been dead. But you got a job to do."

"And I'm just doing it the best way I know how, Mr. Register."

"Yeah, but you're trying to save your ass and convict an innocent young man. Let's sit down and talk about this case."

"I'd rather not discuss the case."

"I know it," Kenny said acidly, "'cause you got no damn case!"

"No," Knowles said patiently, "I'd rather not discuss the case until we have a pretrial, then you can ask whatever questions you like. What you need to do, Mr. Register, is go through your attorney to do all this."

"Well, I sit on my ass long enough, Bill, and my young'un is sittin' in the jail innocent. And I can back it up and I can prove that he is innocent and what y'all got is hearsay, bullshit. I'm gonna put it to you like this here. I'm gettin' fed up. I'm tired to the gills."

"We don't have a bone to pick with you, Mr. Register."

"No, but look a here," Kenny said excitedly. "Y'all got an innocent young'un in there that ain't got to be down there. I know where my young'un was at. My young'un was at home."

"If a jury lets him go, Mr. Register, you'll never hear any qualms from me."

"No, it'll never go to court," Kenny promised. "It'll never go to a jury."

Not knowing what to make of this statement, Knowles said, "Oh, well, however it ends up, you'll never hear a qualm from me."

"No, you'll hear from me," Kenny cautioned.

"Mr. Register, you're entitled to speak your opinion."

"I am speaking my opinion," he replied sharply. "Why did they give the damn car back?" He was referring to his son's car. "They ain't found nothing in it."

"Well, Morgan requested the vehicle," Knowles said.

"All right, who's going to fix it, his car back?" The police had cut fabric out of the car seats to check for blood and semen.

"I have no idea what you're talking about, Mr. Register," Knowles said.

"Who's going to put his seats back in that y'all cut out?"

"There again, you need to go through your attorney, he knows how to handle it. I can't give you answers to the questions you're asking."

"I'm not asking you nothing," he said, sounding distraught. "Except you got an innocent young'un down there who's not supposed to be there."

"And I would respectfully disagree, Mr. Register."

"Well, it'll come out in court."

"There you go, Mr. Register. That's the way to handle it."

"I have been sorta quiet, Bill. I ain't said nothing against you. You got a job to do, and I got a job to do. Ya follow me?"

"Yes, sir."

"But, looka here. My young'un's life is on the line, and if I can probe and break, I'm gonna do it. If I can do anything to help my young'un, I'm gonna do it. And you'd do the same." Kenny was on the verge of tears.

"I understand what you're saying," Knowles said.

"Bill, I don't know." Kenny faltered. His voice cracked. "I'm so damn crazy, I don't know where I'm coming or going. I'm gonna be frank with you. It's rumors out that I threatened you. I've not."

"No," Knowles responded decisively. "I haven't heard or said you threatened me. If I thought you had done that I would come to you and tell you about it."

"Yes, it's rumors out that I threatened you and that's why I called you. I have not threatened nobody. I talked with two people today who said I was going to be arrested for threatening Bill Knowles, but I have not threatened Bill Knowles. But if I wanted to do something, I wouldn't spread it through the county. You follow me? And it's not my nature to do nothing."

"Well," said Knowles, thinking over that last statement, "we've both agreed the court is the place to take care of it. I'm just trying to make a living, doing the job the best way that the Lord gives me the strength and wisdom to do it."

"Well, Bill, the best thing for you to do is get on your knees and pray again, because Ken Register is innocent."

"If he is, the Lord will look out for him, Mr. Register."

"Well, we hope so, Bill."

"Mr. Register," Knowles said, trying to comfort him. "I have no animosity toward you, your family, or even your son."

"Ken's innocent, Bill," Kenny declared, "and if it comes down to the nitty-gritty of it, I'll plead guilty and set him on. I'll say I killed her and that'll be the end of it. I hate to say it, but I will do it." He hesitated. "And I'm a man of my word."

32

With Ken Register's trial for indecent exposure scheduled for September 21, the defense worried publicly about pretrial publicity. "Never in the history of this county has any one defendant received the quantity of media publicity as has Ken Register," argued Morgan Martin, Ken's lead attorney. "All such publicity is in connection with his arrest for the murder of Crystal Todd and has been highly negative and extremely inflammatory."

The indecent exposure trial lasted a day. Ken's testimony was contrary to what the female students had to say. The defense argued that the young women "couldn't see clearly what happened. They thought they saw something they didn't see."

Both of the students said they had clearly seen Ken expose himself and shake his penis at them. Ken countered that he "grabbed on top of my pants and kind of shook it." When asked why he had done that, he said the young women "wouldn't give me the time of day. They made me feel like trash."

Prosecutor Ralph Wilson responded, "You were trash when you came there. That's the kind of person who would expose himself to two young girls he's never met in his life."

Ken finally admitted he was wrong and said he was ashamed of his behavior. When Wilson asked him why he had lied to the police in front of his mother, he said, "I didn't want to break Mama and Daddy's heart."

The jury deliberated for two hours before finding Ken guilty of indecent exposure. Wilson was elated because crimes of moral turpitude reflect on a suspect's character and the conviction had a chance of getting into the upcoming murder trial. Even if didn't, Wilson said, "I think the evidence in that case will stand on its own."

The defense downplayed the importance of the conviction.

"How many kids don't moon somebody?" said Martin. "Ken Register's guilty of flashing a couple of girls at Coastal. There's miles and miles of difference from that and murder."

Wilson spent the rest of the fall preparing for the murder trial. He received the lengthy DNA report from SLED in October and immediately went to work reading the two-thousand-page document and incorporating it into his notes. In November, he was ready for trial and reopened his office after a two-month hiatus from his normal duties. He had spent more than five hundred hours preparing for the case, far more than he usually spent on a death penalty trial. After his victory in the indecent exposure trial, Wilson was confident of his case against Ken in the rape and murder trial. He stood resolutely before the divided community and, despite death threats, vowed to see justice served.

The defense, headed by Martin and his partner, Tommy Brittain, also studied the DNA report. Martin spent hundreds of hours getting ready for the trial, which would be his first courtroom defense of a death penalty defendant, a milestone in his career.

Martin knew contending with the confession and DNA match wouldn't be easy. On the other hand, winning was possible. The prosecution had little or no other physical evidence. Ken had a strong alibi. There were possible flaws in the prosecution's case regarding the gathering of evidence. In effect, SLED's forensic lab was on trial. The Register case would be the first murder trial in South Carolina based on DNA evidence. Lawyers from all over the state closely followed the defense and prosecution strategies. Many of them would attend the trial.

Martin couldn't ask Wilson for a plea bargain. Shirley Register was actively engaged in her son's defense and, as Ken's staunchest supporter, had publicly declared him innocent. They weren't going to seek a plea that required Ken to admit his guilt; in their eyes, he hadn't done anything wrong. With a death sentence possible, the Registers decided to try for a full acquittal.

Bonnie Faye hated Ken and wished him dead. She came out and said a death sentence might not be harsh enough punishment. "He deserves what she got," Bonnie Faye said. Preparations were made to care for the grieving mother in case she was overwhelmed by testimony that described the brutal nature of her daughter's death. A counselor was nearby or on call in the event that Bonnie Faye broke down during the trial.

Despite the protests of those around her, Ken's girlfriend remained loyal during the long wait. Certainly, her friends argued, a fifteen-year-old had better things to do than attend the rape and murder trial of a nineteen-year-old man, particularly after he had been found guilty and sentenced to a year in prison for indecent exposure. Nonetheless, she accompanied Ken's parents in and out of court and once mouthed, "I love you," to Ken from her reserved seat.

Ralph Wilson and Morgan Martin had faced each other several times prior to the Register trial and knew each other's tactics and strengths. Wilson was a large man with an imposing presence and brought a fire and passion to the courtroom. His courtroom demeanor was a product of his humble background. Having grown up with eight brothers and sisters in a two-bedroom house, he had learned early in life that patience and dogged persistence would more than likely rule on any given day. Often loud, and always determined, Wilson knew the task facing him in the trial was akin to "stringing pearls"; each piece of evidence had to be methodically and carefully put in place. Martin's strengths included his ability to negotiate and establish personal connections. Jurors smiled as he spoke to them directly and softly. His country boy voice and style reflected an understanding of the jurors' burden and his grasp of the weighty matters of court. Wilson knew Martin's cross-examination talents were unsurpassed. Witnesses taken in by Martin's natural story-telling ability and friendly banter often found themselves saying things they hadn't wanted to say. They squirmed through relentless and incisive questioning.

Both Wilson and Martin had the local advantage of having attended law school at the University of South Carolina. They graduated in the late 1970s and were well known by the presiding judge of the trial, having met several times before in his court.

Wilson and Martin had skillfully maneuvered through the political process in Horry County and in the state. Wilson honed his abilities in the Public Defender's office, where he was a strong opponent of the death penalty, in private practice, and as deputy solicitor under then-solicitor Jim Dunn. Dunn was known for his courtroom theatrics and Wilson acknowledged having learned a trick or two as he and the other assistant prosecutors labored under a heavy case load. When Dunn retired and endorsed Wilson as his successor, Wilson in 1990 became the first African-American solicitor in South Carolina.

Martin took a different route, but through his experiences he matched Wilson's understanding of defense and prosecution strategies. Shortly after law school, Martin served in the Horry County solicitor's office under Dunn. He handled cases in family court and worked for several months without pay. Upon leaving the solicitor's office, Martin entered private practice and successfully secured a seat in the South Carolina House of Representatives. At the time of the Register trial, he was both a lawyer and a state legislator.

The high profile of the Register case placed Wilson and Martin at the center of attention and established the seasoned lawyers as local legal titans. People were betting on the outcome of the trial based on the lawyers' reputations alone.

Ken Register pleaded not guilty. Jury selection and pretrial motions were held in Marlboro County, the home of presiding Judge Edward Cottingham. Finally, after the largest crime investigation in the history of Horry County, the trial was about to begin.

PART V

THE TRIAL

33

The atmosphere in and around Conway was circus-like, considering the seriousness of the occasion. The *Sun News,* as if calling attention to a church social, carried a story headlined "Attending the Trial?" that gave times for arriving at the courthouse and advice on spectator etiquette. "Circuit Judge Edward Cottingham said he will allow standing-room-only crowds as long as there is order," read the missive. "If the crowd becomes noisy, he said he would remove all spectators."

An unusually large number of people milled about the downtown area and debated in hushed voices whether to brave the crowds at the courthouse and try to watch the trial. Few people knew the details of the crime and few, apparently, gave much thought to what horrible stories they might hear.

Getting a seat required arriving at the courthouse at the crack of dawn and waiting several hours. Even then, many viewers had to stand during the proceedings. Some stood all day, day after day. Business at local restaurants in the downtown area, expected to boom, was down, perhaps because, as one restaurateur noted, people were afraid of losing their seats.

Metal detectors were installed in the courthouse as part of the extensive security measures taken to ensure safety. Perhaps in response to the picture the national media had painted of Conway as a redneck, hick town, someone taped a sign on a door of the courthouse that read, "No knifes aloud."

Horry County hadn't seen anything like this in ten years. The Rusty Woomer death penalty trial, which resulted in his death in the electric chair in 1990, had caused a stir in the county and had drawn large crowds to the courthouse. Woomer and an accomplice had gone on a daylong, drug-induced crime spree through three counties before ending up at a motel in Myrtle Beach. Their car was spotted and when police surrounded the motel, Woomer's partner killed himself. Woomer was captured. Four people died and one was wounded. A young mother who was shot in the face with a shotgun was left for dead. Her testimony at the trial, despite her disfigurement, was shocking beyond words. Horry citizens were outraged at the senseless violence inflicted by Woomer and flocked to the courthouse to see justice served.

The Woomer case, unlike the Register case, didn't involve a long investigation filled with fear and suspicion in a divided community. Woomer wasn't a local boy with extensive ties in the region. No one in Horry County cried when the governor threw the switch.

The courthouse for the Register trial, on the other hand, was filled equally with Ken's supporters and foes in a reflection of the community's sentiments. The trial was unusual because many of the dozens of witnesses called to testify were teenagers, friends of both Crystal and Ken. It was difficult to determine whether the tears shed during and after the trial were of joy or anguish. For the citizens of Conway in 1993, this was the trial of the decade.

A television program that aired on January 14 caused a stir around town. The CBS show *Street Stories* featured a segment, narrated by Deborah Norville, that portrayed Ken as a victim of science and sloppy police work.

Both Dan Rather and Ed Bradley asked the question, "Did science make a mistake?" Bradley pointed out that there were no national standards for personnel or labs conducting DNA tests, and reported that critics said the labs were often wrong.

Norville guided the piece, which consisted of interviews and a tour of Conway. She described Conway as a town where everyone knows each other and lots of people are related. Numerous scenes of downtown Conway and the surrounding rural areas were shown while a country music song whined in the background. An unnamed Conway youth with a thick regional accent proclaimed, "It seems like nothing like that could happen in the little town of Conway. That's big city stuff there."

Norville toured the crime scene as she interviewed Bill Knowles and questioned the evidence collection and preservation process, employing hearsay and editing to inject doubt.

She spoke with Ralph Wilson about a possible motive for the murder and contradicted him concerning the confession and serology results. She interviewed some of Ken's friends and his girlfriend, who said the DNA had to be wrong.

Norville also spoke with DNA experts Barry Scheck and Peter Neufeld, who would become famous in the O. J. Simpson murder trial. Scheck and Neufeld noted that DNA analysis involves statistical probabilities that can be "misleading and misinterpreted." Norville explained how DNA analysis works. "Only small sections of a person's DNA, only a few genes," are tested, she pointed out, and while the chances of people having identical DNA profiles are slim, it can happen under certain circumstances.

Scheck and Neufeld defined the circumstances. In a small town, where everyone is married to their cousins, it would be possible for two people to have the same DNA profile, based on shared genes. In fact, Scheck said, it was probable, in "a small inbred town like Conway."

Scheck and Neufeld questioned the reliability of state-run labs that perform the DNA analysis, which is difficult to perform. Neufeld said an innocent person should not submit a sample for analysis because of the possibility of a false positive. Norville then asked Ken Register what he would have done differently if he could do it all over again. He said he wouldn't have submitted a blood sample.

Residents were insulted by the show. An administrative assistant at the detention center where Ken was being held said, "They made it look like we were Mayberry, that we were some backwoods, hillbilly town. I lived here all my life and I don't know anybody who married their cousin."

A woman on her way into the courthouse quipped, "We *can* get out of the family."

But many people in the community were intrigued by the show's criticism of how the crime scene was handled and the questions about DNA analysis. "DNA has got a long way to go," one resident said. "They've got to have more evidence than just a DNA test to go by. I think they should have had a lot tighter strings on the investigation."

Knowles didn't like the segment and pointed out that he and Ralph Wilson were not free to say much about the investigation prior to the trial. "I would have been more pleased with the story if they would have related the entire story made available to them, instead of bits and pieces," Knowles said. "I think it would have been a much more informative story if they had waited until the end of the trial."

Day after day, the old wooden courthouse creaked and groaned at the seams to fit in yet another curious person. When asked why he was attending the trial, one spectator, a lawyer who closed his office for the entire trial, said, "Are you kidding? This is the best show in town."

34

In his opening statement, Ralph Wilson recognized the burden of the State and gave the jurors pointers on how to do their job. Morgan Martin, speaking for the defense, explained the concept of "beyond a reasonable doubt." Using an analogy of a father protecting his son, he encouraged the jurors to think, "I don't believe he's guilty. You're gonna have to prove to me so I have no doubts." Martin concluded his brief statement by laying out his strategy.

"This boy wasn't there," he said. "There will be a defense of alibi presented in this case proving that at the time the girl was killed, he couldn't have been there."

The jury listened in stunned silence as several witnesses testified about the gruesome extent of the wounds to Crystal's body and described in detail what they remembered about the crime scene and the evidence-gathering process. With each witness, details previously unknown to the public were revealed. Wilson carefully organized the order in which the witnesses appeared so that he could tell the shocking tale as convincingly as possible. He started by questioning the Allen brothers, who had found Crystal's body, then continued with the ambulance driver.

The highlight of the first day came in the afternoon, when detectives Jordan and Knowles testified about the arrest and confession. Jurors and spectators sat on the edges of their seats as Jordan and Knowles described the process. Knowles read the confession, then answered hours of questions about the damning piece of evidence. He admitted upon cross-examination that the interrogation was designed to elicit a confession from Register.

"The reason you're there," Martin said, "is to question the boy about killing Crystal Todd?"

"Or get an alibi," responded Knowles, "or get his version of it, to get a statement of some type from him, yes, sir."

"And he told you up front that he didn't rape or murder Crystal Todd, didn't he?" asked Martin.

"That's correct."

"And he told you repeatedly, throughout the course of the day, did he not?"

"That's correct," said Knowles.

"And you and Officer Caldwell kept telling him, 'That's not so. We know that's not so,' didn't you?" said Martin, looking toward the jury.

"I think Agent Caldwell did more of it than I did, but he was told that, that's correct."

"You told him or Agent Caldwell told him in your presence, 'Son, we've got you. That DNA says you're the man, and you're the only man, so you might just as well come across and tell us what happened'?"

"Yes, sir. That was probably said."

"All right," Martin fired back, "and he told you, 'You've got the wrong man. I didn't do it'?"

"That's correct."

"And you fellows didn't take no for an answer. You kept on talking to him, didn't you?"

"Well, yeah," replied the detective. "There were periods of breaks in there where he was allowed to regain his composure."

"Well, it's 5:30 now," said Martin. "If we sat here until eleven o'clock tonight, how many times you reckon I could tell you I didn't do it?"

"I have no earthly idea," replied Knowles.

"It would be a whole bunch, wouldn't it?"

"Yes, sir."

"And so," continued Martin, "there was a lot of conversation and talking and cajoling of Ken Register to admit that he had killed Crystal Todd, was there not?"

"Yes, sir."

Martin also questioned Knowles about the lies the police had told Ken during the interrogation.

"I thought I heard you say on direct examination that you lied to him?" probed Martin.

"I did not tell him the truth, yes, sir," Knowles answered.

"Well," responded Martin, matter-of-factly, "would you call that a lie?"

"Yes, sir."

"All right," said Martin.

"I don't deny that," said Knowles.

"You lied to the boy and you're a police officer?"

"Yes, sir. I did."

"Because you wanted a confession one way or the other, didn't you?"

"I was using what I had available to me to try and obtain a confession."

"That's an interrogative technique that you use, isn't it?"

"I would just call it a form of interview."

"Would you call it trickery and deceit?"

"I would definitely say it fit in that category."

"How many times did you trick and deceive and lie to him?"

"Twice that I recall."

"You're sure about that now?"

"I'm not sure," replied the detective, "but I recall two times right off."

"How many times did Agent Caldwell, in your presence, lie to the boy?"

"One time that I recall."

"One time," continued Martin. "Well, let me ask you this: Do you recall him being told that there were tire tracks from the scene that matched those on his car?"

"I didn't make the statement," Knowles said. "Agent Caldwell did, but it was something to the effect that there were tire tracks left at the scene and they matched his vehicle."

"And his footprints at the scene, 'that match up to yours'?"

"I don't recall that."

"You don't deny that Caldwell told him that, do you?"

"No, I wouldn't deny anything Agent Caldwell did," replied Knowles.

"Well," said Martin, "you were right there with him, weren't you?"

"And I can't remember everything he said," Knowles shot back.

"That's a good point. You can't remember everything that you said. You fellows talked about setting up a video camera or an audio recording in that office before you ever got Ken Register over there so that whatever interrogation was had of him, whatever he said, whatever you said, could be brought right in here and shown to this jury, didn't you?"

"One was set up," confirmed Knowles.

"And you do not have to have Ken Register's permission to videotape him or audiotape him as you interrogate him, do you?"

"No, sir, but as is customary with anyone else I interview, that is one of the first questions I'll ask, and there have been other occasions where individuals did not wish to be recorded, and I didn't do it then either."

"A meeting of the great law enforcement brains in this state got together and planned the arrest and interrogation of Ken Register, did they not?" Martin asked.

"Now, that's not a proper question," Judge Cottingham interjected. "That's more of a statement. Ask your question."

"Well, this, as you said, was a preplanned arrest?" Martin asked.

"Yes, sir," the detective responded.

"All right, and you had the equipment, and you talked about just setting up a video. Ken Register don't have to know anything about it."

"I don't recall discussing a video camera," Knowles said.

"You could have done that, could you not?"

"Yes, sir, the law says I can."

"And you could have recorded him on an audio on a tape?"

"And him never known it," Knowles said.

"And you ain't above tricking him if you can, are you?"

"No, sir, I'm not."

"So then we would know exactly how he was questioned, what questions he was asked and how he responded, wouldn't we?"

"Yes, sir."

"But we don't have that now, do we?"

"No, sir."

"We've got it down to where it's your word against his, don't we?"

"That's correct."

"And that's the way police like it, isn't it?"

"No, sir," said Knowles. "I would much rather have had it recorded."

"You could have recorded it, couldn't you?"

"I could have tricked him into it, yes, sir."

"Well, you ain't above tricking him," Martin said. "You already said you tricked him twice, and I'm fixing to go down the list of some more tricks now, so you . . ."

"I'm not above it, no, sir," said Knowles.

". . . ain't above tricking him? The long and the short of it, the reason we ain't got it is because you didn't want it?"

"That's not true."

Actually, that was only partially not true. Knowles was following FBI protocol, which is to not videotape or record interrogations. That way, it's the detectives' word against that of the accused when the case goes to trial. In most cases, the jury will believe the police.

"OK. Now, you also told him that somebody had seen him on Elm Street, here in his car on Elm Street, didn't you?" Martin continued.

"Yes, sir, I did," Knowles responded.

"And that was not true, was it?"

"No, sir, it was not."

"And then you told him that somebody had seen him in the Coastal Mall parking lot, didn't you?"

"Yes, sir, I did."

"And that wasn't true, was it?"

"No, sir," admitted Knowles, "it was not."

"All right, and you had told him that someone had seen him with Crystal Todd that night, didn't you?"

"I did not, no, sir," Knowles said. "It was done in my presence."

"Agent Caldwell told him that, didn't he?"

"Yes, sir."

"And these things were to where he would deny it and you would tell him again, 'Son, ain't no need to deny it. We've got you. We've got somebody that saw you with Crystal Todd that night. There's no need to deny it.' Isn't that what you would tell him?" Martin asked.

"Not every time," Knowles responded, "but it was something to that effect."

"How many times do you reckon over the course of that three and a half to four hours you interviewed him was that boy told that?"

"I would say seven, eight, ten times."

"And that boy told you from the time he went in there, several times, that he wanted to talk to his mama, didn't he?"

"Yes, sir, he did."

"And you didn't want him to talk to his mama, did you?"

"No, sir. I did not."

"You didn't want him to talk to any lawyer, did you?"

"No sir, I did not."

"You didn't want him to talk to anybody, did you?"

"We were doing everything that we knew possible to try and get him to give us information about the murder within the legal ramifications."

"You got him isolated, you got him scared," Martin said.

"I didn't get him into anything," Knowles countered. "What he got, he got himself into."

A confession is considered reliable if it is consistent with supporting information. The reliability or unreliability of aspects of a confession don't necessarily indicate whether other aspects are true or false. For example, a person might confess that he had killed another person by shooting and stabbing him. If there are no stab wounds on the victim, that part of the confession would be unreliable. However, that person still might have shot and killed the victim. Morgan Martin hoped to cast doubt in jurors' minds by attacking portions of, and, therefore, the reliability of the confession.

"All right," Martin said to Knowles, "so after he had been there this five or six hours, you finally got him to break and/or open up and tell you what you wanted to hear, and that was, 'I stabbed her,' right?"

"Yes, sir," responded Knowles.

"Now, this is the time when your job really starts and you really get to get some good out of a statement, isn't it?" Martin asked. "But first of all, you don't believe this statement, do you?"

"I believe portions of it," said Knowles decisively, "I sure do."

"But there's no question that there's much of what he told you, you still don't believe?"

"No, sir, I don't."

"What you are taught to do," said Martin, "once he had said, 'I got together with her, we rode off, had sex. I stabbed her. She was screaming. I stabbed her,' then you started asking him about details and trying to find physical evidence which you could bring to this court as a result of what he had told you, didn't you?"

"Yes, sir."

"And so you asked him about the knife?"

"Yes, sir."

"And you never found the knife, did you?"

"No sir, I have not."

"And you asked him about some car keys that you had been looking for throughout this investigation, didn't you?"

"Yes, sir."

"And he couldn't tell you where to find the car keys, could he?"

"No, sir." .

"And as you continued to talk with him there, he couldn't tell you or wouldn't tell you about the wounds to her body, could he?"

"He told me that he was in a frenzy. He didn't remember what he had done," responded Knowles.

"And then you asked him, or Agent Caldwell asked him, 'How about any mementos of this crime?' And he couldn't give you anything, could he?"

"No, sir."

"He was asked specifically about buttons that were torn from the blouse, whether or not he had taken those or they had been in his car and he later removed them?"

"Yes, sir."

"He didn't know anything about those, did he?"

"That's correct."

"He was asked about his bloody clothes, 'What did you do with those bloody clothes?' wasn't he?"

"Yes, sir, and his response to that was he didn't get bloody."

"In sum and in total, Mr. Knowles, when he had broken down and, as you say, the Lord had reached into this situation and had caused him to come forward with the truth, you couldn't get any specific item corroborating the truthfulness of the fact that this boy had stabbed that girl, could you?"

"That's correct, and I didn't expect it. You have to remember, this was three months after she was murdered that he was arrested," Knowles said.

"He was asked, 'You had anal sex with her, didn't you?'"

"I asked him about that."

"And he said, 'No,' didn't he?"

"He denied it."

"Yeah, and somebody did with her," Martin pointed out.

"No question," Knowles agreed.

"And he tells you he never raped her or forced her to have sex, didn't he?"

"He admits to consensual sex."

"Well, but that ain't what you wanted to know anyway, is it?"

"Yeah, because I wanted the truth," Knowles said.

"That's right, but what the truth was as far as the physical evidence showed you is that she had been assaulted forcefully and/or raped?"

"That's correct. We asked him about the sodomizing."

"And you got nothing?"

"No, that's not so," said Knowles assuredly. "We got a confession."

On redirect, Wilson brought up a couple of points that Martin hadn't mentioned in his long cross-examination.

"Did the defendant tell you that he didn't stab her until she got out of the car and started to get herself dressed?" Wilson asked.

"That's correct," Knowles said.

"And when you found the body, tell the jury what condition of undress she was in."

"Her pants were pulled up and her underwear rolled up in them."

"He asked you whether or not Ken Register kept any mementos of this murder?"

"Yes, sir."

"In the Bible at the Register home, tell us what was found," Wilson said.

"Newspaper clippings concerning Crystal Todd's murder," Knowles replied.

35

Darkness was falling on the second day of the trial when Medical Examiner James Downs took the stand. His graphic testimony about the autopsy sent gasps through the courthouse.

An expert in forensic pathology, Dr. Downs used large drawings and a Styrofoam head to describe the extent, size, and depth of each of the thirty-five stab wounds, seven bruises, and multiple abrasions inflicted on Crystal's body and head during the last fifteen minutes of her life. Color-coded charts showed which of the wounds were inflicted before she died, which were potentially mortal wounds made as she lay dying, and which were made to her body after she was dead. There were eleven stab wounds to her face and head, three penetrating the skull and entering the brain, a phenomenon never seen before by the medical examiner or any other pathologist at the Medical University of South Carolina.

Downs had determined that Crystal was conscious while she was being stabbed repeatedly in the head and face. A stab wound just above her left ear paralyzed the right side of her body, yet she continued to fight off her attacker with her left hand, which suffered multiple cuts. She was nearly decapitated. A necklace was embedded in the cuts. Some of the cuts in her chest were made after she died and provided more evidence, a juror later said, of the sick mind of the killer as he played among her remains, partially removing her stomach from her body.

Blunt force trauma bruises in the anal and vaginal regions were consistent with forced sexual activity, testified the medical examiner. This was supported by the existence of sperm in Crystal's anus and vagina. The muscles of her anus were stretched out, not having contracted before she died, indicating that a foreign object was inserted into her anus up to and after her death. The courthouse spectators sat in stunned silence as the doctor explained that Crystal was anally raped while being stabbed, while bleeding to death, and after she died.

One juror starting crying during the explicit testimony and a recess was called so she could compose herself. The middle-aged woman sniffled quietly into a tissue and repeatedly damped her eyes. As the testimony continued, Ken sat emotionless through the matter-of-fact explanation of Crystal's death. The audience, closely heeding Judge Cottingham's warnings, remained still and quiet, needing no reminders from the two dozen officers posted around the courtroom.

When Morgan Martin, on cross-examination, asked if the attack was frenzied or deliberate, Downs responded, "There was a lot of force involved, a lot of power. This was a very controlled and deliberate attack in a lot of ways."

The State's case included testimony by a SLED serologist, Agent Emily Reinhart. She testified that she had examined the tires and swabs from the search of Ken's car and found minute traces of blood on one of the tires and on the gear shifter, steering wheel, inside door latch, and outside door handle. Martin pointed out on cross-examination that there hadn't been enough blood in any of the locations to perform typing and that the blood could have come from anywhere.

Ronald Paul James testified that Ken Register had brought his car to James' Tires just after the murder for a thorough washing and a set of new tires. The tires were ordered around November 22 and received by James on December 5. The car was washed inside and out, even though it appeared to only need an exterior washing. Ken again had the inside and outside of the car washed at James' Tires on December 19.

Ken's whereabouts on the night of the murder were reported by witnesses, who were not happy to be called by the prosecution. One witness, who had spoken with Ken the morning after the murder, had to be referred to a statement he had given police regarding the conversation.

"What did Ken Register tell you he did the night before?" asked Greg McCollum, a prosecution lawyer.

"He gave no specifics," said the young man, "but he told me that he was with his girlfriend. He stayed with her or there at her house until around midnight and was at his home at around 12:30."

The direct examination also revealed that Ken had phoned him on Sunday morning at 9:06 and asked if he had seen Crystal the night before.

"He called you at 9:06?" McCollum asked.

"Yes, sir," replied the young man.

"And asked you if you had seen Crystal Todd?"

"Yes, sir."

"OK, and what was your response?"

"No, I hadn't. My girlfriend and I went to the beach to get something to eat, and then we came back to my house to watch a movie."

"Do you remember him saying anything to you about her possibly being missing?"

"Yes, sir, that's what he was referring to. Crystal's mom had called him and asked him to help her find her, and he just wanted to know if I had seen her anywhere that night because he knew I had been at the beach."

Testimony later revealed that Ken had hung up the phone and, at 9:15, called Bonnie Faye to ask about Crystal. Ken had apparently asked his friend if he knew Crystal was missing without first confirming that she was, indeed, still missing.

Deena James, Kevin's mother, testified about Ken's nervousness about giving blood. Winnie Dale Bessant testified about Ken's relationship with Bonnie Faye before and after the murder. Bessant had stayed with Bonnie Faye for three weeks after the murder, until Bonnie Faye returned to work. She then visited during the week and stayed with her on weekends. She reported that Ken, after the murder, suddenly became Bonnie Faye's best friend and visited more frequently than he had before the murder.

"He would stop by real often to see Bonnie Faye and talk with her, asking her what she had found out, were the police getting any leads, real concerned and consoling her," Bessant said.

"Do you remember whether or not you saw Ken Register at Crystal's funeral?" asked McCollum.

"I saw him on more than one occasion there," she replied.

"And how did Ken Register appear to you that day as the

man from Goldfinch's [funeral home] was pinning the flower on his lapel?" McCollum asked.

"I noticed the side of his face was so red and he had a white splotch," she answered. "I was looking at him and I said, 'My Lord, the blood is about to come out of that poor boy's face.'"

"After Crystal's death, did Ken Register ever come over and console Mrs. Todd?"

"Many times," Bessant said. "Every time he left, he always hugged her, and there was one occasion I remember well. She was really upset that night, and he stood there for approximately, I'd say two minutes, and just held his arms around her, and she was crying and said, 'Ken, I don't think I can live without her,' and he was just rubbing her up and down her back and patting her and saying, 'Yes, yes.'"

More testimony filled in the gaps and strengthened the prosecution's case. T.R., Ken's long-time friend and coworker at Santee Cooper, testified about conversations he had with Ken after the murder. T.R., however, was a reluctant witness and didn't want to say what he had told the police just after Ken's arrest. Holding a transcript of the taped interview, McCollum convinced the witness to confirm that Ken was sleepy the day after the murder and that he often slept during his half-hour lunch breaks. T.R. confirmed that Ken had told coworkers the Wednesday following the murder that Crystal "was cut from the throat down to her vagina and stabbed in the head." This knowledge indicated Ken's guilt; the police hadn't released details about the wounds.

Forensic serologist Emily Reinhart's testimony also included an explanation of the process of examining blood and semen samples.

"Most people characterize people on their height, weight, and hair color and eye color," Reinhart said. "Well, in forensics, we have a way of characterizing a person by properties that we can detect in a laboratory. These aren't things that can be seen with the visual eye. These are things that must be detected by chemical procedures."

The semen found inside of Crystal had been compared to the blood sample donated by Ken and a blood sample from a T-shirt found at the Registers' house during the search. Reinhart explained that she was able to type Ken's blood from his semen because he was a Lewis Secretor.

"The population is divided into two groups of people," she said. "You're either a secretor or a non-secretor. A person that is a secretor has the ability to secrete their blood type into other body fluids. For instance, if a male is a secretor, I would be able to determine his blood type from a semen stain. However, a non-secretor does not secrete their blood type into other body fluids, so, there's two groups in relation to this test." Ken Register was a secretor with blood type O, the same as the donor of the semen found inside Crystal.

Reinhart explained to the Court how she had matched an enzyme found in the semen, phoscoglucomutate (PGM), to Ken's blood. "The PGM sub-type test is totally independent of secretor status," she explained. "This is a test that is done on the blood where a sub-typing is found. In Johnnie Register's case, the PGM sub-type was one minus two plus."

The semen donor had a blood type of O and a PGM sub-type of one minus two plus, as did Ken. Since forty-five percent of the population has a blood type of O, and five percent of the population has a PGM sub-type of one minus two plus, and these characteristics exist independently in the population, 2.25 percent of the population has both of the characteristics. Since the blood was typed and sub-typed from a semen sample, ruling out females, the probability was reduced to 1.1 percent of the population. The probability of Ken's blood type matching the blood type of the semen donor by chance was only about 1 in 90. This unlikely match convinced SLED to further process Ken's blood by DNA analysis.

The serological evidence wasn't contested by the defense.

Agent Lori Johnson, a SLED forensic analyst, spent more than an hour outlining for the jury how Ken's samples were analyzed, explaining in laborious detail each step of DNA processing. Morgan Martin spent another hour systematically tearing apart her explanation, hoping to make the jurors doubt the validity of the new science.

Ralph Wilson had anticipated the defense's attack on the competence of the relatively new forensic lab. During discovery, Wilson had offered Martin the remainder of Ken's forensic material so he could have his own DNA analysis performed. The defense declined the offer and chose, instead, to question the competency of SLED's analysts, perhaps hoping to simply overload the jurors with technical jargon.

Then Bonnie Faye took the stand and told the jury about the night Crystal disappeared.

"At some point in time that night, did you call the defendant?" Wilson asked.

"Somewhere right after one, I think," she said.

"What conversation did you and he have?"

"Well, I asked him if he knowed any party that she might be at. He told me two parties. I couldn't remember the last one he told me. We went by the first one and they was already broke up."

"What time did y'all go to look for her, the two of y'all?"

"It was somewhere around 1:30 until 3:30. I know it was about 3:30 when we got back home. I think we went down every street except where her car was at."

"All right, and did you find Crystal that night?"

"No."

"Do you know what time it was or did you go to bed?"

"I didn't ever go to bed. I walked all night, what time I weren't hunting her."

"OK. Now let me go to something else and ask you this: Now, Kenneth Register had been kind of a friend of your family's for a while, had he not?"

"Yeah."

"And he would come over kind of frequently?"

"All the time. I mean, he come a lot."

"OK. After Crystal's death, did Kenneth Register continue to come to your house?"

"He come more then."

"And at some point did he stop coming?"

"Yeah."

"When was that?"

"After he come back and told me they had pulled his blood," said Bonnie Faye. "He quit coming."

* * *

Agent Streater's testimony ended the prosecution's case and proved to be highly significant. Streater had been present for parts of the interrogation and Ken's confession.

"We went over his statement several times, and at approximately 3:30, Agent Caldwell and Detective Knowles left the interview room to have the statement that he gave us typed into a statement form," Streater testified. "I remained in the room with Ken Register, and he made several statements to me. He said, 'I just got scared, and I don't know why I did it. I'm glad it's finally over. Every time I saw a police car, I got scared and thought I was going to jail. Since this happened, I couldn't eat or sleep. I would sleep at work on breaks and at my girlfriend's house, and I'd eat only enough to stay alive,' and after the funeral at Bonnie Faye's house, some lady gave him some punch. He tried to drink it and ran outside and threw up in the bushes. He said, 'My life is ruined now. I've lost everything that I cared about, my job, my boat, my girlfriend.'"

Ken's conversation with Streater corroborated evidence obtained through interviews with his friends and coworkers. For at least one juror, Streater's testimony validated the confession.

"When the boy said he was so glad it was over with, and that every time he saw a police car he thought about being arrested, I don't think he [Streater] would have made that comment up," the juror said.

36

The defense began its case on January 20, 1992, the day Bill Clinton was sworn in as the forty-second President of the United States. That morning, the front page of the *Sun News* carried side-by-side pictures of Ken and the President.

While Morgan Martin was considered the lead attorney and handled most of the cross-examination, his partner, Tommy Brittain, was responsible for preparing Ken and the other defense witnesses to testify. Born in South Carolina and, like Martin and Ralph Wilson, a graduate of the University of South Carolina Law School, Brittain sharpened his skills in the Army at Fort Hood, where he served as a JAG officer and processed courts-martial for four years. Martin and Brittain were churchgoers and family men who had become friends and then partners. They had worked several big cases together.

The first several witnesses for the defense testified that Crystal's car was parked at the Conway Middle School at 11:30 p.m., before or just as Ken had left the go-cart racetrack in Aynor, thirty minutes away. The prosecution countered that the witnesses were confused or wrong about the time. Ken's girlfriend, Tammy, testified that he had left the go-cart racetrack at 11:40 p.m. Brittain made certain she got her point across.

"Let's go through that piece by piece and find out exactly how you know it is twenty minutes till twelve," Brittain asked her. "Are you approximating this?"

"No, sir," she said. "This is about dead on the head because I went to Ken's car to say goodnight, and I seen his digital clock in the car, and when we got in the car, it was 11:32, so we always stay in the car about ten or fifteen minutes, and I looked at the clock and told him to be careful and that I loved him, and I kissed him goodnight and I seen the clock, and it was like 11:40. I mean 11:38, 11:40. It was right there."

"You spent time with Ken Register from November the 16th until he was arrested, I take it?" Brittain asked.

"Yes, sir."

"All right. Your relationship with him during that period of time, was it the same as it had been?"

"Yes, sir."

"Did you notice any significant differences in his conduct or anything?"

"No, sir, I didn't."

"How frequently were you with Ken Register during that period of time?"

"Last year I was a JV cheerleader, so I had games on Thursday nights, and he would go to my football games and basketball games, and then we were together every Friday, Saturday, and Sunday, and then once in a while like if I thought I was gonna go to church or if something was going on in the community that was on a week night, we would go together."

"During all of this time," continued Brittain, "did you see him on weekends?"

"Every weekend."

"During any of this time, did you notice anything unusual or different about the way he was acting?"

"No, sir, I didn't."

"How long does it take to get from your house or the go-cart track to Conway, roughly?"

"Roughly thirty minutes."

"How about his eating habits? Did they change in any way that you could see?"

"No," she responded. "He still eats a lot."

"And sleeping habits, did they change in any way that you could see?"

"No. He started working at Santee-Cooper, and he had to get up at 5:30 in the morning and drive down to the beach and work, and we'd talk on the phone, so on weekends sometimes, I would be tired, Ken would be tired, and sometimes we would lay around on weekends and sleep, on Sunday evenings, but other than that, no."

The testimony of the next two witnesses corroborated that Ken was at the racetrack at 11:30, and that Crystal's car was in the parking lot in Conway at 11:30. A neighbor testified that he had seen Ken arrive home on that Saturday night. On cross-examination by Ralph Wilson, however, the man revealed that he hadn't actually seen Ken or his car that night. Though Ken wasn't identified as a suspect until three months later, the man remembered that specific night and knew the time of Ken's arrival home because he had heard the sound of Ken's car and saw the glow of his headlights through closed curtains.

"You saw some lights, and you heard a sound, and there ain't no question in your mind that that was Ken Register's car, is that right?" Wilson asked.

"No, sir, no question, no question about it," replied the neighbor.

"All right," continued Wilson, "and when is the first time that you went down to the police station and said, 'Hey, look fellows, let me tell you right now, I know old Ken Register got home at 12:25 because I heard his car and I saw his lights'?"

"I hadn't been," said the man.

"Hadn't been?"

"No, sir."

"Even till this day as we speak, you hadn't been?"

"No, sir."

"Well, when is the first time in this whole world that you ever told that story?"

"Right now," replied the man.

The defense devoted the rest of the day to examining the DNA evidence. Two experts talked at length about the complicated process. The defense's strategy was to question the state lab's techniques. If the DNA analysis was shown to be unreliable, or at least incomprehensible, the prosecution would have to rely heavily on the circumstantial evidence in the case and the testimony supporting Ken's alibi would appear stronger. That would still leave the confession, but Martin and Brittain hoped to convince the jury that Ken was confused and scared and that the police had lied and coerced him into confessing.

"What's your full name, son?" Tommy Brittain asked the witness.

"Johnnie Kenneth Register," he said.

Brittain loudly clapped his hands and yelled, "Did you kill Crystal Todd?"

"No, sir. I did not kill Crystal Todd," he responded.

"Did you rape her?" Brittain said loudly.

"No sir, I did not rape her," Ken said.

"Did you meet her that night?"

"No, sir. I did not meet her that night."

"Approximately what time did you get home that night and how do you know that's what time you got home?"

"Well," he began, "Mama, she always waits up on me. She never goes to sleep until I get home. When she seen me pull up, she got up from the den and started walking in the kitchen to me and I met her about halfway in the kitchen, and when I walk in my door, the kitchen, you know, the bar and everything is here, and then the kitchen table, and there is a clock right above the kitchen table, and she looked there and said, 'You're home a little early, ain't you?' so we know it was approximately, I can't say exactly 12:15, but it was approximately 12:15."

"You say your mama always waits up on you. What do you mean by that?"

"Well, you know, I go to work early in the morning-time. I get home and me and Tammy, you know, I'd go like if she had football games or basketball games during the week, I would go, so I never spent that much time with my mama during the week, and so she would always wait up on me on weekends, and when I would get home, we sort of made that time for us to sit down and talk, and that's just the time we set over the time with me dating Tammy. Saturdays, I'd go to the river and so when I get home on weekends, she's there; she's waiting on me, and we talk. You know, we don't have any specific thing to talk about. We just talk about anything."

Ken testified about his arrest and the ride to police headquarters in Conway. He said he had tried several times to explain to the arresting officers that a mistake was being made, but the officers kept telling him, "Shut up. We're taking you to the homicide office and there you can talk with somebody."

"They wouldn't let me talk or anything while they was transporting me," Register recalled. "Once they got into the homicide office, they took the handcuffs off of me, and then Bill Knowles and David Caldwell come in to talk to me."

"How were you feeling then?" Brittain asked.

"Well, I was scared. I didn't know what to expect, you know. I was thinking, you know, 'Hey, I can set here, I'm gonna tell them the truth, tell them what happened,' you know, and it would be over with, but it didn't turn out like that."

"How long were you there?"

"Probably about six hours."

"What did Officer Knowles and Agent Caldwell say to you and what did you say to them in the first thirty minutes?"

"Well, you see, they come in and, you know, they was asking me like, 'Son, why don't you go ahead and tell us what happened that night,' and I told them, I said, 'Sir, I don't know what you're talking about, you know. I didn't do this,' and they kept on and, I mean, I told them over and over, you know, that I didn't do it, but every time I told them no, I mean, they would just keep on and say, 'Yes, you did it, you know. We know you did it.' I mean, they like lied to me and told me they had people that seen me, you know, with her, and they told me they had people that seen me at Laurel Street and people that seen me at the mall and stuff with her, and I knew all this was a lie, you know.

"They told me about they had the DNA, said that I was a positive match on the DNA and that it was, you know, it was a good test and it's never been beat in a courtroom before, and they told me, said, 'Why don't you just go ahead and quit lying to us, you know. We've got all this stuff. We know you did it,' and I told them over and, I mean, I told them a bunch of times I didn't do it, and they just wasn't taking no for a answer. They just kept on and kept on with me."

"You say at some point in time they told you that they had witnesses that had seen you with Crystal Todd that night?" Brittain asked.

"Yes, sir."

"Well, I mean, come on, son, you knew that wasn't true, didn't you?"

"I knew it wasn't true, but, I mean, I was setting in yonder and they was telling me this stuff over and over. I mean, after so long of hearing it, you know, I knew that they hadn't seen me, but I knew these people had to be making a mistake. You know, you just had to be there in that situation with they there and you in here and, I mean, they're telling you this over and over. You know they're lying to you, but, I mean, you can't get to nobody to talk to. I mean, they've just got you there by yourself, I mean."

"Did you ever tell them that you knew they were lying to you?" Brittain asked.

"Yes, sir."

"What did they tell you?"

"I told them, 'You know, I know you're lying to me. You know, just quit lying to me,' and Bill Knowles, he looked at me, and Caldwell told me, said, 'Son, we can't lie to you. We're police officers. You know, our Constitutional rights tells us that we cannot lie to you,' and when he told me this, you know, I didn't know what to believe. I was confused. I just didn't know."

"At some point in time, did you begin to ask for somebody?"

"Yes, sir," Ken replied. "Like when they first handcuffed me at, you know, at work, I asked them, I told them, I said, 'I want to talk to my mom,' and they wouldn't ever say anything to me about it, and when I even got there, you know, they just kept, you know, going on about this. I told them, I said, 'You know, I want to talk with my mom,' and David Caldwell looked at me and said, 'Son, we're trying to get up with her. We don't know where she's at right now, but just as soon as we do, we'll let you talk with her,' but he never did, you know. He never would let me call or anything."

"Well," Brittain asked, "at some point in time, did they leave you alone and tell you they was going to see your mama?"

"Yes, sir. That morning, they had been telling me about all the stuff they had and everything they supposedly had, and, you know, they tried to make it feel like, make me feel like I just needed to go ahead and tell them the truth, you know, and they just kept telling me that if I wanted to live the rocky road, you know, that would be fine, and Bill Knowles, he like leaned back in his chair, and cocked his leg up, and he looked at me and said, 'Son, I've been in this business thirteen years. People that's cooperated with us and stuff is out living productive lifestyles now.' And he said, 'People that ain't, they're in jail,' and, you know, I could spend the rest of my life in jail, you know, or I could either get the electric chair for this crime, and I remember when they was going out, you know, told me, said,

'We're gonna go talk with your mama,' but he said, 'Now, remember what we're telling you, you know, you help us out, you know, we'll go talk to the judge and tell him that you cooperated with us and stuff.'"

"What, if anything, did they tell you about your mama's attitude about this?"

"Well, they come back, you know. You see, they had told me that my mom, you know, she was kind of upset, and they said my dad was so enraged that they couldn't even talk to him, you know, and they said they couldn't hardly talk to my mom, but he said the few words they did get through my mom, she said that she loved me and she wanted me to go ahead and tell them what happened that night, and they told me about my girlfriend's parents and stuff. They said that they had all of them convinced that I had did it, and they said, my girlfriend, you know, said that I stood her up that night, that I never even showed up."

"Now," continued Brittain, "this is taking place over the course of several hours?"

"Yes, sir."

"Was there ever any suggestions made to you by either one of the officers that Crystal may have done something to cause this?"

"Yes, sir. David Caldwell, he looked at me in some point of the thing and he told me, he said, 'Son, I can't put my feelings in the report.' He said, 'I have to put facts in it.' He said, 'You need to go ahead and tell us what happened.' He said, 'You're a good kid.' He said that he can't find anybody to talk bad about me, and he had told me, he said, 'You know, you don't remember it. You must have blacked out that night, you know.' He said, 'She must have done something for you to lose it and stuff,' and, you know, I looked at them and said, 'No, I wasn't there, you know,' but he suggested that it was her fault and that I had lost it and all this stuff."

"How many times do you reckon you told them that you weren't out there and you hadn't done it?" Brittain asked.

"Over five or six hours, probably a hundred times or more. I don't know. It was, you know, I mean, it was quite a lot."

"Now, at some point in time you quit telling them that you weren't out there?"

"Yes, sir."

"At some point in time, you quit telling them that you weren't guilty?"

"Yes, sir."

"Tell me what happened. What brought you to that point and what did you do to come up with this statement that's been introduced into evidence?"

"Well, you know," Ken said, "it's kind of hard to understand, but, you know, they took me in there, they lied to me, they told me that everybody was against me. They told me they had people that seen me there. They told me they had DNA on me. It was like they had me isolated from everybody. They wouldn't let me talk to nobody. They made me feel like and think that everybody was against me and they were my only friends I had. They just made me feel like I had to trust them. They made me feel like they was my only hope out, you know, like it was my only way, just to do what they wanted me to do."

"Well, how did you come up with this statement?" Brittain asked.

"Well, like I say, when they left me in yonder for that forty-five minutes to an hour, you know, they had already, you know, talked with me from the things they told me in that room from that morning until the time they left me in there. I took those things, the things they suggested to me, the things that was in the newspaper, and I set there and I thought up, just a plain lie."

"All right," Brittain said, "let me hand you this. It's been marked State's Exhibit Number 47, and it's got your name on it right down here at the bottom. That's your name isn't it?"

"Yes, sir."

"Johnnie Kenneth Register, II?"

"Yes, sir."

"You signed it?"

"Uh-huh."

"OK. Let's go over it sentence by sentence. 'On the night Crystal Todd disappeared, I left the go-cart track and drove to Conway.' Is that true?"

"Yes, sir, that's true."

"The second sentence, 'I saw Crystal in her car at the red light close to the Middle School.' True or false?"

"That's a lie."

"All right. Why did you say you saw her at the Middle School?"

"While I was in there, they had told me that her car was at the Middle School and it was parked, I don't know. I just told them I saw her there."

"'I tooted the horn to get her attention.' True or false?" Brittain asked.

"That's false."

"'She couldn't leave her car right there, so I followed her to the Middle School and she got in my car to go riding around.' True or false?"

"That's false."

"'We ended up parked on the dirt road.' True or false?"

"That's false."

"'We started kissing, and one thing led to another, and we started having sex.' True or false?"

"That's false."

"'I didn't have a rubber.'"

"That's a lie, too. I mean, the whole thing is a lie."

"'She said, 'Don't shoot off in me,' but I couldn't help it,'" Brittain continued.

"That's a lie."

"'She started screaming and hitting me in the chest, and she said if I got her pregnant, she'd say I raped her.'"

"That's a lie."

"'I was scared. I didn't know what to do. My knife was between the seats. She got out of my car and started getting dressed and was still screaming.'"

"That's a lie."

"'I stabbed her outside of the car and threw the knife as far as I could.'"

"That's a lie."

"Then there's a little scribbled out thing right here. It looks like it had something to say, something like about 'Tammy gave me a knife,' or something like that. Are those your initials there?" Brittain asked.

"Yes, sir."

"OK. How did that happen?"

"Well, they brought the statement back to me and it had Tammy's name in it, and . . ."

"Well, did that surprise you?" Brittain asked.

"Yes, sir."

"Why did that surprise you?"

"I mean, because, when I was making up this lie here, I never said anything about Tammy."

"All right," continued Brittain. "What was their attitude about it?"

"I said, 'Tammy?' and they said, 'Oh,' and they said, 'Here, go ahead and change that.' You know, it was like they put it there for me to change."

"All right. 'I left Crystal there and headed home.'"

"That's a lie."

"You know," Brittain said, "why didn't you tell them about the wounds that this girl had?"

"Because I didn't, I didn't kill the girl. I had no idea of, I mean, how many times she was stabbed or where she was cut. I didn't know."

"How about the car keys?"

"They asked me, 'What did you do with the keys?' I mean, I didn't know what to tell them because I wasn't there, and I told them, I said, 'I guess they're in her pocket. I don't know.'"

"You supplied no details about anything that went on out there that night?" Brittain asked.

"I didn't know any," Ken said. "I didn't kill the girl."

On cross-examination, Wilson asked Ken about the arrest and interrogation and got him to admit that he had been read his rights.

"And there ain't no question about the fact that you understood them rights, right? You understood them?" Wilson asked.

"Well, you see, sir, when they read me my rights, they read them to me when they picked me up. I mean, what I thought my rights was, I mean, when I got in yonder, I didn't think I had them, my rights. I mean, because I thought that when I got in yonder, I could use the phone. They would never let me, so I didn't know what was going on at the time."

Wilson showed him the confession.

"Ain't no question, son, that that's your signature on there, isn't it, three times?" he asked.

"Yes, sir. At 4:10 p.m., as you can see right here on the bottom, that was at the very end of the thing. I had done told them everything, and they come to me and they bring me this at 4:10. They set down, read them to me, have me initial them that evening, sign here, sign there and there."

"Now, back to my original question," continued Wilson. "There's no question but that's your signature on that document?"

"Oh, yes, sir, it's right there."

"Now, no question they told you had the right to remain silent? They told you that, didn't they?"

"Yes, sir."

"They told you anything you say can and will be used against you in a court of law?" continued Wilson.

"Yes, sir."

"They told you you had the right to talk to a lawyer and have him present with you while you're being questioned? No question they told you that?"

"Yes, sir, they told me."

"Told you if you cannot afford to hire your own lawyer, one will be appointed to represent you before any questioning, if you want one? They told you that?"

"Yes, sir."

"They told you if you desire to make a statement or answer questions, you have the right to stop at any time?"

"Yes."

"They told you, and then they turned around and gave you a copy of this statement?"

"Yes, sir, as I was walking out the door."

"And not only did they do this at 4:10 p.m., when you were originally arrested, son, they sat down with you when they put the handcuffs on you, the first thing they did was tell you what your rights were and the officer read them to you, didn't he?"

"Yes, sir. Like I said, when I was standing at the table, I stood up, and I think Russell grabbed my right hand, and the other guy grabbed my left hand."

"How much education you got, son?"

"I've got a twelfth grade degree."

"A twelfth grade education, and y'all have to take some kind of achievement test to get out of high school, these days, don't you?"

"Yeah, exit exam."

"And you took it and you passed it and got out of school, so you can read and write?"

"Yes, sir."

"And you understood? Ain't no question about that, is there?"

"I understood my rights, but, I mean . . ."

"All right," continued Wilson, "you understood, so any statement you gave, you gave of your own free will and accord after having been told what your rights were?"

"No, sir," Ken said, "I didn't give that statement under my own free will."

"Well, tell this jury who it was that forced you to give a statement? Which one of these officers—point him out to us—forced you to give a statement?"

"Well, see, I know it's hard to understand, but, I mean, nobody hit me and nobody slapped me, but when they get you in yonder and they make you feel like you have nobody, they make you feel like they are your friends. I mean, you've got one guy over here that is getting like this close in your face, hollering at you, telling you, 'You did it. You did it.' Then you've got this other man back here; he's kicked back and he's relaxing. He acts like your friend. I mean, just the way they go about doing it, I mean, after a while, so long of it, they make you believe that nobody is on your side. I mean, it's hard to believe, but they'll break you down."

"Who hollered at you, son?" Wilson asked.

"David Caldwell."

"What did he say to you in hollering at you?"

"He'd look at me and say, 'Why don't you quit lying,' and stuff like that."

"Was he the one that you was gonna fight?"

"I was never gonna fight any of them," Ken said.

"I'm talking about in the interrogation room, do you deny that you got angry and that you were getting ready to fight?"

"Yes, sir," said Register, "I don't deny getting angry. I mean, I was setting there. I mean, he was like this close to my face, and you know how people talk real hard and loud and spit comes from their mouth? I mean, you could feel it hitting on the side of your face."

"And you got angry about that?"

"Yes, sir, it got me a little upset."

"And what were you gonna do because you were angry?"

"I wasn't gonna do nothing," Ken said. "There wasn't nothing I could do."

37

The defense knew its best hope was to convince the jury that Ken Register had been forced into confessing, and that his confession was unreliable. For that reason, one of its key witnesses was Dr. Richard Ofshe, a sociology professor from the University of California at Berkeley. Interrogations, Ofshe explained, are not random question and answer questions, but designed to elicit an admission and a confession.

"It's an art form in which police officers learn how to manipulate and lead people to do what they want them to do, which is to confess," he said. "Clearly, some techniques that sometimes appear in interrogation are improper. If you threaten that you're going to beat someone if they don't confess, that's improper, but there is a well-recognized area of police interrogation that's entirely legitimate, and that's what one sees principally in the analysis of police interrogation, the use of legitimate tactics."

Ofshe introduced the concept of false confessions, which he said occurred frequently. The question wasn't whether Register understood his Miranda rights. The police had concocted a plan that minimized the chance that Register would invoke his rights but isolated him from anyone who might support him. Ofshe offered that the police had overstated the evidence when they told Ken they knew he was guilty and had irrefutable DNA evidence.

"If these techniques are effectively done, an individual who knows that he's not guilty may reach the conclusion that I have no hope, that all of these mistakes are going to get me convicted," Ofshe said.

"Explain what police are taught to do once they get a statement," Martin said.

"Often what happens in interrogation," Ofshe said, "is that an individual is brought to the point at which they will conform and say, 'Yes, I did it.' Now, the real work of building a good case begins. That's when they go for corroboration. Corroboration consists of an accurate description of the crime, including details that only the killer could know."

"What about in this particular case, the type of confession that Ken Register has described to you?"

"Well, in this case, Mr. Register agreed that he did it and Detective Caldwell describes that after that agreement, he attempted to get corroboration on ten points and I find it extremely important that that sort of information was not elicited, especially since Detective Caldwell did a professional job in attempting to elicit it."

"Do you have an opinion of the reliability based on the corroborative details of this statement signed by Ken Register?" Martin asked.

"My opinion would be that this is an unreliable statement."

On cross-examination, Ofshe insisted that the confession was unreliable because it lacked corroborative information. The confession appeared to be made up, a confabulation; it incorporated many facts that had been suggested to Register.

"These are standard elements that one sees in interrogations all the time," Ofshe said. "They are elements that Detective Caldwell used in trying to structure a statement that would be relatively easy for Mr. Register to agree to. Once you get that far, now you try to get an accurate statement, and that's where the interrogation breaks down. Mr. Register was apparently trying to come up with a minimal statement that he thought would satisfy them so that they would go to the solicitor and intercede on his behalf, and that would, in the short run, get him out of this situation which was intolerable to him."

"Let me ask you this," Wilson said. "People who make false confessions, after they finish making the false confession, do they say after the fact that, 'Every time I saw a police car, I got scared and thought about going to jail'? Is that customary after the person had just made a false confession or a fabricated confession?"

"I don't know, and I don't know of any research that goes into this." Ofshe replied.

"Well," Wilson continued, "what about the person saying after the funeral that, 'I got sick and went outside and threw up'?"

"My answer is the same."

"What about, 'I just got scared. I don't know why I did it'?"

"My recollection of Mr. Register's testimony is that he doesn't remember having said those things," Ofshe said.

"So again, you're basing what you're testifying to solely on what the defendant has told you, not on what everybody else has told you?" Wilson asked.

"No," Ofshe said. "I'm basing it on the fact that I have been involved in cases in which both police officers and defendants have lied, and, therefore, I try to avoid statements that are in dispute in basing my reasoning and analysis one way or the other."

Later, during the state's rebuttal case, when it got to respond to the defense, Wilson wanted to question the psychiatrist who had performed a competency evaluation of Ken. His goal was to rebut Ofshe's testimony that Ken's confession had been coerced. Wilson had asked Ofshe whether a guilty person might make up a false confession that would later be found reliable. Ofshe said it was possible, but that he had never seen a defendant "crafty enough" to purposely fake an unreliable confession. Wilson wanted the jurors to hear psychiatric evidence from the competency evaluation that Ken had a "fake-good personality." Someone with a fake-good personality, Wilson explained, was "capable of that kind of manipulation and that kind of trickery."

Judge Cottingham denied Wilson's request because of a previous ruling that precluded using the competency evaluation against Ken. Besides, he added, that type of testimony would be dangerously close to personality profiling, which was not allowed in South Carolina courts.

The last witness for the defense was Shirley Register. She described Ken's behavior on the evening of November 16 and said nothing was unusual about him, his clothes, or his behavior when he got home at around 12:15. She said they had talked for a while until she went to bed at about two o'clock. She knew Ken went to bed shortly after that because he stopped by the door to her bedroom and said softly, "Good night, Mama. I love you."

The cross-examination was brief and gave Shirley a chance

to express her love and concern for her son. Wilson questioned her about the note she had written to Ken that wasn't given to him during his interrogation. The prosecution believed the note was a reminder to Ken of his alibi.

"And that's your handwriting, isn't it?" Wilson asked.

"Yes, it is," she replied. "Would you like for me to read it?"

"Yes, ma'am, if you would."

"'Ken, I love you. I know where you were at. We know when you left the racetrack and I know when you came home. I'll stand by you. I love you, Mama.'"

"OK, and there ain't no question about the fact that he's your son?"

"Yes, he's my son."

"All right, and you love him just as much as Mrs. Todd out here loved Crystal, I'm sure." said Wilson.

"Yes, sir, I'm sure she loved Crystal with all her heart and I love Ken with all my heart, Mr. Wilson."

"I know you do, and . . ."

"But," she continued, "I'll tell you one thing, Mr. Wilson, and I don't mean any disrespect to you, and Your Honor, I don't mean any disrespect for you, but I can't sit here in this stand today and say one thing or tell you a lie . . ."

"All right," said Wilson.

". . . because there's a day coming when I'm not gonna have to sit before you . . ."

"All right," Wilson said again.

" . . . and there's a day coming that these nice lawyers over here is not gonna have to defend me . . ."

"Ma'am," interjected Cottingham, "just answer the question, please."

". . . and I can't say anything here today that one day somebody would tell me to 'part from me because I don't know you,'" she continued.

"I understand," Wilson said. "Ma'am, the only thing I wanted to ask you other than that was, that that was your son, you love him . . ."

"Yes, sir," she responded emphatically, "with all my heart, and if you love somebody, you don't lie for them."

"All right," continued Wilson, "and you certainly don't want to see anything happen to your son?"

"No, I don't want anything to happen to him."

Wilson had no more questions. Shirley Register had nothing else to say. The mother of the accused stepped down. And the defense rested.

All of the expert witnesses in the trial had impressive credentials, but Dr. Park Dietz, a forensic psychiatrist with the FBI, was virtually a celebrity. His résumé included numerous academic achievements and testimony in such high-profile cases as the John Hinkley, Jr. and Jeffrey Dahmer murder trials, the trial of the freeway killer in California, the trials of dozens of serial killers and mass murderers, and hundreds of other criminal cases. He was one of the most recognized and respected men in forensic science.

Ralph Wilson called Dietz to rebut Richard Ofshe, who had testified that Ken Register had given a "coerced compliant confession." As Dietz explained, a coerced compliant confession is given when a person feels the intense pressure of an interrogation and wants it to end. The confession can be completely true, completely false, or somewhere in between.

"What is an unreliable confession?" Wilson asked.

"An unreliable confession is one that's contradicted by other facts or where a defendant contradicts himself by telling different stories at different times."

"Doctor, is there anything in the defendant's signed statement of February 18th that you consider unreliable?"

"Well, looking only at the signed statement and comparing that to all the other evidence independent of Mr. Register, the only element in it that I believe can accurately be called unreliable is Mr. Register's suggestion in that statement that while still at the scene, he threw the knife as far as he could. That is not corroborated in that a thorough search by law enforcement failed to produce the knife, and that suggests that it was not within throwing distance."

"Well, Doctor," continued Wilson, "when he talks about other things in that statement, such as Crystal Todd having consented to sexual intercourse, is that a falsehood or is that true, or how do we know?"

"Truth or falsity is not for me to say," said Dietz, "but as to reliability, we cannot say that that's an unreliable statement. It may be merely an incomplete statement since what the evidence indicates is that Crystal Todd was raped vaginally and sodomized. That does not tell us whether she also had consensual sex."

"Is there anything that the defendant told the police on the day of his arrest in giving the statement that you consider unreliable?" Wilson asked.

"There are elements of the statements given that day, other than the signed statement, that I consider unreliable, yes."

"What are they, Doctor?" asked Wilson.

"Well, the defendant's denials that he killed Crystal Todd, which he made many times, are, of course, contradicted by his admission that he killed her, and so that is an unreliable issue. Secondly, the defendant's statement that he never had sex with Crystal Todd is contradicted by the presence of his semen in her vagina and her rectum, and thirdly, the defendant's statement that the agents who had come to speak to him earlier, Investigator Dale Long and a SLED agent, accused him of killing Crystal Todd, in my opinion is unreliable with respect to contrary evidence that they did not accuse him."

"Doctor, aren't there aspects of this offense that the killer would know but that the defendant never volunteered to the police?"

"Yes," Dietz said. "Well, some things that the killer would know that Mr. Register did not volunteer to the police were that there had been oral penetration of Crystal Todd, as indicated by the presence of spermatozoa in her mouth, that there had been forced vaginal penetration, as indicated by the trauma showing that her vagina had been forcibly entered, and the killer would know that there had been sodomy, as evidenced by the tissues surrounding her anus and by the presence of semen in the rectum. The killer would also know that there had been a large number of stab wounds and would know their general vicinity."

"Doctor, why would a guilty suspect fail to volunteer these details while admitting the murder?"

"Those details, would, of course, make a murderer sound more extreme, would make a killer sound more evil and would reveal perversions that a guilty party would be ashamed to admit to," Dietz said.

"Have you encountered this before in your experience with criminals?" Wilson asked.

"Yes, I have," Dietz replied, "especially with sex offenders. It's quite common for there to be an admission, where there's any admission, to the most violent aspects of the behavior, but great hesitancy, reluctance, sometimes silence, when asked to talk about the sexual parts, because while they can talk about killing someone and still appear macho, to reveal the sordid sexual things that they do would make them less of a man in the eyes of those they're talking to, and they don't want to admit that. They're ashamed of it."

"Doctor, did you hear Dr. Ofshe list Lieutenant Caldwell's efforts to get corroborative information from the defendant about certain physical evidence?"

"Yes."

"Do you recall what that effort consisted of?" Wilson asked.

"I recall Dr. Ofshe's list in which he mentioned nine features. He said that Lieutenant Caldwell had tried to obtain corroborative evidence about where was the knife, where were the keys, did the defendant take any memento, where were Crystal's missing buttons, where were the killer's bloody clothes, how did the killer get bloody, how bloody did the killer get, a description of the wounds beyond that which could be learned through general sources, newspaper and so on, and information about cleaning blood from the car."

"Doctor, why would a guilty suspect giving a confession hold back that kind of information?"

"Well, that information relates to evidence of a crime taken from a scene, and the whereabouts of the knife, the keys, any mementos, buttons, the bloody clothes, blood in the car. What happened to that physical evidence is damning information that will make it clear exactly what happened, and killers, despite confessing, may withhold information on the presence of such physical evidence that's been disposed of, discarded or otherwise hidden, in order to protect some other party who helped them dispose of the evidence and in order to prevent the corroboration from being found."

The largest crowd heard closing arguments as Judge Cottingham allowed spectators to pack the courtroom even tighter than before. The emotion of the trial became apparent in territorial disputes over vacated seats. The strain of remaining absolutely still and quiet during the trial began to show on the faces of spectators. After two days of jury selection in Bennettsville, South Carolina, then two days of pretrial motions, the main phase of the trial was now in its seventh day of testimony. Jurors, some of whom had been sequestered for nearly two weeks, appeared worn and tired. Additional officers were posted through the courtroom and instructed to arrest anyone creating even the slightest disturbance.

Wilson began his closing statement by arguing that the issue was clear: "Who do you believe?" he asked the jury. "If you believe the defendant, Johnnie Kenneth Register, then he's not guilty, but in order to believe him, you have to disbelieve every law enforcement officer who took this stand and who testified. You have to believe that every single one of them at some point in time all banded together to make up a lie on Johnnie Kenneth Register."

Wilson scoffed at the notion of a conspiracy among the law enforcement officers and said he was "galled" by the defense's claim that police officers hadn't done things right.

The jury listened intently for the next hour as Wilson's voice boomed through the courthouse, getting louder and louder as he attacked the defense's case and countered its anticipated arguments. Wilson pointed over and over to the DNA evidence linking Register to Crystal, hammering at the brutality of the crime confessed to by the defendant.

"You have seen a great deal of smoke," Wilson said. "You have heard a great deal of puffing, but the issues are relatively simple and the question is simple. The question is, who do you believe?

"Ladies and gentlemen," Wilson said softly, "my responsibility in this case is over. I have done my job. I make no apologies for that. The people of this county deserve nothing less. They deserve justice, and this defendant deserves justice, and that justice for the people of this county and for this defendant is exactly the same. Justice in this case is a verdict of guilty on all counts. Anything less than that violates the oath that we all took. This defendant is guilty, and he has earned the right to be convicted."

Both Brittain and Martin closed for the defense. Brittain verbally walked the jury through Ken's alibi. Carefully tracing the defendant's movements on the evening of the murder, Brittain reminded the jury of the testimony that placed Ken eighteen miles from Conway just after 11:30 and after the sighting of Crystal's car.

"I can't imagine," Brittain said, "trying to convict a man of murder when for two days, witnesses have gotten up on this witness stand and proven, though there's no obligation to, that he was somewhere else when this crime was committed. This poor child was with her killer at 11:30 and where is Ken? He is miles away in Cool Spring. The witnesses got up on this stand, one after another, and told you that, and not just his girlfriend and the cousin. You know, the preacher's daughter, she's lying, too," Brittain said sarcastically. "They're all lying. Witness after witness is lying.

"Now, it doesn't take anybody with a whole lot of sense to realize if that car is sitting there and parked at 11:30, and she's not in it, where is she? She's with the man that took her out of there, and it's not Ken Register. He's at the go-cart track for another ten minutes, and then he's got to drive another sixteen or seventeen minutes. Now, just follow through on that for just a second. He has to drive from that go-cart track to come into Conway, so let's say he could do that and get here by five minutes till twelve o'clock. Now, he's got to find her and take her away from somebody 'cause she's already gone, but let's say he does that in five to ten minutes. Now he's at 12:05. Then he's got to drive eleven minutes to get to the crime scene, so it's 12:16 or 12:17 to get to the crime scene.

"Now, that pathologist has told you what went on with this poor child. You can figure that any way you want to. You're looking at an hour's worth of the saddest mayhem that could possibly occur, so that's 1:16 or 1:17 and he's twenty-five minutes from home. The victim's mama is talking to him on the phone at one o'clock! If that don't walk you out on something like this, when can you prove your innocence, and there my man [Ralph Wilson] sat and never addressed one little syllable of it. Never did he talk about it.

"Unfortunately, from what the pathologist tells you, she probably had to endure a lot and for a long period of time, and this is without believing Miss Shirley, whose credibility has never been questioned in this courtroom. She had him home by 12:15, which means if he had anything to do with it, she's in on it. It just ain't that way.

"The reasons to doubt in this case are so numerous that it's a frightening thing that something like this could come this far. I'm telling you, if there's not a reasonable doubt in this case, then let's just tear the courthouse down, because when alibi witnesses that put you somewhere else when the crime was committed that have never been challenged don't create a reasonable doubt, then Thomas Jefferson and George Washington, and all that crowd, don't know what they were talking about.

"What's going on here is a situation that's bigger than all of us. It's how we determine if a person is guilty, and if we get to the point where the lab technicians of the world are going to have the say-so, then we have dismantled our freedom in this country."

Morgan Martin had the final say for the defense. He asked the jurors, as he had in his opening statement, to consider whether the evidence would convince them of guilt if their child was on trial.

"Do you feel any hesitation?" he asked. "If you do, there's no question what you do. You find him not guilty. If they came to you or to any parent, and said, 'Your child did this,' what would it take for you to believe it beyond a reasonable doubt, so that you convict and his life is ruined forever?"

Martin systematically analyzed the evidence presented by the state and said he agreed with Solicitor Wilson that common sense was necessary as the jurors examined the evidence. "Don't leave your good common sense at home," he said. "Please take it with you into the jury room, 'cause it proves the boy's innocence if you want to look at it that way."

The evidence that was most important, Martin told the jurors, was the evidence that the state didn't have. They didn't have a time of death that was consistent with Ken's activities. They didn't have any corroborating evidence for the confession. There wasn't any fingerprint, hair, or fiber evidence linking Ken to Crystal. There wasn't any evidence that Crystal had been in Ken's car. There was no footprint or tire track evidence linking Ken to the crime scene. There were no witnesses that saw Ken and Crystal together that night. There were no scratches or anything on Ken to indicate he had struggled with someone. Nor were there, according to defense witnesses, any changes in Ken's behavior from before to after the murder.

"This boy has not been proven guilty," Martin argued. "As a matter of fact, he's given you evidence proving his innocence. Well, he don't act like he's sorry. 'He don't do this, he don't do that,' says the solicitor. Maybe he's not guilty. How do you act when you sit where he sits today? How do you look? Arrested almost a year ago, has it changed him in any way? How can it not? Has he suffered, has his family suffered? If he's not guilty, what have they been through?

"You folks go back into the jury room and you deliberate, and if you feel a hesitation in your heart, you can't convict this boy. We'll be satisfied with justice and what justice is."

The jury was dismissed for deliberations at 6:30 p.m. Despite Judge Cottingham's invitation to the audience to move about and talk quietly, most of the crowd of four hundred stayed close to their seats, willing to wait into the night for the jury's verdict.

Kenny Register smoked heavily during the break and stayed outside nearly the entire time. Kenny was upset about the trial and spoke about it in his colorful style. Finally, the police escorted him into the courthouse for a meeting with Judge Cottingham. Cottingham tried to ask Kenny whether he had actually threatened to kill Ralph Wilson if the verdict came back guilty, but saw firsthand what the police already knew about the angry man: He wouldn't be quiet. Kenny cursed and rambled about the "frame-up job being pulled" on his son. Cottingham tried to talk with Kenny about the serious charge, but became frustrated and threatened to hold him in contempt of court. The judge warned Kenny that if he didn't calm down, he would find himself in jail for six months. Kenny continued to mouth off. As he was escorted from the courthouse, he again dared Cottingham to put him in jail.

Just after eleven o'clock, four and a half hours after deliberations began, the jury sent word that it had reached a verdict. The last of the spectators scrambled back to their spots as the bailiffs locked the doors inside the courthouse.

At 11:10 p.m., Judge Cottingham returned to the courtroom. The audience watched silently as the jury foreman handed the verdict forms to the Clerk of Court. Shirley Register reached out and took the hand of her daughter. Kenny Register leaned forward, rested his elbows on his knees, and clasped his hands. Ken slipped his feet back into his loafers and stood with his lawyers. The moment everyone had waited for since the discovery of Crystal's body fourteen months earlier arrived as the Clerk read the verdicts.

The Clerk read: "As to count one of the indictment, being murder, we, the jury, find the defendant, Johnnie Kenneth Register, II, guilty.

"As to count two of the Indictment, being criminal sexual conduct in the first degree, we, the jury, find the defendant, Johnnie Kenneth Register, II, guilty.

"As to count three of the Indictment, being kidnapping, we, the jury, find the defendant, Johnnie Kenneth Register, II, guilty.

"As to count four of the indictment, being buggery and sodomy, we, the jury, find the defendant, Johnnie Kenneth Register, II, guilty."

Sighs of relief spread through the courtroom. Bonnie Faye was gleeful at first as nearby supporters squeezed her hand and patted her on the shoulder. Ken became angry and displayed the first real emotion he had shown during the trial. Staring menacingly at the jurors, he muttered loudly. Wilson turned and watched as Morgan Martin stepped in front of Ken and tried to calm him. The guards positioned around the courtroom shifted toward the crowd as an unspoken warning for them to remain quiet and still. Bailiffs, carrying handcuffs, moved efficiently toward Ken as the jurors rose and hurriedly filed out.

Shirley sat in disbelief, shook her head, and watched as Ken, red-faced, was hustled from the courtroom. Kenny was unusually quiet, but he scowled at the departing jurors. Ken's girlfriend sat and sobbed, unable to contain her emotion. The teenager's loved ones couldn't console her.

Bonnie Faye was smiling when she left the courthouse. Although it was late at night, she went directly to Crystal's grave to tell her daughter about the conviction.

"I wanted to tell her they had found him guilty," she said later.

38

In South Carolina, a guilty verdict for murder is punished by either death in the electric chair or life in prison. A jury can spare a convicted murderer for any reason, even if aggravating circumstances are shown, but cannot sentence a murderer to die in the electric chair if aggravating circumstances are not shown.

Although Ralph Wilson was tense when the verdict was read in the first phase of the trial, he was optimistic about getting a death verdict in the second phase. He would be allowed to introduce evidence that he wasn't allowed to introduce earlier, but that he thought would sway the jury. That the jury hadn't needed the evidence to find Ken guilty made him even more optimistic.

The convenience store manager testified about Ken buying pornographic magazines. The woman's testimony was corroborated by a second witness, who testified that Ken brought the magazines to work and kept them in the work truck to look at during the day. Another witness provided a short video clip showing Ken at Crystal's funeral placing a flower on her coffin.

The next three witnesses were the two college students Ken had exposed himself to two months prior to the murder and the university police officer that had processed the students' report.

Then came the shocking testimony of a young woman and her mother, who said they had each received at least one hundred obscene phone calls from Ken when he was fifteen years old.

"The thing that's important is not the fact that the calls were made but what was said," Wilson had argued earlier in the trial in an unsuccessful attempt to enter the evidence. "The reason it's important is because exactly what was said allegedly by this defendant in those obscene phone calls is what happened to this victim in this case, almost verbatim."

In 1988, a young woman, C.C., had taken her car for a repair where Ken worked. She left her unpublished phone number at the business and, that night, received the first of over a hundred obscene phone calls. The menacing calls were descriptive and included numerous references to murder, mutilation, and rape. C.C.'s mother also became the recipient of calls.

Alarmed, C.C. and her mother contacted the phone company and the police. The phone company tried to trace the calls, but merely determined the general direction they were coming from. C.C. was frightened and angry that the male caller could fill her life with fear. She and her mother were receiving up to ten calls a day and were afraid to go to the store or the movies or to pay bills.

After a while, C.C. started responding to the caller. She told him he was sick and asked him to get help. She listened for sounds that could give clues to his identity. The caller told her he was calling other girls, too. Her strategy finally paid off when she heard a familiar background noise and correctly recognized it as coming from a garage. Realizing the calls had started just after she had her car repaired, she bravely went to the automotive repair shop. Ken's uncle, who owned the muffler shop, was alarmed and apologetic when he heard the story, but doubted whether one of his employees was making the calls. Unconvinced, C.C. spotted the person she had spoken with during her original visit and found out his name. When she returned home, she looked up the boy's phone number. That evening, when she received another call, she hung up and quickly dialed Ken Register's number. When he answered, she heard a familiar voice.

C.C. went to a judge in Conway and swore out a warrant against Ken. She returned home, fortified by her decisive action, and waited for the next call. When the phone rang and the caller told C.C., "I'm coming to get you," she said angrily, "No, I'm coming to get you."

C.C. was so mad that she got in her car and drove to the repair shop. During the entire ride, she wondered whether she was doing the right thing. She almost turned around several times, but felt that if she was ever going to have peace of mind, she had to continue. When she arrived at the shop, she saw Ken and yelled, "Ken, get over here!"

Ken saw the irate woman approaching. Before C.C. even opened her mouth, he said, "I didn't do it. I didn't do it." C.C. lit into him. She scolded and yelled at the embarrassed teenager, releasing her frustrations, and demanding an apology.

"I'm sorry, I didn't mean to," Ken said.

C.C. demanded that Ken call her mother and apologize to her, too. Ken protested, then picked up the phone and, without being told or having to look up the number, called C.C.'s mother and apologized to her for having made the obscene calls. Ken's uncle watched Ken's confession and apologies.

C.C. contacted the police and identified the caller. A Conway police officer served Ken with an arrest warrant for unlawful use of a telephone on July 12, 1988. Ken again admitted to making the calls, this time in front of his uncle and the police captain. Ken was taken to the J. Reuben Long Detention Center, where it was discovered that he was only fifteen years old. He was immediately released into the custody of his sister. The police officer turned over the arrest warrant to the Department of Youth Services.

Nearly four years later, C.C. was watching TV when the newscaster reported that Ken Register had been arrested for murdering Crystal Todd. Hearing that Register had no prior arrest record, C.C. called the police department to find out what had happened to the obscene phone call charges she had made against him in 1988. The police were puzzled by C.C.'s questions and asked her to come down to headquarters. The day after Ken's arrest for Crystal's murder, C.C. gave the following voluntary statement to Agent David Caldwell:

It must have been about three years ago when I took my car to Register Mufflers. I left my mother's phone number so they could call me. That night we started getting the obscene phone calls. This went on for weeks. I would sometimes listen in an attempt to figure out who he was and to encourage him to get some help.

He terrified my mother. I was scared too and called the police and they got involved.

In the calls he would say things like, "I'm going to tie

you up and spread your legs. I'll make you scream. I'm going to hurt you. I know where you live and I'm going to get you."

He told my mother, "I want to fuck you. I'm going to cut you open. I'm going to kill you."

He spoke to me with a lot of anal references like, "I'll ram my dick in your ass and your pussy." He said, "I'm going to ram the gear shift in you." I finally found out that it was Ken Register and confronted him at his uncle's muffler shop. He admitted it and I made him apologize. He admitted it to his uncle also. The City Police were involved and I left it with them. I don't know what ever happened with it.

I told Ken Register's mother that Ken would end up raping and killing some girl.

Wilson was interested in C.C.'s statement and asked the police to find out what had happened to her case. Ken's aunt, an administrative specialist at the Department of Youth Services, acknowledged that the department had received the report, but there was no file on the matter. Wilson was suspicious of the family connection and ordered an investigation into the missing records. In the end, he blamed sloppy recordkeeping.

Dr. Robert Hazelwood of the FBI Academy in Quantico, Virginia, was one of the most controversial witnesses called in either phase of the trial. He provided testimony about sexual sadism and sexual homicide and the reasons killers commit sexual violence. Hazelwood was one of the original behavioral profilers. He worked closely with members of the FBI's elite serial crime unit, including John Douglas, the model for one of the lead characters in the movie *The Silence of the Lambs*.

Morgan Martin objected to Hazelwood's qualifications and his testimony, which, he believed, would introduce profiling into the trial. Cottingham overruled the objection, finding the witness eminently qualified, but reaffirming that profiling would not be allowed. His reason was simple: profiling is an inexact science. It is not a description of the person who committed the crime, but of who the person who committed the crime might be. Obviously, not every person who fits the profile of a suspect is the person who committed the crime.

Hazelwood had consulted on thousands of homicides and

sexual assaults and had interviewed dozens of rapists, murderers, and sexual sadists, and their families and victims. In prepa-
ration for the Register case, he reviewed three hundred
thirty-two cases he had worked that involved multiple stab
wounds and demonstrated overkill—much more violence than
necessary to end a person's life.

"It's indicative of a great deal of anger, a great deal of hostility being vented upon the victim," Hazelwood testified.

"What can cause that kind of behavior?" Wilson asked.

"It's caused by something the victim either said or did to the
killer," Hazelwood said.

"And what would multiple stab wounds to the head indicate?" Wilson asked.

"That would indicate a tremendous amount of rage and
anger personally directed toward the victim."

"And what about facial battering?"

"Facial battering is also indicative of rage and anger directed
toward the particular victim of a homicide."

"Now," continued Wilson, "let me ask you, in regards to disposing of bodies, has the FBI classified the types of body disposal?"

"Yes, we have," Hazelwood answered. "We have classified
the methods that killers have disposed of bodies in three different ways. The first is concealment. That is where the offender
takes a great deal of time and effort, drives great distances or
goes to great effort to ensure the body will never be found. An
example would be weighting it down with heavy weights and
disposing it in a lake or in the ocean.

"A second type of body disposal would be displaying the
body, placing the body where it is certain to be found so as to
shock the individuals who find the body and to further inflict
trauma on society. That's a very intentional act. That takes a lot
of time.

"The third method of disposal is what we call body dumping, that is hastily disposing of a body more in an effort to just
simply disassociate yourself, the killer, from that body and get
away from the scene as quickly as possible. That would indicate the individual was in a hurry and did not have time to properly dispose of the body and left in a very rapid manner."

"What, then, does the term paraphilia mean?" Wilson asked.

"Paraphilia is a professional term for what you and I would call sexual deviation," said Hazelwood. "It consists of several different types. Fetishism, sexual attraction to an inanimate object. Other forms, common forms, are telephone scatology. That's what you and I would call obscene phone calls. Exhibitionism is a paraphilia or sexual deviation. Sadism is a paraphilia. Necrophilia, having sex with the dead. All of these would be classified as paraphilias or what you and I call sexual deviations."

"And can an individual have more than one paraphilia?" Wilson asked.

"Yes," replied Hazelwood. "As a matter of fact, every time I lecture on the subject, I always remind my audience that when you have documented the presence of one paraphilia or sexual deviation, you can be assured there's at least one or possibly more sexual deviations involved."

"Would you explain to us what you mean by telephone scatology?" Wilson asked.

"Telephone scatology is the making of a telephone call to an individual typically unknown to the caller or known on a very brief basis. It is done to instill fear. They generally use obscene or sexually obscene or sexually threatening terminology and the motivation is to instill fear in the recipient of the phone call."

"What is, then, meant by the term exhibitionist?"

"Exhibitionism is the exposure of one's genitals in a public or semi-public place to a stranger," Hazelwood responded.

"And how would that differ from sexual sadism?"

"A sexual sadist," continued Hazelwood, "is an individual who is sexually aroused, one who is sexually stimulated from the suffering of his victim. The suffering of his victim can be either physical suffering or it can be emotional suffering. An example of emotional suffering would be keeping a woman in captivity, for example, or making obscene phone calls to her, or exposing oneself to her. Physical suffering would be, of course, the suffering of pain as a result of injury that the killer inflicts on the victim."

"Would you explain to us what the term trophies means?" Wilson asked.

"A trophy is an item which the offender associates with the

occurrence of the murder. A trophy can be an article of clothing he took from the victim, a driver's license, a piece of jewelry that he took from the victim, or it can be something like newspaper clippings. The purpose of a trophy is to relive the experience for masturbatory purposes."

"Well," said Wilson, "what about just a regular person who was interested in the crime. Couldn't they also make clippings?"

"Oh, certainly. You'll find very frequently that individuals who knew the victim may clip the newspaper articles out and save those. Now, there might be a second reason that the article might be clipped, to keep an idea of what the progress of the investigation is."

"Is there a continuum of sexual sadism, and, if so, explain that to us?" Wilson asked.

"Yes. All sexual crimes, regardless of the type of sexual crime, originate in the mind. It originates with fantasy, mental images of a sexual nature. All of us fantasize, but our fantasies do not necessarily deal with violent activities. All sexual crimes deal with some form of violence, either physical or emotional violence inflicted on a victim, so they begin with fantasy. You'll find some offenders that will then begin to act out those fantasies through writings or through drawings or through images of one type or another, photographic images, video images of one type or another, or begin to act out against inanimate objects, actually begin to act out against dolls or clothing or photographs, that type of thing.

"You may also find some offenders that act out their sexual violent fantasies against paid prostitutes, paid partners, or consenting partners such as wives, girlfriends, that type of thing, and then finally, the end, of course, in a continuum is that they act out against non-consenting individuals."

"You mentioned earlier that sexual fantasies precede sexual crimes," Wilson said. "How important is fantasy to those crimes?"

"Fantasy is extremely important because an offender, a person who has committed a sexual crime, has demonstrated what his fantasy is, what his masturbatory fantasies, what his images are, what stimulates him sexually. If you see a crime, look at what happened to the victim and you'll see what his fantasies or what his thoughts about doing to victims were prior to the commission of the crime."

"Are obscene phone calls one way in which an individual can verbalize his fantasies?" Wilson asked.

"Yes, they are," replied Hazelwood.

"Have you spoken with the young woman and her mother who received the obscene phone calls and have you had an opportunity to read the police report and complaints in this particular case?"

"Yes, sir."

"Were you also present during their testimony and were you also present when the young ladies from Coastal Carolina University testified?"

"Yes, sir."

"Have you been able to arrive at a conclusion as to what may have motivated the defendant in this particular case to make these calls?"

"Yes," responded Hazelwood. "I believe that the individual who made those calls did so from a sexually sadistic motivation. I believe some themes come across very strongly as to what his fantasies were or what his motivation for making the calls was, and those fantasies include forced and painful sexual acts, degrading women, instilling fear in the recipient of those phone calls, using a knife to inflict harm, taking life, and basically his overall motivation in making those phone calls was to get even with women for real or imagined wrongs. In other words, to inflict fear in them, to have them suffer emotionally as a result of those phone calls."

"What about these conversations lead you to believe that the defendant would be a sexual sadist?" Wilson asked.

"A number of things," Hazelwood replied. "Again, it's important to remember that a sexual sadist is an individual who is sexually aroused from the suffering of his victim, either physical or emotional suffering. It's also important to remember that these phone calls are nothing more than a reflection or a verbalization of what his fantasies are. Each one of those calls was intended to instill fear, and I'll give you some direct quotes from the victims. 'I'm coming to get you and I'm going to kill you.' 'I'm going to cut you open.' 'I'm going to fuck you and make you scream,' and those are just a few, all of which were designed to instill fear in the victim.

"The second thing is that I noted that the caller's sexual preference is anal sex, and I'll quote, 'I'm going to ram that gear shift up your ass. I'm going to fuck you in the ass. I'm going to ram the gear shift up your ass and pussy.' Thirdly, he has a great deal of hostility, a great deal of animosity, a great deal of anger toward women. He never once referred to them as sweetheart, honey, darling, nothing endearing. Instead, he used terms like bitch, whore, slut, and cunt.

"Next, he has a great interest in using foreign objects on the women as stated, 'I'm going to slit your throat, cut you open, and I'm going to ram the gear shift up your ass and pussy,' end quote. He's also interested in sexual bondage, that is binding the victims to get a helplessness and a hopelessness feeling on the part of the victims. He stated, 'I'm going to tie you up, gag you, and fuck you.' He only referred to the use of a knife or a cutting or a sharp instrument. He never referred to any other type of weapon such as a ligature, strangulation, shooting, anything like that. He always referred to a cutting type of instrument during his conversations."

"Do you have an opinion as to what motivated Mr. Register to expose himself to these young women?" Wilson asked.

"Yes, sir," Hazelwood answered. "All of the illegal actions of Mr. Register display a motivation of hostility and anger toward women, a desire to degrade them and cause them to suffer. Public exposure is no exception to that. Whether or not they were intimidated or fearful, the purpose was to instill fear in those victims by exposing himself to them. He wanted to get even with them for making him feel like less than a man. For example, he stated in response to Mr. Wilson's cross examination at that trial, quote, 'They kind of shunned me off, sort of looked at me, you know, you know, who are you? It kind of got me a little upset, you know, they wouldn't give me the time of day to talk to me or nothing. They started walking off.'

"Page 198 of that same transcript: 'They started walking off, you know, and it kind of hurt my feelings.' Then during redirect by Mr. Martin on page 214 of that same transcript, Mr. Register stated, 'It made me feel like, hey, you know, you, who are you,' to which Mr. Martin asked, 'Made you feel like what?' The response from Mr. Register on page 215 was, 'Like I was trash.'"

"Do you find any continuity of Mr. Register's sexual fantasies and obscene phone calls to the young woman and her mother and the indecent exposure to the young girls and to the murder of Ms. Todd?" Wilson asked.

"Yes, I do."

"What is that?"

"For example, there is a consistency in the desire in all three of these to punish and humiliate women. That's very obvious to me in the obscene phone calls to the young woman and her mother, also a desire to get even for real or imagined wrongs by the two young ladies at the university. Finally, there's a great deal of consistency between the fantasies exhibited verbally by Mr. Register in a phone call to the young woman and her mother, and, in fact, the murder of Crystal Faye Todd.

"Just a few of those consistencies include a knife as the desired object to inflict damage in both situations, the calls and the murder. The desire to cut a woman open is evident in both situations, the calls and the murder. The desire to rape anally is evident in both situations. The desire to rape vaginally is evident in both situations. The desire to inflict pain is evident in both situations. The desire to make the victim scream is evident in both situations. Those are the consistencies that I noted."

The last witness for the prosecution was Bonnie Faye. As a long-time advocate of victims' rights, Wilson put the grieving mother on the stand to remind the jury of the devastation produced by Ken's actions. Bonnie Faye started crying when she was shown Crystal's high school senior picture.

"Mrs. Todd, tell this jury how Crystal's death, how her murder has affected you as her mother," Wilson asked.

The courtroom was silent. After a long pause, Bonnie Faye finally answered.

"I'd rather be dead than sitting here right now," she said. "I'd crawl in the grave now and let her go. She was the only thing I had."

She damped her bloodshot eyes with a tissue. "I've got nothing left," she said.

Martin simply stood, put his hands on his hips, and looked at the crying mother. After Martin said, "No questions for Mrs. Todd," Wilson moved to the side of the witness stand, took Bonnie Faye's arm, and helped her down and to her seat. Everyone in the room watched in silence.

Defense witnesses addressed Ken's lack of a violent criminal history and his suitability, or lack thereof, to prison life. Two of Ken's teachers and his minister told the jury that they had never known Ken to do anything wrong. They had been surprised when they heard about Ken's troubles because they had never seen that side of him. Ken was, according to his minister, "just the finest young man that I have ever met or has been to my church."

Both Ken's sister and his mother told the jury that Ken had been a normal little boy, doing normal little boy things, and enjoyed normal relationships with all of his family members. His sister said she loved Ken a lot and did not want to see him die in the electric chair. Shirley talked about her family's life and touched the jurors' hearts with stories about camping with the kids when they were little, Ken's love of swimming and fishing, and how he rode on the tractor while his father farmed to earn extra money for the family. When asked how she felt about her son facing either life in prison or death in the electric chair, she proclaimed that she and her God knew of Ken's innocence. When asked by Martin what sentence she wanted to ask of the jury, Shirley said, "Well, as any mother would, I don't want to see my son die."

Wilson summed up his case by arguing that Ken deserved what Crystal got: death. Brittain argued otherwise.

"If an eighteen-year-old has had problems with sex and these types of things since he was fourteen, and if he's lived a life where he took care of handicapped children and he played on a football team, and people that knew him thought he was good, and he had this other side to him, and out there on that little road, he could stab and kill and cut like you've seen, then don't tease yourself," Brittain said. "He is one sick human being, and we don't kill sick people in the United States of America. No, sir, not nineteen-year-old sick people."

Finally, Ken exercised his right to speak to the jury. The

statement he chose was simple and direct. Ken stood, turned to face the jury, and said: "I don't know what to say to y'all. I know y'all found me guilty. I ask you for your mercy. That's all I can do. Thank you."

Ken's chair creaked as he sat down. Sniffles and muffled sobs filled the courtroom. The long ordeal of the trial had taken its toll on the jurors and spectators. A confused numbness settled upon the room. Cottingham's brief instructions were heard through the rustling of uncomfortable bodies.

The jury needed only an hour and fifteen minutes to reach a verdict. It unanimously found aggravating circumstances of criminal sexual conduct, kidnapping, and torture. Ken had held Crystal against her will and raped and tortured her to death.

Hearing this, Ralph Wilson nodded his head in satisfaction. He was convinced that Register deserved to die for his crimes. Wilson was stunned, though, by what he heard next: "We, the jury, unanimously recommend that the defendant, Johnnie Kenneth Register, II, be imprisoned in the state penitentiary for the balance of his natural life."

Wilson felt the jury had choked. It was unable to do what was right and necessary. The jurors couldn't make Ken Register pay for his crimes with his own life. He would now become a ward of the state and live at the taxpayers' expense.

Judge Cottingham, who had earlier promised to follow the recommendation of the jury, did just that. Register stood before him as his sentence was handed down: life plus thirty-five years in prison.

The courtroom crowd was subdued. Still stunned by the graphic testimony regarding the phone calls, the spectators couldn't take their eyes off of Ken as he was escorted out of the room. Cottingham gathered his papers, stood with the jurors, and prepared to exit the courtroom. The ordeal was over. The need for strict crowd control was at an end. Bonnie Faye glared at the jurors, seemingly unable to understand the sentence.

"I don't know how anyone could have any mercy on him," she said. "He certainly didn't have any mercy at all on Crystal."

Wilson watched in disbelief as the jurors were led out. In his mind, he began formulating questions for the debriefing, when he would speak to the jurors and find out what persuaded them in the trial. How could they not have sentenced Register to death? Life plus thirty-five? That meant Register would one day be eligible for parole. What were they thinking? What could possibly have convinced them to spare someone capable of committing such a heinous crime?

PART VI
THE AFTERMATH

39

The verdict angered those in the community with strong allegiances to Ken Register and his family. Having heard enough of the complicated and often conflicting testimony to support its reasonable doubts, the disgruntled minority moved quietly off of the courthouse grounds and immediately began sorting through the dramatic moments of the trial, seizing on isolated pieces of testimony to express its emotional declarations of Ken's innocence.

The jurors had heard evidence enough to satisfy any doubts they might have had and said so afterwards in the debriefing with Wilson. The DNA, they reported, was too complex to decipher up front, but fit the overall picture of Ken's guilt considering the confession and circumstantial evidence. They were impressed with the expert testimony. The additional testimony during the sentencing phase cemented the jurors' beliefs that they had reached the right decision.

One juror had watched the defendant closely during the trial and wanted Ken to somehow say that he didn't do it, that he couldn't have been responsible for the brutal rape and torture of his friend. Instead, the juror saw an emotionless young man answering questions as if he were reading from a script. He saw Ken sitting impassively, even while others in the courtroom reacted with horror, as the medical examiner explained the gruesome extent of Crystal's wounds. He watched as Ken handled the bloodied clothes of the person he once dated and said, "I didn't kill the girl."

Wilson believed that Ken's emotionless demeanor hurt him in the first phase of the trial. "His lawyers did a really good job in preparing him," he said. "Almost too good a job because he was so calm. Being that calm in a murder trial is not rational, not something that the average person can understand and believe is real."

Nonetheless, the jurors couldn't sentence him to death for his crimes because he was just too young.

Wilson was further infuriated when Ken was assigned to a medium security prison, the Allendale Correctional Institution in Fairfax, South Carolina. "He's conned people all his life," Wilson said to a *Sun News* reporter, "and now he's up there conning those people. At least they have the benefit of hindsight, which Crystal Todd didn't. What are they going to do when Ken Register escapes?"

The controversy didn't end with the trial. Talk show host Sally Jesse Raphael devoted an hour-long show to the case and arranged for Bonnie Faye to face Ken, via live video, for the first time since the trial. The viewing audience in the television studio quietly watched the monitors as Sally Jesse summarized the case. Pictures of Crystal and Ken hanging out at a swimming pool were followed by the startling account of Crystal's death. A description of the arrest accompanied a video of Ken placing a rose on Crystal's coffin at her funeral.

Looking forlorn, Bonnie Faye repeatedly cut her eyes past where Shirley was seated to the large television screen where Ken's image appeared. Shirley wore an enigmatic smile as Sally Jesse announced Ken's appearance from his new home, a state correctional institution. Bonnie Faye's chest heaved as she anxiously waited for her first opportunity to address Ken since just before his arrest, almost two years earlier. She glowered at the screen. Ken seemed to look back. Ken's blue shirt matched his eyes. He appeared rested and calm. Seated alongside Bonnie Faye, Deena James softly placed her hand on the leg of the shaking woman.

"What makes you think that Ken killed your niece?" Sally Jesse asked Deena.

"Well, number one," Deena said matter-of-factly, "he signed a confession. And number two, his DNA matched correctly." After a deep breath, Deena summarized the evidence for the audience.

"But do you, Deena, think he did it?" Sally Jesse asked pointedly.

"I certainly do," she replied.

"And you think he did it," Sally Jesse followed, "because the DNA from his blood matched what?"

"It matched the DNA found in the semen in Crystal's mouth, her anus, and her vagina," Deena said.

Sally asked Bonnie Faye if she had something to say to the person convicted of murdering her daughter. Bonnie Faye angrily called Ken a "baby-faced, baby-talking monster." Her rapid-fire delivery expressed what she had wanted to say for almost two years.

"You was hugging my neck the next morning," Bonnie Faye told Ken. "How could you do it? And be a pallbearer at her funeral? I know your momma wants you home, but she don't want you home as bad as I do. Ken Register, I want you to come home in a box in so many pieces, it'll take an hour to pick 'em up and put 'em in it. You enjoyed what you done to Crystal. All the time hugging my neck. You're the worst monster. There's nothing on earth that could crawl as low on their stomach as you."

Deena held Bonnie Faye as she leaned toward the screen and unleashed her fury. Shirley Register smiled and listened.

"You'll break one day, buddy," Bonnie Faye snarled. "You'll break good one day, I know."

When Ken tried to defend himself and called Bonnie Faye, "Mrs. Todd," she snapped, "Don't call me Mrs. Todd. Call me 'Mom,' like you used to."

Sally Jesse then turned to Shirley, who answered questions in her characteristically calm way.

"Shirley, you believe your son is innocent," Sally Jesse asked.

"I know my son is innocent," Shirley said.

"Now, he is in prison for life," Sally Jesse said. "I would think it is very hard to see a twenty-two-year-old son in prison for first degree murder. You do believe, however, he didn't do it. Based on what?"

"I know that Ken did not kill Crystal Todd," Shirley said calmly. "Ken couldn't have committed the crime that he was charged with. Ken was with his girlfriend that night, there was witnesses where he was at . . ."

"That was never brought out in court," Deena interrupted. "The time was never documented that he left the racetrack at a certain time. Nobody but his mother knew that he was there at a certain time."

"There were people there at the trial that had the time of each race," Shirley added. "When each race was over, and these people testified to that."

"But it was never proven in court," Deena said.

"No," Bonnie Faye said.

"At 11:30, Crystal Todd's car was already parked and she was gone from that car, and at twenty minutes to twelve Ken was still with his girlfriend," Shirley insisted.

"That was never proven except for what the mother says and the ex-girlfriend says," Deena said.

Bonnie Faye leaned towards Ken's image on the TV screen. "Ken Register, let me tell you something," she sneered. "You tried to date her ever since she was fifteen. She made you feel like trash, didn't she, Ken?"

"Oh, no, ma'am, I never tried to date her," Ken replied.

"Oh yes you did," Bonnie Faye said.

"You did date her," Deena said.

"Her friend Carla was with her that night," Bonnie Faye said, "and if they'd let me bring her she could prove it. You've been trying to date Crystal since she was fifteen. She told me all you wanted was sex and you stunk is the reason she wouldn't date you."

"Bonnie, hold on a minute," Sally Jesse said, trying to restore order. "Shirley, the night of the crime, tell me what happened with the times as you understand them."

"When Ken got home that night, it was twelve-fifteen," Shirley said.

"Did you see him when he came home?" asked Sally Jesse.

"Yes I did. I was up waiting on him."

"Was he dressed the way he was dressed when he went out?"

"He was dressed in the same clothes he left in," Shirley said, nodding her head.

"Was there any blood on the clothes?"

"No, there was no blood on him. At one-thirteen, Bonnie was calling my house and she spoke with Ken," said Shirley.

"What did you ask Ken at 1:13?" Sally Jesse asked Bonnie Faye.

"I asked him if he might know any party where Crystal was at," Bonnie Faye replied. "You see, he stalked 'em all. He told me the next morning. Made out like he was going to church. And hugging my neck." Bonnie Faye looked at Ken. "And you didn't have Crystal's blood from under your fingernails when you was hugging my neck."

"Mrs. Todd, the thing about this thing is, you're not paying attention to the facts of this case," Ken said.

"You forget that you were convicted by twelve jurors," Deena said.

"Yes, listen to me," Ken said.

"You're guilty," Deena said.

"Ken . . ." Sally Jesse said.

"You say the DNA matches me . . ." Ken said.

"It does match you," Deena said.

"The DNA expert says it don't," Ken said.

"Ken . . ." Sally Jesse said.

"They say the confession, but they tricked me," Ken said.

"Tricked you?" Deena said.

"Yes," Ken said, sitting back. "Twelve jurors felt those guys that beat Rodney King was innocent, too, didn't they?"

"Ken," began Sally Jesse again, "how did they . . ."

"We got somebody setting right back there . . ." Bonnie Faye interjected.

"Bonnie, wait a minute. Now, Ken, how did they trick you?"

"Yes," said Bonnie Faye, "tell us."

"Just like you told us that they treated you awful," Deena said. "I asked my son and he said you were acting like a baby when you said the police were treating you awful . . ."

"He told me the same thing," Bonnie Faye said.

"All right," said Sally Jesse, with her arm outstretched to silence Deena and Bonnie Faye. "Just let him talk."

"Can I have a chance?" asked Ken.

"Sure you can," answered Deena.

"Tell us some more of your lies," said Bonnie Faye.

"Mrs. Todd, you can take . . ."

"Don't call me Mrs. Todd," snapped Bonnie Faye.

Sally Jesse's attempts to balance the exchange were useless. Bonnie Faye looked as if she would burst into tears one moment, then became angry and frantic the next. Ken sighed heavily and exhaled forcefully through pursed lips. Shirley's reserved demeanor seemed unsuited for the caustic verbal battle. She sat smiling, with her hands folded in her lap, without speaking for the remainder of the show.

Sally Jesse tried to get Ken's side of the story. "Now where were you the night of the murder?" she asked.

"I picked up my girlfriend, we went to a turkey shoot," Ken said. "We left the turkey shoot, we went back to her house. Then we left and went to the go-cart track. I stayed there until the last race. And it's not only me saying this. There's five or six different people. People I don't even know."

"But it was never proven, that time. Remember that, in court, all those people and it was not proven," Deena said.

"You returned home what time?" Sally Jesse asked.

"I got home at 12:15," Ken said.

"It was thirteen minutes after one o'clock when I called you and you said you just got home," Bonnie Faye said. "Remember?"

"And keep in mind," Deena added, "that his mother is the only one that saw him come home at 12:15, supposedly with no blood on him."

When Ralph Wilson joined the conversation, Sally Jesse asked, "Has justice been served?" The audience burst into applause when he answered, "Probably not. The thing that probably should have happened in Ken Register's case is he deserved the death penalty."

Wilson spoke forcefully, clearly, and captured everyone's attention. When he described how Crystal had been mutilated and nearly decapitated, the shocked spectators gasped. A split television screen pictured Ken listening without apparent emotion as Wilson relayed the FBI forensic scientists' explanations for the post-mortem wounds to Crystal's body.

"The person, whoever it was, that killed Crystal Todd, did it for sheer enjoyment," Wilson said. "They got a great deal of satisfaction from feeling the knife against her skin."

Then another guest entered the fray: Jane Spillane, the wife of mystery writer Mickey Spillane.

Mickey Spillane is known internationally as the creator of the character Mike Hammer, who has appeared in more than a dozen novels. Spillane's Hammer, a tough-guy private investigator who had an eye for pretty women but was hard on criminals, was highly popular from the late 1940s through the 1950s. Spillane's work is largely responsible for the private investigator/detective novel genre that has flourished since then. Many of Spillane's Hammer books were best sellers, responsible for over 140 million copies sold worldwide, and have been turned into successful movies or adapted for television. At 80 years of age in 1999, Spillane continued to write and had retained the rugged good looks that enabled him to step into his own character and play the Hammer role in the 1963 movie *The Girl Hunters*.

Several months prior to the Register trial, Jane and Mickey Spillane were contacted by a woman whose son had been arrested for rape. The case had languished for months in the court system and she had been unable to convince anyone to examine her son's alibi. Intervening on the young man's behalf, the Spillanes asked Wilson to get involved in the case. When a DNA analysis came back negative, the charges were dropped. The assistant solicitor who had originally handled the case was demoted and two police officers were punished. In a letter of apology to the mother of the falsely accused man, Wilson recognized the Spillanes as a determining factor in justice being served.

Following Ken's arrest, Mickey saw Ken on television and was immediately convinced the police had the wrong person. To Spillane, Ken didn't fit the profile of a murderer. Mickey couldn't attend the trial, so he asked his wife to go for him. At first, Jane was convinced of Ken's guilt and thought going to the trial would be a waste of time. But she stood in line each day and fought the crowds to attend the trial and heard every word. Day by day, she became increasingly concerned over what she thought were problems with the prosecution's case. Where was the evidence—the fibers, footprints, fingerprints, and tire tracks—to link Ken to the crime scene? And why should the DNA experts of SLED be any more believable than the defense experts who all said SLED's conclusions were incorrect? By the time the trial ended, she was no longer convinced of Ken's guilt.

"I definitely would have found him not guilty, and I did not know he was not guilty," she said. "I just knew there was an awful lot of doubt."

When she walked from the courtroom the evening of Ken's sentencing, she knew she had to get involved.

"I came home at the end of it and called Mrs. Register," she said. "'I don't know if your son is guilty or innocent,' I told her, 'but let's find out.'" The Registers accepted her offer.

Jane Spillane and Shirley Register began their own investigation with the conviction that they wouldn't quit until the whole truth was known. The stalwart women worked tirelessly, recruiting additional help, and pored over police reports, phone records, and thousands of pages of documents. An ad was placed in the newspaper to solicit information about the case. Dozens of freedom-of-information requests were written. As their investigation expanded, Jane became more convinced of Ken's innocence and grew confident that new or reevaluated evidence would force a new trial.

It wasn't long before the word "conspiracy" began popping up in newspaper and radio interviews. "I believe [Crystal] had gotten herself in a very, very bad situation, maybe drug-related, and she couldn't get out of it," Jane said on the national television show *Inside Edition*. "I believe she expected to be murdered. I had a lot of threats against my life, and that's what really convinced me that someone out there is really upset that we are looking into this case."

Jane's outspoken involvement with the case continued. She ran for solicitor on an anti-corruption platform, believing, based on her investigations, that the "good-ol'-boy" political system in Horry County had led to widespread abuses. As a non-lawyer candidate, and therefore one not entrenched in the system, she believed she stood the best chance of cleaning up the abuses. She opened her candidacy by stating, "I am Ralph Wilson's worst nightmare." Jane was true to her stated goal of seeing Ralph Wilson defeated in the race. She didn't win, but she garnered a respectable percentage of the primary vote, particularly in Georgetown County, just south of Horry, where she and her husband are permanent residents.

The new Register investigative team had several confrontations with Bonnie Faye on radio and TV. Prior to the first of Ken's appeals before the South Carolina Supreme Court, Shirley appeared at a news conference with Ken's new lawyer and announced the establishment of a fund to cover legal costs.

"I have spent tens of thousands of dollars for Ken's defense," Shirley said. "I owe thousands more and there are yet more fees and costs to appeal Ken's convictions."

Bonnie Faye spoke from the crowd and urged listeners to donate money to the Crystal Faye Todd Scholarship fund that had been established at Conway High School.

"I think it's a bunch of bull," Bonnie Faye said of the fund to support Ken's appeal. "I can pay my bills. I've had to pay all my funeral bills and everything else."

Emotions peaked during a press conference that the Spillanes called to distribute an artist's sketch of a person whom they believed knew something about Crystal's murder. Maintaining that the police were not releasing information about the real killer, Jane and Mickey stood outside the courthouse, distributed pamphlets, and asked for public support to pressure Wilson to come clean about the case. One of the Todds' supporters asked the Spillanes, "How long are you going to go on with this three-ring circus? It's Mickey Mouse."

"It might be to you," countered Mickey Spillane, "but an innocent boy is in jail."

The Spillanes remained calm. For ten minutes, as workers and deputies looked out of the courthouse windows, they explained their view that the wrong person had been arrested and convicted of Crystal's murder. Tempers evened and the crowd drifted off until Bonnie Faye suddenly showed up.

"Your son killed my daughter," she screamed at Kenny Register.

"You're only saying that because the real killer threatened to kill you, too," Kenny said, taking a step forward.

A sheriff's deputy quickly stepped between Bonnie Faye and Kenny. "OK, now," the deputy said, "let's just settle down."

Bonnie Faye accused the Spillanes of trying to profit from Crystal's death. The Spillanes maintained their only motive was to see justice done and an innocent boy freed.

A Todd supporter then asked the question that had come up repeatedly: If there is any real evidence that proves Ken's innocence, why doesn't it come to light? What would be so difficult about taking it to the police? So far, those questions haven't been answered.

Ralph Wilson called any claims of new evidence "hogwash."

"They aren't raising any questions that weren't raised at the trial," he said. "Anybody can make allegations. To be frank, I'm very tired of them talking about the police in a conspiracy, all to converge on poor Ken Register."

Jane Spillane once again asserted her controversial accusations on the Sally Jesse Raphael show. When Sally Jesse asked why Crystal was murdered, Jane responded: "I think that Crystal got involved with some very unsavory characters."

"Why would someone want to kill Crystal?" Sally Jesse asked.

"Because Crystal may have double-crossed someone," Jane said. "Crystal Todd was involved in drugs. And Bill Knowles knows it and so does Ralph Wilson."

"That's the first I've heard of that," Bill Knowles said from the audience.

"This is the first I've heard of that," Wilson said.

"Prove it," Deena said. "Prove it."

"We met with you and Shirley Register in Ralph Wilson's office," Knowles said, shaking his head, "and you come on national television, and this is the first time you have ever said it."

"Jane, you say you know who did it," Sally Jesse said. "Do you know who the killer is?"

"I never said, 'I know who did it,' " Jane said. "I think I know who did it, yes, ma'am, one of them. I think I do, but I won't say it on national TV at this point."

She never did say who did it. And Ken remained in prison.

The South Carolina Supreme Court's response to Ken's appeal brought more controversy. Ken's appeal consisted of seven points centering on the confession and the DNA analysis: Was Ken denied right to counsel and right to silence and should the confession have been admitted? Is DNA testing scientifically reliable and should it have been admitted? Should the defense have been allowed more time for DNA discovery? Did Cottingham err in admitting the confession and DNA evidence?

Each of the points was precisely addressed in the Supreme

Court's reply: There was little or no confusion about the issues. DNA was accepted as scientifically reliable by the courts in South Carolina. The defense had ample time for discovery prior to the trial. There was no error in admitting the confession and DNA evidence.

Ken's argument that he had been denied his right to counsel and his right to silence was more interesting. Wilson had carefully gotten Ken to admit several times during the trial that he had received and understood his rights. The Supreme Court noted Wilson's plan and, through several references to the trial transcript, ruled that Ken understood he could remain silent and wasn't subject to self-incrimination.

In addition, the Supreme Court ruled that Ken saying "I want to call my mama" did not constitute an invocation of his right to receive counsel. In a lengthy explanation, the Supreme Court pointed out that "the lawyer is the one person to whom society as a whole looks as the protector of the legal rights of a person in his dealings with the police and the Courts. Thus, a request for a third party who is not an attorney is not sufficient to invoke a right to counsel during police custodial interrogation. Unless a parent is trained in the law, there is no reason to think she can give legal advice or act as a legal advocate."

The Supreme Court pointed out that Ken was neither a juvenile, as were the defendants in the case law he cited in his argument, "nor was this Register's first encounter with police questioning or the criminal law system. The conclusion is inescapable that, when he was arrested in February 1992, Register was not only emancipated, but also he had sufficient experience in the world to know the function of lawyers in the criminal law system.

"Register also never hinted that his purpose for wanting to see his mother was to discuss legal counsel. To the contrary, the facts seem to indicate he sought to confer with his mother as an alibi witness. Register asserted he would not tell police 'what happened' until he had conferred with his mother. When asked to write her son a note telling him to be honest or truthful, Register's mother refused. Instead, she attempted to assure him of her support for his alibi by writing him a note and telling him she would stand by him.

"Besides her note supportive of Register's alibi, circumstantial evidence makes it possible to infer that Register's mother helped him conceal his role in the murder and that she must have actively participated in the construction of his alibi. Therefore, police were justified in their decision not to let him see his mother to help him remember details when he started getting confused.

"There was no error in this remarkably well-tried and adjudicated case," the Court ruled. "The conviction and sentence of the lower court should be affirmed."

Ralph Wilson chose not to pursue charges against Ken's mother. As of the summer of 1999, Ken Register was still locked away in prison. And the Registers and Spillanes were still trying to prove his innocence.

EPILOGUE

Knowles slowed his car and pulled up to the mouth of the lane. Rather than sitting in the car, as he usually did, he switched off the engine and, almost from habit, got out and walked toward the spot where Crystal had died. Stepping over a knee-high cable stretched between two posts sunk in the ground, he noted with satisfaction that the voices that had plagued him on earlier trips were gone. As if to satisfy himself, he stopped several times to listen. Each time, he heard only the sounds of the woods.

The brush to the left of the lane had grown thick over the last several years, changing the balance of the scene to accentuate the clearing on the right where scrub oaks and pines had stood at oddly placed angles. *Good*, thought Knowles. The extra space somehow seemed cleaner, more ordered. The absence of cars had allowed the path to grow over.

A flash past the corner of his eye caused him to stop. Despite the owner's attempt to keep out intruders, someone had recently visited. Nailed to a stake on the opposite side of the ravine was a large bow placed near the spot where Crystal's body had been found.

"Well, I'll be," he said, stepping closer for a better look. The ditch had eroded from years of rain. All that was left was a flattened gulch, still deep, but covered with such thick foliage that rain water had to snake around the roots. Adjusting his head to see around the bushes, Knowles smiled as he saw that the burnt orange curves of the wide ribbon blended well with the crimson and browns of the remaining leaves. He'd almost missed it. *Perhaps*, he thought, *the remembrance would remain undisturbed, as someone had obviously intended.*

"This is the last time, Crystal," he said, turning to scan the scene. "We've now got the complete story. It's all over after this."

In his mind, Knowles saw the blue Plymouth Sundance roll to a stop, just before the spot. This time, he saw clearly through the windshield. He saw the murder as he knew it had to have happened.

Ken turned his body toward Crystal and hovered over the console, his face inches from hers. The vacant stare on his face looked menacing in the dim moonlight.

"What are you doing?" Crystal said, placing her hands on his chest to stop his advance and pushing weakly. "Ken, stop now, you're scaring me," she said, laughing nervously.

Ken suddenly reached forward and pulled Crystal's face toward him. He kissed her roughly on the mouth. She squirmed and pushed harder on his chest, but his strength was overpowering and he held her fast.

"Ken," she said, alarmed, when he broke away. "What are you doing?"

He kissed her again, holding the back of her neck firmly. She pushed away from him and tried to lodge her arms between them, but he was too strong.

"Geez, Ken," she said angrily, her voice filling with panic. "What, did your girlfriend turn you down tonight? Stop it, we're not doing this!"

Jerking her forward, Ken wrapped his right arm tightly around her shoulders and began to squeeze. Her arms were pinned between them. "I told you not to say that!" he growled.

"Whoa, wait, wait, Ken. C'mon, now!" she said. Crystal's mind raced. Oh my God! What do I do? "It don't have to be like this. You're hurting me. If you'll tell me what's wrong . . ."

"Just shut up! I ain't talking no more." With his right arm around her shoulders, Ken held Crystal's right arm and twisted her, allowing him access to the front of her body with his left hand. The buttons on her shirt popped off as his hand moved roughly down from her breasts to tug at the button on her pants.

"Whoa, Ken, you're tearing it up!" Crystal slipped her left hand down and tried unsuccessfully to hold his hand. "Listen Ken, listen for a minute. Whatever it is, Ken, I'm sorry. I shouldn'a mentioned her."

"Get those pants off, bitch," he demanded, ignoring her increasingly frantic pleas. "And don't give me that crap like you ain't done this before."

"You're hurting me, Ken. Please stop, that hurts!"

"You think this hurts?" He tightened his grip around her shoulders.

"Stop it, stop it!" Crystal whimpered, then cried. Her voice changed to a plea. "Ken, stop for a minute and I'll help you! Just stop hurting me." Her body went limp and she began to sob.

"I told you to get those pants off." He eased his grip around her shoulders, but kept his body above her and to the side. Crystal awkwardly fumbled with the button and zipper of her pants.

"The bra, too," he panted, his breath hot against her cheek and ear.

"I need to sit forward a little bit," she said nervously.

Ken slipped his body back over the console and freed himself with his left hand. Crystal unfastened her bra and slipped her left leg out of her shoe, pants, and panties. Ken slid on top and entered her forcefully with a grunt.

Crystal sobbed and thought of her promise to Carla to avoid getting herself into situations she couldn't handle. But how could she have prevented this? Ken was her . . . her . . . her what? The word friend suddenly seemed so absurd. Strained sounds filled the car as Ken thrust his hips downward.

"Ken, don't shoot off in me," Crystal moaned. "I'm not on the pill no more."

Ken suddenly gripped the seat tightly and bucked spasmodically several times, grinding his full weight into Crystal as his body tensed and shook.

"Too late," he said with a shudder, then he pulled out of her.

"What?" she said quickly. "What did you say?"

"You heard me," he said, laughing.

"Did you say too late?" She shoved her hand down and felt the sticky warmth between her legs.

"Damn you!" she said bitterly. Her frustration emerged as intense anger and she struck her clenched fists at Ken's face and chest. Raising his body as she wedged her knee between them, he rolled back over to the driver's seat.

"You son of a bitch!" she screamed.

Ken leaned back from the raging young woman, easily fending off the blows with his hands.

"I can't believe you!" she yelled, pulling herself up in her seat. "You practically rape me and now I'm supposed to worry about getting pregnant by you? You asshole!"

Ken sat with his hands raised and made a plea of his own. "Crystal, wait. Now just stop that! It weren't so bad."

"Weren't so bad? Fuck you!" Nearly hysterical, she leaned forward and screamed into his face. "We'll see how bad momma thinks it is when I tell her what happened!"

Ken growled. His body tensed. He forcefully pushed away the raging woman. "Better watch yourself now," he warned, twitching with irritation.

"If I get pregnant," Crystal screamed, her face distorted, "I'm going to tell everyone you raped me! How do you think that will sound? The high and mighty Ken Register!" Crystal reached through Ken's raised hands to claw at his face, but he grabbed her wrists and thrust her back against the door. She swung again clumsily with her fist and then reached down to the floorboard to retrieve her shoe. "I'm gonna tell everybody!"

"Shut up, I'm warning you. You ain't saying nothing to nobody!" Ken said, pounding his fists on the steering wheel.

"Oh, you don't think I will?" Shaking her shoe at Ken, she cursed again and said, "And guess who I'll tell that you raped me? That's what I'll do. See what she thinks of you then!"

Ken cried out as he lunged at Crystal, wrapped his hand around her throat, and yelled, "Shut up, you little slut! I told you to stop talking about her." Tightening his grip around her throat, he screamed, "You won't tell anybody anything!"

He picked up Crystal off the seat by her throat and pushed her against the door, hitting her head against the metal bar at the top of the window. Several seconds passed before he released his grip, allowing her to crumple in the seat, choking and gasping.

Ken, panting heavily, leaned back and suddenly burst out laughing when he realized he was still fully erect. He stared at his thick forearms and hands as they tightly wrung the steering wheel.

Crystal slowly reached over and opened her door, bathing

the interior of the car with light. Lifting her legs one by one, she swung them out the door and leaned forward. Pulling herself to her feet, she stood unsteadily, holding on to the door with one hand as she awkwardly slipped her leg back into her panties and her pants leg.

"Damn you," she muttered.

She sat back down on the car seat and her anger emerged again. Leaning forward out the door, she fumbled to tie her shoe. "I am gonna tell," she told him.

Ken's hand fell on a knife he kept in the center console. He opened the serrated blade into position and stared numbly at Crystal's exposed back. Crystal finished tying her shoe and slowly slumped back in her seat, dizzy from leaning over. She was exhausted. Over a ringing sound in her ears, she heard a growl and rolled her head to the left. Ken was holding a knife in his clenched fist.

"What are you gonna do now?" she said weakly as she rocked forward and reached to pull herself up by the door. "Kill me?

"Oh my God!" she suddenly groaned. She felt a searing pain in her back, then a second and a third stab. The force of the blows drove her forward and down to the ground. She tasted dirt as her face ground into the hardpack of the lane. Her wounded body involuntarily slumped to the side and she sputtered to clear her mouth of damp debris mixed with oozing blood and saliva.

And then he was there, astride her, easily pinning her wrists with one strong calloused hand. Summoning her flagging strength for a frantic effort, she twisted out from under him, crawled under the opened door, and dragged her body forward toward the front of the car.

Then he was there once more, and the depraved assault on her body continued. The bloodied knife moved forward again and again, past an upturned hand placed futilely in harm's way as a pitiful defense against a monster intent on silencing her cries of betrayal.

Turning away from his kill, Ken walked to the car, opened the door, took out a towel, and wiped his hands and the knife. Taking precautions against creating a blood trail came naturally from years of hunting and skinning game. Working quickly, he efficiently covered the car seat. He started the car, careful to touch only those things essential to operating the vehicle, and backed down the lane. He stopped suddenly though, when Crystal's body appeared in his headlights. Anyone who turned into the lane, maybe even anyone who looked down the lane while riding by, could see her. He left the car running, lifted Crystal's lifeless body, dragged it across the lane, and heaved it into a ravine. The corpse landed on its side, with one foot sticking up grotesquely over the rim of the ditch.

Ken got back into the car. He never had any question about where he was going. He sped along the familiar country roads headed for the one place he knew he would be safe. Where he could count on protection, and comforting, and help, just like always, so he could figure out what to do.

Rounding the last corner, he rejoiced in the sight of his destination. I have to figure out what I'm going to say, he thought. As he slowed the car and pulled into the driveway, he realized he already knew. The Lord had long ago given him what he needed. He would use the explanation he'd used before, the one that always began with, "Oh, Mama . . ."

"So, that's it, Crystal," Knowles said. "May you rest in peace."

APPENDIX

Ken Register remains in the Allendale Correctional Institution in Allendale, South Carolina while waiting for his appeals process to end. After the United States Supreme Court refused to hear his case in February 1997, ruling that it lacked merit, his lawyers filed a Post-Conviction Relief appeal to the Horry County Circuit Court of Common Pleas in January 1998. Part of the PCR was predicated on the theory that Ken's attorneys failed to have a second DNA test performed. Recognizing the newness of forensic analysis, Ralph Wilson had offered Morgan Martin leftover blood and semen samples for an independent analysis at the state's expense. Martin ostensibly declined, choosing instead to attack the credibility of SLED's procedure.

But in the depositions for the PCR, Martin revealed that he had, in fact, taken advantage of Barry Scheck's expertise by sending him SLED's DNA results. Scheck was impressed by the cross-matches between the various samples and determined that SLED's tests and results were sound. He decided that his involvement with the case was over.

Publicly, Martin had declined Wilson's offer to have an independent lab analyze the DNA. Secretly, however, Martin wanted to have the tests done. But Ken said he didn't want blood samples sent for processing.

"You aren't going to do a complete test, are you?" Ken asked his lawyer. "I don't want a complete test."

Martin understood. "It's got to make it more difficult," Martin said in the deposition, "for you to attack the work that they [SLED] did if your test confirms it." The simple serology test performed by an independent laboratory confirmed SLED's finding that Ken's blood contains the rare enzyme found in the semen samples obtained from Crystal's body. In retrospect,

Martin had made a smart strategic decision to decline Wilson's offer.

As of the summer of 1999, the PCR ruling was still pending.

After a few dutiful visits to the prison, primarily at the request of Ken's parents, Ken's girlfriend sent Ken a "Dear John" letter, which explained that she had decided to go on with her life without him. She is attending college and plans on becoming a health professional.

Lieutenant Bill Knowles is still with the Horry County Police Department. He recently participated in a television feature on profiling that highlighted David Caldwell's work in South Carolina. Knowles said Crystal's murder was the case that had the most impact on his professional and personal life. He still visits the crime scene.

After losing a 1998 bid for reelection as solicitor, Ralph Wilson opened a private practice in Conway. Wilson acknowledges that although he has been involved with twenty death penalty murder cases, the Register case is the only one he is ever asked about.

The high visibility of the Register case promoted the careers of Morgan Martin and Tommy Brittain, considered two of the top criminal defense attorneys in South Carolina. Martin left the South Carolina House of Representatives after the case, but has since reentered public service as part of the Democratic administration of Governor Jim Hodges. Martin and Brittain have an office in Conway.

Carla Allen was killed in an automobile accident a year and a half after Crystal's death.

Two years after Crystal's murder, Sophia, the convenience store clerk who sold the pornographic magazines to Ken, was murdered in a robbery of the convenience store where she worked. Her attacker was wielding a wooden board with a nail protruding through one side. The case remains unsolved.

The Todd case and the reality of big-city crime signaled a loss of innocence for Conway. Knowles admitted that, given what he sees every day as a part of his job, he is perhaps overprotective of his loved ones.

The Todd case also signaled a new era of cooperation for law enforcement entities throughout Horry County. Knowles cites the handling of the Todd murder investigation as a textbook example of how law enforcement can work together to a single end.

DNA analysis has become a reliable and valid forensic tool and is now largely unchallenged in its routine identification of murderers and rapists. The DNA analysis in the Todd case was featured on the television program *Discovery* in 1998 and was cited as an example of how far public acceptance of the techniques have come in a few years.

Bonnie Faye Todd continues to mourn her daughter's death. Crystal's car, shiny and looking as if it were new, still sits in the driveway of her home.

Kenny and Shirley Register sit by the phone in late afternoons, waiting for Ken's calls from prison, hoping for a miracle that will reunite them. Faded yellow ribbons sag around the old oak tree in front of their quiet country home. Ken's car, faded and rusty, sits unattended in the weeds under a weathered shed. His high school graduation tassel still hangs from the rear view mirror.

ACKNOWLEDGMENTS

Projects such as this result from the contributions of many people. We would, therefore, like to thank everyone who knowingly or unknowingly provided information that made its way to the pages of this book. We express our sincere apologies if we have missed someone or have included someone who did not want to be recognized.

Detective Bill Knowles served as our guide for the story and, despite a busy schedule, willingly met with us on numerous occasions. He patiently answered our questions and provided what materials he could. In addition, Bill graciously gave us feedback on portions of the manuscript.

Many other people provided source material. Ralph Wilson, Morgan Martin, and Tommy Brittain were inspirations with their professionalism as we probed into sensitive areas during interviews. All are gentlemen and fine representatives of the Horry County legal system.

One of the first things we heard as we began putting this book together was that, "If you tell a good story, somebody, and maybe even everybody, will end up mad at you." There is, in our experience, truth to this statement. Our thanks for information about the case go to Bonnie Faye Todd, Jane Spillane, Kenny and Shirley Register, and a few others who have asked to not be identified.

Information was obtained from local newspapers, including The *Sun News*, *The Horry Independent*, *The Coastal Observer*, and *The Barefoot Messenger*. The trial transcript was obtained from court reporter Bettye S. Gum. We appreciate the diligence associated with transcribing information. Thanks, also, to the personnel of the Horry County Library for their assistance during our many visits.

Information on the history of Horry County was obtained

from *An Illustrated History of Horry County*, by Rod Gragg; *Horry County, South Carolina: 1730-1993*, by Catherine H. Lewis; and from conversations with Alice Floyd.

Thanks to Kathy Ropp, editor of *The Horry Independent*, for making available the newspaper's photo library.

Thanks to Cindy Caison for clerical help, and thanks to various readers who offered advice on portions of the manuscript. Among our readers were Carolyn Hills, Jim Hills, Peggy Bates, Richard Causey, E. W. Hudson, and Jane C. D.

In addition, we want to warmly recognize our publisher and our editor. Thanks to Lonnie Herman of McGregor Publishing for the encouragement, for the confidence shown in our work, and for allowing us to be a part of the overall process. As we've found, there's a lot more to writing a book than putting words on a page. Thanks also to Dave Rosenbaum for his patience and creative insight into the telling of the story. His editorial suggestions and comments guided our efforts and kept us moving forward in what was a new process for us. Thanks, y'all. We value the new friendships and we're not unappreciative of the opportunity we've been given.

And, of course, our heartfelt thanks to family members and friends who have provided love and support over the last couple of years.

Dale Hudson and Billy Hills
Conway, South Carolina
August 1999